MEMORY, CONSCIOUSNESS AND TEMPORALITY

NEUROBIOLOGICAL FOUNDATION OF ABERRANT BEHAVIORS

Editorial Board:

MICHAEL MYSLOBODSKY
Tel-Aviv University & Howard University

STANLEY D. GLICK
Albany Medical College

SEYMOUR S. KETY
Harvard University & McLean Hospital

MORRIS MOSCOVITCH
University of Toronto

DANIEL R. WEINBERGER
National Institutes of Health / National Institute of Mental Health

MEMORY, CONSCIOUSNESS AND TEMPORALITY

by

Gianfranco Dalla Barba
Institut National de la Santé et de la Recherche Médicale
France

KLUWER ACADEMIC PUBLISHERS
Boston / Dordrecht / London

Distributors for North, Central and South America:
Kluwer Academic Publishers
101 Philip Drive
Assinippi Park
Norwell, Massachusetts 02061 USA
Telephone (781) 871-6600
Fax (781) 681-9045
E-Mail <kluwer@wkap.com>

Distributors for all other countries:
Kluwer Academic Publishers Group
Distribution Centre
Post Office Box 322
3300 AH Dordrecht, THE NETHERLANDS
Telephone 31 78 6392 392
Fax 31 78 6546 474
E-Mail <services@wkap.nl>

 Electronic Services <http://www.wkap.nl>

Library of Congress Cataloging-in-Publication Data

Dalla Barba, Gianfranco, 1957-
   Memory, consciousness, and temporality / by Gianfranco Dalla Barba.
      p.cm.—(Neurobiological foundation of aberrant behaviors; 3)
   Includes bibliographical references and index.
   ISBN 0-7923-7525-4 (alk. paper)
   1. Memory. 2. Consciousness. 3. Phenomenology. I. Title. II. Series.

BF3171 .D35 2001
153—dc21   2001038562

Copyright © 2002 by Kluwer Academic Publishers

All rights reserved. No part of this publication may be reproduced, stored in a retrieval system or transmitted in any form or by any means, mechanical, photocopying, recording, or otherwise, without the prior written permission of the publisher, Kluwer Academic Publishers, 101 Philip Drive, Assinippi Park, Norwell, Massachusetts 02061

Printed on acid-free paper.   Printed in the United States of America

The Publisher offers discounts on this book for course use and bulk purchases.
For further information, send email to <michael.williams@wkap.com>.

Contents

AKNOWLEDGMENTS vii

PREFACE ix

CHAPTER 1. THE PROBLEM OF THE PAST AND THE PARADOX OF THE TRACE 1
   1. Knowing and remembering: a phenomenological description 1
   2. The paradox of the trace 5
   3. Memory and representation 13

CHAPTER 2. THE *HOMUNCULUS* FALLACY 27
   1. Memory and control systems 27
   2. The homunculus fallacy 32
   3. The foundations of consciousness 43
      a) The problem of the foundations of consciousness 43
      b) The neurobiological anthropomorphization of the unconscious 45
      c) Psychoanalytic anthropomorphization of the unconscious 57
      d) Functionalist anthropomorphization of the unconscious 61
   4. Science and materialism 71
   5. Conclusions 83

CHAPTER 3. VARIETIES OF CONSCIOUSNESS 87
   1. Consciousness cannot but be defined as consciousness *of* 87
   2. Consciousness is not passivity 89
   3. Becoming conscious means becoming conscious of something in a certain way 92
   4. Varieties of consciousness 94
   5. Where does the originality of the modes of consciousness come from? 97

6. Memory as a particular type of consciousness 10

CHAPTER 4. TEMPORALITY 10
1. Phenomenology of temporality 10
   a) The past... 10
   b) The present... 11
   c) The future 11
2. Ontology of temporality 11
   a) The before-after relationship 11

CHAPTER 5. KNOWING AND REMEMBERING 12
3. Ontology of knowledge 12
4. Ontology of memory 13

CHAPTER 6. MEMORY AND CONSCIOUSNESS 14
1. Is a scientific theory of consciousness possible? 14
2. A hypothesis on the relationship between memory and
   consciousness 15
3. Towards experimental phenomenology 16

CHAPTER 7. CONSCIOUSNESS AND REALITY 18
1. Amnesia 18
2. Confabulation 19
3. Consciousness and existence 20

REFERENCES 21

INDEX 22

AKNOWLEDGMENTS

I am indebted to a great many people for many different reasons. Over the past years I had the good fortune to talk extensively about memory, consciousness and temporality with many colleagues and friends from a variety of different disciplines. I also had the opportunity to read a number of papers and books dealing with several topics of this book from one point of view or another. All of the people I discussed with and authors I read were influential in some way, either because they directly helped my ideas to evolve or because their ideas seemed to me so at odds with my that I felt strongly encouraged to pursue my way of thinking. I will not mention their names but I am really grateful to them all.

There are, however, a few people to whom I am particularly indebted. Paolo Brigenti and Valeria Zeviani were the first people to read an early draft of the book. They questioned me, criticized, encouraged and humbled me over the course of a most pleasant Thai meal. Catherine Tzortzis read a more advanced draft of my work. Her comments and her editing work were invaluable.

If I asked Paolo Bartolomeo to write the preface of the book it is because he probably knows the book as well as I do. With him, I had the opportunity of discussing most of the ideas expressed in the book. As a cognitivist on the way to repentance (I hope!), Paolo is probably the best person who can evaluate the merits and the flaws of my work.

Franco Denes and Lisa Cipolotti introduced me many years ago to cognitive neuropsychology. I am sure there is scarcely a word in this book of which they would approve. Nevertheless they encouraged me, showing great respect, friendship and loyalty.

François Boller has been Head of the laboratory where I have been working now for 12 years and where intellectual freedom never lacked, which is not always the case in other labs. François often lent me encouragement, which has helped me in this work.

There are two more people who deeply influenced my work The first is Jean-Paul Sartre, who I never met, but who has inspired my intellectual life.

The second is Endel Tulving. I am particularly grateful to Endel for encouraging my work and for reminding me what science is, or should be: an always incomplete attempt to discover some aspects of nature. I have heard him saying on various occasions: "I am wrong, we are all wrong. In one or two centuries scientists will laugh reading our papers and books on memory. Nevertheless we must keep trying, because if we don't, they will have nothing to laugh about". Thank you Endel!

PREFACE

It is not frequent to come across a book announcing a major paradigm shift in its discipline. And yet, such seems to be the case for this book. Gianfranco Dalla Barba argues that any understanding of memory must pass through an adequate consideration of the operations of consciousness, and urges to reconsider these issues in the light of the phenomenological tradition. One could see this position as an invitation to give proper credit to a first-person perspective, after decades of exclusive reliance on third-person descriptions of 'objective' performance. In this 'ecumenical' sense, the return of phenomenology to cognitive science might be welcome as an addition to the now more traditional methods of behavioural and neurophysiological research. Converging, mutually constraining evidence from these three sources might ultimately contribute to a better understanding of consciousness[1]. But Dalla Barba's position appears to be much more radical than that. His arguments on memory and consciousness imply that the very foundations of cognitive science, that is, the idea that "thinking can best be understood in terms of representational structures in the mind and computational procedures that operate on those structures"[2], are wrong. There are no such things as mental representations, or memory engrams, because there is no homunculus there to interpret them and to provide memory traces with their relationship with a past event. Following coherently his line of reasoning, Dalla Barba raises doubts about the very possibility of a science of consciousness. The aim of science is to achieve objective knowledge by establishing quantitative relationships. On the other hand, "[c]onsciousness, by definition, is subjectivity that describes itself according to rules of quality and not quantity" (ms p. 198). It follows that any attempt to objectivate consciousness inevitably transforms it in something radically different. The necessary conclusion is that an

---

[1] Flanagan, O. (1992). *Consciousness reconsidered.* Cambridge, MA, US: MIT Press.
[2] Thagard, P. (1996). *Cognitive Science.* In: Stanford Encyclopedia of Phylosophy (E.N. Zalta, Ed.). Available at: http://www.illc.uva.nl/~seop/contents.html.

(objective) science of (subjective) consciousness is not logically possible. This conclusion is not, however, explicitly stated by Dalla Barba, who is himself a thoughtful and productive cognitive scientist. A more lenient perspective for the future of cognitive science could be that you may take the risk and make inferences on what is going on in somebody else's consciousness, and perhaps discover lawful relationships, from his/her verbal reports or other behavioural evidence (see, e.g., Dennet's heterophenomenology[1]). Dalla Barba seems to adhere to such a perspective. Also, changes in brain functioning during cognitive activities may provide hints concerning the neural correlates of consciousness[2] (despite Dalla Barba's claim that the brain has no special status for the operations of consciousness!). Though, as he points out, it is unclear how to establish causal relationships between these phenomena, finding neural activity which is both necessary and sufficient (within a given context) to the development of a determinate subjective experience[3] would be an exciting result, and could perhaps offer insights for developing rehabilitation strategies for brain-damaged patients.

A fruitful domain of interaction between phenomenology and cognitive science could be the building of taxonomies of consciousness operations. For example, the fact that one can detect a briefly presented array of letters as made of letters, but can verbally report only a subset of the array[4], suggests a distinction between phenomenal consciousness (the experience of seeing the array of letters) and reflexive consciousness (supporting the capacity of verbally reporting the letters)[5], a distinction already hinted at by Husserl, Sartre and Ricoeur[6]. In the memory domain, Dalla Barba proposes yet another taxonomy of the modes of consciousness, that between 'knowing consciousness', 'temporal consciousness' (remindful of Tulving's distinction between semantic and episodic memory), and 'imaginative consciousness'. This distinction receives support from the performance of

---

[1] Dennett, D. C. (1991). *Consciousness explained*. Boston, MA, US: Little, Brown and Co.
[2] Rodriguez, E., George, N., Lachaux, J. P., Martinerie, J., Renault, B., & Varela, F. J. (1999). Perception's shadow: long-distance synchronization of human brain activity. *Nature, 397*(6718), 430-433.
[3] Kanwisher, N. (2001). Neural events and perceptual awareness. *Cognition, 79*(1-2), 89-113.
[4] Sperling, G. (1960). The information available in brief visual presentations. *Psychological Monographs, 74*(11), 1-29.
[5] Block, N. (2001). Paradox and cross purposes in recent work on consciousness. *Cognition, 79*(1-2), 197-219.
[6] Vermersch, P. (2000). *Conscience directe et conscience réfléchie*. Available at: http://www.es-conseil.fr/GREX/.

brain-damaged patients showing a selective deficit for one of these modes of consciousness. These two examples underline the fact that first-person phenomenology and third-person observation of someone else's performance need not give rise to incompatible results, even if third-person observation is inevitably contaminated by a functionalist framework. More generally, it is not to be excluded that logically flawed assumptions, such as those underlying functionalism, may lead to genuine progress in science, whereas rigid methodologies may hamper it[1].

Be that as it may, this book represents a radical and carefully articulated criticism of functionalism in cognitive science. Shall it ultimately be the small child pointing to the shallowness of "the mind's new science"[2]? Perhaps only time will say. Certainly, this book has the capacity of forcing cognitive scientists to a critical evaluation of the assumptions underlying their research, as its drafts did for me during the past few years, and its central arguments continue to do now.

Paolo Bartolomeo

Paolo Bartolomeo is senior research scientist at the French institute of health and medical research (INSERM).

---

[1] Feyerabend, P. K. (1988). *Against Method*. (Rev. ed.). London; New York: Verso.
[2] Gardner, H. (1985). *The mind's new science: A history of the cognitive revolution.* New York, NY, US: BasicBooks, Inc.

One fact is limpid and clear: neither the future nor the past exists. It is inexact to say that there are three kinds of time: past, present and future. Maybe it would be more exact to say that time can be conceived of in three ways: the present of the past, the present of the present, and the present of the future.

Augustine, *The confessions of Saint Augustine*

CHAPTER 1

THE PROBLEM OF THE PAST AND THE PARADOX OF THE TRACE

1. KNOWING AND REMEMBERING: A PHENOMENOLOGICAL DESCRIPTION

What is memory? If you look it up in the dictionary, you soon discover that this term is used to refer to very different aspects of human experience. Robert[1], for example, defines memory as: 1) the faculty used to preserve and recall past states of consciousness and that which is associated with them; 2) a combination of psychical functions through which the past is pictured as past; 3) the preservation in the brain of impressions which continue to influence our behaviour in the form of habits. The polysemy of the concept of memory is found in these definitions whose origin lies in general use. Therefore memory is not only the faculty to preserve and recall past states of consciousness, or the faculty to picture the past as past, but it is also the expression, in the form of habits, of past experiences which are preserved in the brain. If then you look directly at how the term memory is generally used, it is evident that it refers to the ability to remember episodes or information of every sort. We say, for example, "I remember the name of the person I met yesterday, I remember several lines from Dante, I remember how I spent my last holiday, I remember the chemical formula for water", etc. Therefore the word memory is commonly used to denote the faculty to use any type of acquired information. It is easy to see though that this polysemous term is used to refer to at least two substantially different phenomena. Indeed, memory refers both to the act of recalling episodes and personal events as well as to the capacity of using acquired information

---

[1] Robert, P., 1972.

which has no personal or temporal connotations. For example, the idea of memory refers both to the memory of your last holiday and to the knowledge of the chemical formula for water. The term memory is therefore ambiguous because of the substantial difference in the meanings it is used to express. Let's see.

Here is a book, on the table in front of me. What knowledge do I have of this book? First of all, I recognise it *as* a book, that is I know that the object in front of me is a book and not, for example, a bicycle or a coffee machine. Quite early, in my childhood, I realised that a book, a bicycle and a coffee machine were distinct objects. At first I distinguished them without being able to give them a name or function. I then learnt to indicate these three objects with three different sounds, "book", "bicycle" and "coffee machine". I also understood that a book is something that belongs to a distinct category, that of books, that is that there are a quantity of objects in the world called by the same name because they share certain characteristics: they are sheets of paper bound together, on which words and images are printed. What else do I know about this book? Well, for example, that it belongs to a certain particular subcategory of books. Indeed, it's a novel and not a handbook of physics, it's a paperback edition and not a hardback, it was written over a century ago and not today, I know what it's about because I have read it, unlike many other books that I have never read. I could also add that I know it is made out of ink, glue and cellulose, that some people have enjoyed it while others have enjoyed it less, that the author belonged to a certain literary school typical of the time and place in which the book was written, that the publisher is an important one that is now in economic straits. How come I know all these things about that book, where does all this knowledge come from? My past experience will be held responsible. Certainly, it is probable that over the years my continual interacting with the world around me has enabled me to deposit certain more or less stable "meanings" that now enable me, for example, to state all that I know concerning this book which is on the table in front of me. It is easy to see though that my knowledge of that book, though it is based on my past experience, is not exclusively mine, but is, or could be, common knowledge to all the members of the society to which I belong. In other words, everyone knows or could know what I know about this book because, like me, everyone in the course of their lifetime has had access to the information necessary to form a more or less complex idea of book.

But there is something else about this book in front of me. Something this book means *to me* and which does not belong, nor could ever belong, to any other being in the universe other than me. Indeed this book is *mine*. And not only because I bought it and now possess it, but because it is part of my personal past of which I alone am at the same time protagonist and sole repository. I have had direct experience of this book in the past and continue to do so in the present direct experience, which makes the book an element of what I have been and of what I now am. In other words, not only do I know what other people know or could know about this book, but I also have certain memories of it which no one else has or could ever have. I remember in fact having bought it in that certain bookshop and of having found it after spending ages looking for it among the bookshelves. I remember having read it during the summer when I was on holiday in that certain place, the moments of boredom and of satisfaction while reading it, etc. In short, that book evokes in me certain memories, pictures of the past in which I was the protagonist, which belong exclusively to me. But you may object that I can tell you about my memories of this book, as I am in fact doing at the moment, and so they are not only mine but belong to whoever, in one way or another, learns of them. Certainly, anyone may learn the date, the place, the name of the bookshop and the exact position on the bookshelf from which I took this book, if I choose to tell him. He may also learn which pages bored me and which enthralled me, under which tree and at what time of the day I would read. But his knowledge of it will always be impersonal and atemporal, of the same type as the rest of the knowledge he possesses about that book and the world in general. While for me, this book represents an element of my past. A past which I can consciously evoke by transcending the present and placing myself and that book *down there* in the past, in *my* past. In no way can my experience of this book become someone else's past, even if, hypothetically, someone knows all about that experience down to the smallest detail. Indeed, in that case, my experience of this book will not become experience of this book in someone else's past, it will quite simply be a memory, however detailed, of *my* experience of this book. It seems clear then, that if we trust what our direct experience of the world reveals to us, we must recognise a substantial difference between phenomenal experience which characterises the memory of one's own personal past and that which is associated with the use of acquired knowledge.

But what is the nature of the difference between what I remember and what I know about that book? After all, both memory and knowledge stem from my past experience. Phenomenal experience reveals to us that the subjective experience which accompanies the recollection of a personal episode is completely different and unlikely to be confused with the experience which accompanies the putting to use of knowledge; but is this really such a substantial difference? The reflective data which, for example, makes it clear that knowing that water in chemical terms is H2O, gives rise to a subjective experience which differs from remembering an evening spent with friends at a restaurant; should this data be taken seriously or can it be quite easily overlooked? The notion concerning the chemical formula of water, even though it comes from my past experience, lacks any temporal connotation whatsoever, while the memory of an evening spent with friends sends me immediately back to the past; is this only an illusion or a bizarre memory epiphenomenon, or does it reflect the very structure of memory? Let us say at once that what direct experience of phenomena reveals must not be taken lightly and certainly not be neglected. That which direct experience of the world reveals to us cannot be considered useless, the by-product of a hidden world by which it is preceded and determined. Sending the "explanation" on to somewhere else means preferring the abstract to the concrete, negating the reality of experience by referring the essence of concrete experience back to an abstract world which is only experienced indirectly. Nietzsche had already warned against the "illusion of hidden worlds". The cup which is in front of me at this moment does not refer me to any hidden essence. The cup is neither the atoms of which it is composed nor a hypothetical representation of cup which I carry around with me as content of my consciousness, or of my physiological or psychological unconscious. The cup's appearance, that is my perception of cup, encompasses and refers me to a whole physical and psychological series of events which cannot lay claim to any priority over the cup as it appears to me now. Of course I can go beyond appearances, as indeed one tends to say in everyday language. By means of another operation, on another level in that it excludes my direct perception of cup, I can say that the cup is a man-made china object, the perception and knowledge of which is possible thanks to some representation or unconscious mental act or some computational treatment of the input "cup". It is only too clear that this type of operation does not permit us to go beyond appearances, but rather creates an infinite series of appearances. The china object, the representation or the computational treatment of the input are nothing other than the actors on a stage, in a play which I use to explain the cup's appearance. In other words, this cup does not appear *because* it is made of china, but it appears *as* made of china. If the relation between it's being made of china and its appearance were a causal one, then there would be no way to distinguish the cup from any other object made of china. One may want to argue that it is not just a question of materials. The china was, in fact, worked in order to attain the shape of a cup. But it is not that the material plus the work of man or of a machine will lead us to the appearance. That which appears cannot be the sum of nothing, or one could say it is the sum of everything which is the same thing. The cup, indeed, appears to me not only as man made and of china, but as an object which is in front of me, here and now, in this room, in this city, with this certain light, an object among the objects of my experience. The cup is, first of all and irremediably, its being here in front of me, in front of this consciousness that I am, and it is not the appearance of a hidden essence or the result of a causal chain. If we were to see the cup's appearance as depending on something beyond what it is, we would end up by being strangled by a causal chain which starts from the china object and ends up losing itself in the infinity of the universe. Even though the appearance of cup does not coincide with its essence, which, as we shall see later, is to be found in the consciousness to which this cup appears, it cannot be overlooked in favour of other appearances, which in turn would send one on to still other appearances in a *reductio ad infinitum*. If now instead of the cup we take memory into consideration, or that which is commonly indicated by this term, it becomes clear that the difference between memory and knowledge, which is a difference of appearance, cannot be done away with just like that, relegating it to a peculiar epiphenomenon or memory illusion. Knowing and recollecting appear as different to experience, and this different and unmistakable appearance must be taken into account. Every theory on memory must therefore inevitably give an answer to this phenomenal diversity between memory and knowledge.

2. THE PARADOX OF THE TRACE

An assumption common to many old and new theories on memory is that of considering a memory as the result of the preservation of the past in the organism which remembers. Accordingly, if I now perceive the image of this cup of coffee on the table, tomorrow I will be able to remember it because this image has, so to speak, been deposited in some part of my brain in the form of a *memory trace*. In other words, the event of "cup-on-the-table-on-such-and-such-an-afternoon" has caused a modification in the equilibrium of my brain which I call memory trace of the event, or, to use more elegant terminology, an engram, in which the event is deposited in the form of representation. The activation of the trace, that is, its subsequent passage from a passive to an active state, will result in recollection of the event. Present-day versions of this now classical way of thinking have been reformulated more or less explicitly in current functionalist theories. These substitute the physical trace with a functional trace which is preserved in the architecture of a system which is no longer physical (the brain), but virtual (the cognitive system). It is easy to see that, however reformulated, any theory which bases the ability to recollect on the preservation of an event inside a trace contains a paradox, fruit of a misleading assumption, that is the belief that time can exist in things. The past event which I now remember, for example my dinner yesterday with Paola, is present to my consciousness as a past event, in that the event was contained in the memory trace whose activation produced the recollection. In other words, the past of that event, or its "pastness" as Bergson[1] says, is already there, enclosed in that "thing", physical or abstract as it may be, which I call memory trace of the event. But it should be clear that "things" as such are not temporal. Objects of the world are neither present, nor past, nor future, but they acquire a temporal dimension only in the presence of a person who goes to the trouble of making them temporal. Time cannot even be found in a "thing" like the brain, however much one would like to give it a particular status in the universe. This erroneous assumption, on which theories of memory are founded, is directly reflected in the paradox to which these theories fall victim. The paradox of the memory trace, as we shall call it, consists in seeing memory, that is what is given to consciousness as past, as originating in elements borrowed from the present. Let's see why.

The event which I now perceive, for example, the glass which is on the table in front of me, is without doubt a present event. This event of glass-on-the-table, determines a modification in the equilibrium of a system, be it

---

[1] Bergson, H., 1896.

physical (the nervous system) or virtual (the computational level), which I call memory trace. What is the temporal nature of this modification, namely of the memory trace? Without doubt present. The glass-on-the-table which I now perceive is present and if one accepts that this event produces a modification somewhere between my brain and my mind, one will have to accept that said modification will be present, and that the event represented by that modification will also be present. In short, depending on the ideology that one wants to adopt, be it a case of the synthesis of new proteins, of the growth of new dendritic spines, of the activation or the reinforcement of synaptic circuits, or of the particular codification of information, it will always be a matter of present modification of something. What happens when that event contained in the trace is recollected in memory? When the event of "glass-on-the-table" is recollected it happens in the present, that is as the result of the reactivation of the modification that the event caused on a physiological, biochemical, neuroanatomical, neurocibernetical or functional level. And so it is not at all clear how memory, whose basic characteristic is being memory of the past, can stem from a combination of present phenomena, perception, the preservation of the trace and recollection. Activation of the memory trace should, if anything, coincide with a new perception of the event contained within the trace, not with its memory since the event contained in the trace was present as it ended up in the trace and continued to be so for as long as it remained enclosed in the trace. The paradox of the memory trace which current theories on memory overlook had already been clearly reported over fifty years ago. Merleau-Ponty [1] wrote: "...our very best reason for rejecting physiological preservation of the past is also a reason for rejecting 'psychological preservation', and this reason is that no preservation, no physiological or psychic "trace" of the past can enable comprehension of consciousness of the past. This table carries traces of my past life, I have carved my initials, I have left ink stains. But, alone, these traces do not refer back to the past: they are present; and, if I find there signs of some 'previous' event, I find them because, by other means, I have a sense of the past, because I carry in me this meaning. ... a preserved perception (in a 'physical' or 'psychic' trace) is a perception, it continues to exist, it is always in the present, it does not open behind us that dimension of escape and of absence that is the past." If, on the other hand, I recognise that particular event as past, this happens because I attribute a precise meaning

---

[1] Merleau-Ponty, M., 1945.

to it, that of being past, a meaning which by definition cannot be contained in the trace since, in every moment of its existence, it has never ceased to be present.

This does not mean that events do not cause modifications in our brain or in our cognitive system, but these modifications cannot be used to explain recollection. Besides, any object in the universe undergoes modification on account of events. Any object carries with it the marks of the past, and yet, if not metaphorically, no one would think of attributing the possibility of recollection to objects. The signs that events have left on objects acquire the meaning of *past* only by virtue of a consciousness which attributes it to them. Even the impression on the cushion on the sofa in front of me bears witness to past events, but in itself it is present and has never ceased to be so in any single instant of its existence. If I find in it signs of some past event, if I remember the thousands of times that my guests and I myself have sat on that sofa, it is because I attribute a meaning to those marks, that of being past. The "meeness" of memory of which Claparède [1] speaks, the warmth and intimacy with which James[2] describes memory, or Bergson's "pastness"[3], describe certain characteristics of memory well, but tell us nothing about its nature. Indeed, they either describe only one present characteristic of memory, and so they remain in the present, or else if they are already dealing with the past, they presuppose that which they want to explain.

As support for the hypothesis of the memory trace as a condition for recollection it could be stated that it is not at all necessary for the episodes to be contained in the memory trace *as past*. Indeed, for recollection to be possible it is enough for "something" in the trace to indicate that its content concerns some past event. In short, it would be enough for the episodes registered in the trace to be in some way marked, for example, with a type of tag stating the date they took place or simply indicating that what is contained in that trace is past[4]. It is easy to see how, yet again, a hypothesis of this type presupposes the past instead of explaining it. Any tag or indicator added to the episode contained in the trace will indeed be present, as is the episode which it accompanies. The date or the "past" information

---

1 Claparède, E., 1911.
2 James, W., 1890.
3 Bergson, H., 1896.
4 See for example Morton, J., Hammersley, R.H., & Berkerian, D.A., 1985.

of the indicator, in themselves, tell us nothing; they are not past, they become so only if the past is already taken for granted by the consciousness which selects that indicator. In other words, the tag or indicator of pastness of an episode does not precede nor, even less so, does it create the past. On the contrary, it is in some way the consequence of it, it assumes its function of indicator of pastness because I already carry in me this meaning and am capable of attributing it to it. The knot I tie in my handkerchief to remind me that yesterday I made an appointment with Paul is not past and if I ignore it is not even present. When I put my hand in my pocket to take out my handkerchief and I realise it has a knot, I attribute a meaning to that knot, that of being an indicator of a past event which I have to remember so as not to cut a poor figure with Paul. If I did not *already* possess the past as meaning, that knot would simply remain what it is, and not an indicator of something past. The date, the indicator of pastness or what have you, say absolutely nothing about the past, nor do they bear witness to it. If I am able to recollect the appointment with Paul, this episode will appear to me in the past not because of its date but because of the meaning I attribute to that date, namely the meaning of the past that I attribute to that episode. In short, for however many tags, indicators or whatever else you may choose to attach to the memory trace, it will never ever contain the past.

On the other hand, it would be pointless to attribute the order of succession to the contents of the trace, that is something that specifies that episode B took place *before* episode C and *after* episode A. The order of succession, the very idea of a *before* and of an *after* precedes the episode, it is not part of it. If I say that B comes after A and before C, I am temporalising A, B and C according to an order of succession that does not depend on the elements themselves, but on the temporalising act which I perform in accordance with an idea of succession which I *already* possess and which precedes the elements themselves. In other words, for however hard one tries, it will never be possible to draw the past from the memory trace. We shall see later the nature of the past and how this cannot be understood if not within a global temporality. But there is another problem to be resolved with regard to the memory trace. The problem of knowledge and of its preservation.

You could say that, if not the past, at least knowledge will be stored in some part of the brain or else in a functional system as the functionalists claim. Indeed, since knowledge is timeless and impersonal, it could very well be preserved in some trace without this implying the risk of falling once again into the paradox described above. But knowledge, just like the past, is not "something" that necessarily has to be somewhere. It is not a question of *res extensa* which has to occupy space and which can therefore quite happily be placed in a memory trace. Indeed, knowledge cannot prescind from he who knows, that is from the consciousness of he who knows. It is in the consciousness of he who knows that knowledge is to be sought. But, yet again, it is not a question here of drawing knowledge as a "thing" from the unconscious of the memory trace in order to bring it to the light of consciousness as content of the latter. Indeed, consciousness, but we will go into it in more detail further on, has no content, but as consciousness *of*, it is already, for example, cognisant consciousness of this glass. And in order for there to be a cognisant consciousness there must also be consciousness of the cognisant consciousness. It is not a question of Spinoza's *idea ideae*, nor of the well-known formula "knowing is knowing you know". Both these positions would lead in fact to infinity (idea ideae ideae etc.). In order for there to be knowledge there must be consciousness of consciousness as cognisant. What is absolutely unthinkable is the passive existence of knowledge, as it would appear if it were contained in a memory trace, that is knowledge that remains in the limbo of the unconscious or of the physiological. Under these conditions, it is absolutely incomprehensible how non-conscious knowledge can perpetuate itself and still find the strength to produce cognisant consciousness. Later, we will clarify how the relationship between cognisant and known should be seen without falling into the trap of idealism and of realism. For now let it suffice to have clarified that if consciousness were a place, that would be the only possible place for knowledge, and that knowledge shut up in a memory trace is unintelligible.

If, as we have seen, memory and knowledge cannot be contained in a memory trace or in any other place in as far as their existence outside consciousness is unintelligible, how come, you will object, the past continues to influence an individual's present even if he is not conscious of it? Indeed, it is easy to see that most of the gestures I execute reflect and presuppose an acquired knowledge but they are carried out without my necessarily being conscious of this knowledge. For example, a linguistic act does not require consciousness of the syntactic structure of the sentence pronounced, a structure that he who carries out the act generally knows, but of which he is not conscious at the moment in which he pronounces the sentence. Or else, much more simply, I can be conscious of what I am writing and at the same time not of the gesture I am carrying out to bring a cigarette to my lips. And yet this gesture that I perform automatically while my consciousness is directed elsewhere, implies a certain amount of various kinds of knowledge: for example, I must know that cigarettes are brought up to the lips and not, let us say, to the ear; I must know the appropriate gesture to avoid bringing the cigarette to my ear instead of to my lips, I must know that once it reaches my lips it should be smoked and not eaten, etc. All this knowledge determines my present behaviour even though it remains outside my consciousness. Are these not perhaps examples of the influence of an unconscious past, at least in the shape of knowledge, if not of memory, on an unconscious present. And besides, has it not been established, at least since the time of Claparède, that amnesic patients, who from one minute to the next lose all conscious memory of their past experience, as a rule acquire and use knowledge in the so-called "implicit", that is not conscious, way? In the light of these observations it would seem that knowledge can exist outside of consciousness. And if therefore, it is permissible to consider it separable from consciousness then it could even be somewhere, for example, in a memory trace.

Actually, that is not how it is. First of all, we must clarify that the knowledge that accompanies my behaviour and in someway determines it, like the sentence uttered or the cigarette brought to my lips, are certainly beyond the consciousness of that moment, but *can* become conscious if only I give them my attention. And so I can become conscious of the syntactic structure of the sentence I utter or of the gestures I perform to bring a cigarette to my lips. *Only* when this knowledge is present to consciousness as consciousness of knowledge does it acquire its shape as knowledge, that is, it becomes meaning that consciousness thematises. And earlier, what was and what is the knowledge that amnesic patients are able to acquire but not clearly express in the form of meaning? You will admit, without doubt, that it is the result of experience or, to use a more modern term, of information which has been accumulated. But is saying that it is a matter of accumulated information the same as accepting the notion of memory trace? Not at all. That experience, or quite simply the passage from a previous state to a present one, is responsible for modifications in any system does not indeed mean that said modifications are in any way specified, as, on the other hand, one presupposes them to be in a memory trace. I can call these modifications information which accumulates but it is still, one way or another, a question of ìneutralî information, that is non-specified in terms of meaning, knowledge or memories since these exist only in consciousness, or rather, as we shall see, are original and irreducible forms of consciousness. The notion of memory trace requires, on the other hand, that accumulated information be already specified in its phenomenal aspect within the trace, that is, that knowledge, meaning, memories be already within the trace. However, if I observe these modifications from close up, depending on the magnifying glass I choose, I will find, let us say, subatomic participles, atoms, molecules, cells, electro-physiological phenomena, computation symbols etc., but I will never find knowledge, meaning, or memories. It is very likely that the brain, and not only the brain but the whole body, like any physicochemical system, changes with the passing of physical time and that therefore the modifications caused by the passage of physical time are recorded by the system. But this is in no way proof of the existence of the memory trace, and even less so of the influence of the past on the present. Although the present state of matter, of any matter including the brain, is the result of its previous state, it is not at all necessary to make reference to the influence of the past since there is no present state of matter which cannot be explained with the normal means of mechanistic determinism. The example quoted by Sartre[1] clarifies the matter: These two nails look exactly the same. However, one is new while the other was bent and then straightened with a hammer. With the first blow, one of them will go right into the plank while the other will bend yet again: influence of the past, result of experience "of nail bent and then straightened "? No, quite simply the exterior appearance of the two nails is similar but their present molecular structure is different. The present molecular state is, at every instant, the effect of the past molecular state but this does not at all mean that there is a passage from one instant to another with the persistence of the past, nor that the nail bends because it "remembers" its own past or because it "knows" it should bend under the blows of a hammer because of its present molecular state.

Some time ago, in one of the most prestigious international scientific magazines, there was an article entitled "Metallurgy: extraordinary alloys that remember their past". It states: "There is a class of alloys which, like patients coming out of psychoanalysis, remember their past."[2] It is about

---

1 Sartre, J.P., 1943.
2 Robinson, A.L., 1976.

alloys bent at high temperatures and then straightened cold, which when reheated assume once again the bent structure that they had originally. We may well attribute then, metaphorically, memory, knowledge and any other type of intentional act to all finite beings. Certain alloys "remember" their past, the thermostat "feels" variations in temperature, the photoelectric cell "sees" variations in light, the thermos flask "knows" whether it is keeping the liquid hot or cold. However, it is always a question of metaphor, just as only metaphorically can it be said that memory and knowledge are contained within cerebral traces.

We will now try to demonstrate how both the problem of memory and that of knowledge have been overlooked by current theories on memory based on the paradox of the trace.

3. MEMORY AND REPRESENTATION

At the beginning of this century, Claparède [1] made the following observation on an amnesic patient: "It is a case -he wrote- of a forty-seven-year-old woman committed to the Bel Air Asylum. Her illness began 5 years ago. Her old memories are intact, for example, she can list the European capitals without making a mistake, she can carry out various mental calculations etc. Yet she does not know where she is even though she has been in this home for five years. She does not recognise the doctors of the asylum even though she sees them every day and not even her nurse who has been with her for six months. When the latter asks her if she recognises her, the patient answers: -No Madam, with whom do I have the honour of speaking?- What strikes one here -continues Claparède- is her inability to recollect at will her recent memories and, when these are recollected automatically, to recognise them.... I made the following rather odd experiment on this patient: to see if she would retain more easily an intense impression which brought her emotional life into play, I pricked her hand hard with a pin I had hidden between my fingers. This small pain was quickly forgotten as though it were a matter of an indifferent perception and a few instants later she no longer remembered anything. However, when I again approached my hand to hers, she withdrew it in reflex, without

---

1 Claparède, E., 1911.

knowing why. When, indeed, I asked her why she had withdrawn it, she answered with astonishment: -why, isn't it perhaps my right to withdraw my hand?- and if I insisted she would say:- is there perhaps a pin hidden in your hand? – and to my question: - who has made you think that I want to prick you? - she would answer with a refrain: - it's an idea that crossed my mind – or sometimes she would try to justify herself saying: -sometimes there are pins hidden in hands" (pp.84-85).

In this observation of Claparède's we already find, more or less explicitly, the idea that human memory is made up of a combination of distinct functions. In the case of amnesia, some of these are lost, others are retained. Claparède's patient demonstrated that she could use certain general knowledge correctly, that which she had acquired before the beginning of her pathology, and that she was able to take in new information, as her behaviour to avoid another pin prick demonstrated: when faced with the examiner whose hand again approaches hers, she withdraws it, "without knowing why" says Claparède. Indeed she does not "know" why she withdraws her hand, or at least not consciously. Certainly, she knows that it has something to do with pins and the painful pricks that these give when hidden in the fingers of a hand you're about to shake, but this is "an idea which crosses her mind", an impersonal idea and one which in her mind has no connection whatsoever with her own personal past. The episode itself of the prick disappeared from her consciousness while continuing to influence her behaviour. She is not consciously aware of her own past even though she carries the signs of it in her reactions. On the other hand, in this patient, the possibility of conscious memory of past episodes has been irremediably lost.

Claparède was not the only one, nor was he the first, to observe dissociation in the behaviour of amnesic patients. Ribot[1] and Korsakoff[2] had made similar observations, but theirs were mostly clinical observations and so were not taken seriously by experimental psychologists. They only began to "rediscover" what had already been observed at least fifty years earlier towards the end of the fifties[3]. It was only in those years that psychologists realised that memory, recollection, learning and similar

---

[1] Ribot, T., 1882.
[2] Korsakoff, S. S., 1889.
[3] Milner, B., 1958; Milner, B., 1965; Warrington, E.K., & Weiskrantz, L., 1968; Warrington, E.K., & Weiskrantz L., 1968.

concepts could not be disposed of as monolithic and integral phenomena. Indeed, the amnesic were capable of learning many things even in compliance with rigid experimental criteria.

The idea that memory was organised in various systems, which were more or less independent, started to be accepted among psychologists with those studies. According to this hypothesis every memory system is the function of nervous structures which are specific to that system, and is organised according to operative rules which are different from those of every other system. Moreover, the various memory systems are among themselves *functionally incompatible*[1] in the sense that every system is in charge of resolving specific memory problems which can only be resolved by that system. Among the various distinctions, that between the semantic memory system and the episodic memory system is the one of most interest to us. This distinction was first proposed by Tulving[2] to distinguish the ability to remember specific episodes of our personal past from comprehension and language use in general, which was described as semantic memory, where the term "memory" is used too loosely according to Tulving. "Episodic memory –writes Tulving- is a system which receives and stores information about temporally dated episodes and their spatio-temporal relations". Semantic memory, on the other hand, is "the memory necessary for the use of language. It is a mental thesaurus; the organised knowledge that a person has of words and other verbal symbols, of their meaning, of their relationships, as of formulas, rules, algorithms to manipulate symbols, concepts and relationships[3]. Tulving also emphasises the fact that episodic memory depends on conscious recollection of the personal past of he who remembers and that "conscious awareness even if only in the form of a vague sensation of the episodic source of the information recalled, is the hallmark of episodic memory"[4]. It is conscious awareness that connotes episodic recollection and assimilates it to an act, that of remembering, which is completely different from knowledge in *itself* which is identified with knowing. The episodic-semantic dichotomy which emphasises recollection and knowledge as opposing poles of the activity called memory, has been taken up by various authors who, even if with different terminology, have reproposed it without in reality having changed

---

1 Schacter, D.L., & Tulving, E., 1994.
2 Tulving, E., 1972.
3 Tulving, E., 1972.
4 Tulving, E., 1983.

its characteristics by much[1]. Furthermore, Tulving affirms that episodic memory represents, both phylogenetically and ontogenetically, the most advanced stage of evolution. Episodic memory is seen as a subsystem of semantic memory and its functioning therefore depends on the soundness of the latter. In short, there can be no conscious recollection if semantic knowledge has been lost.

Tulving's schematisation has without doubt a merit, that of distinguishing recollection from knowledge and of therefore pointing out what immediate experience of the world already tells us apodeictically, the unmistakable difference between the act of recollection and that of knowledge. Another merit of Tulving's is his having sensed intuitively that the relationship between recollection and knowledge is not one of clear-cut separation, but rather a relationship in which one of the two elements blends into the other. And so we accept that knowledge has both phylogenetic and ontogenetic priority over recollection and this in some way stems from knowledge as a more original and more evolved way of addressing the world. Another, by no means secondary, merit of the distinction between episodic memory and semantic memory is that of having provided a theoretic base capable of explaining, at least in part, some clinical-experimental observations on amnesia. It has been known, at least since the times of Claparède[2] that in the amnesic knowledge, impersonal knowledge of the world, well, in short, semantic memory is often preserved, while conscious recollection of one's personal past, episodic memory, is lost[3].

However, the merits of Tulving's theory end here and at this point its limitations emerge, the first of which is linked to the very idea of a memory system. According to Tulving, every memory system differs from every other, essentially because of the type of information or of representation that it contains. The semantic system is said to contain the representation of the world in the form of meaning, rules, relations, algorithms, in other words, the "meaning" of the world, that which enables one to know it. The episodic system, on the other hand, is supposed to contain the representation of specific episodes from the personal past of each of us. But, even though the

---

1 For example Weiskrantz (1987) distinguishes between memory and events and system and cognition, Hintzman (1978) between episodic memory and generic memory, Baddeley (1982) between conscious recollection and automatic recollection.
2 Claparède, E., 1911.
3 We will come back to the problem of amnesia and its interpretation.

episodic system is said to be dependent on the semantic, what is not clear is how and when a semantic representation becomes part of the episodic system since recollection, which is a function of the episodic system, requires knowledge, which is a function of the semantic system. In other words, if to remember the cup from which I drank tea yesterday I have to have a semantic representation of "cup", when and how does the generic representation of cup become part of my episodic system to then become "that-cup-from-which-I-drank-tea-yesterday"? If it is simply a process of multiplication of the representations in which the episodic representation comes into being at the moment the event is experienced and is detached, so to speak, from the semantic system to become part of the episodic, we would find ourselves with two representations separated by a void. The episodic representation will no longer refer one back to the semantic, but will become isolated from it, lost forever in its being episodic and an orphan to any meaning whatsoever. And so it is pointless to assert the existence of a relationship of dependency of episodic representation on semantic if from the start a relationship of separation has been established. In short, once the two representations have been separated, either where this relationship of dependency comes from is explained or else the possibility of lending "meaning" to recollection will be forever lost. It is obvious that the simple assertion of dependency does nothing but presuppose that which needs to be explained. But even if we accept the existence of two representations, an episodic and a semantic, and the dependency of the first on the second based on a relationship which is given but has not been clarified, our problems are in no way over. Indeed, accepting the existence of an episodic representation, even if in relation to a semantic one, means falling back into the paradox of the memory trace. The episodes represented in the episodic representation cannot, as we have already seen, be past nor can they in anyway refer back to the past. Tulving, however, seems perfectly aware of this problem, but the solution he offers remains unsatisfactory. Indeed, it is pointless to have recollection, that is the conscious experience of recollecting the past, stem from a process of *ecphoria*[1], that is from the interaction between episodic representation and present information. In this way, yet again, you find yourself trying to create the past from elements which do not contain it. Episodic representation, the information which triggers off the process of ecphoria and ecphoria itself are indeed all present

---

1 Tulving, E., 1984.

elements which do not in any way refer back to the past. Yet again, therefore, the latter is presupposed and not explained.

The situation does not seem to improve in the slightest if, rather than two separate representations, the episodic and the semantic, the existence of a single representation, or of a single memory system, is hypothesised[1]. According to this hypothesis the difference between recollection and knowledge does not reflect the existence of two separate representations, but of two different ways of dealing with the same information. Even though the idea that the past is contained in a memory trace has more or less been explicitly rejected, a satisfactory explanation of the relationship between consciousness and past is not provided. According to this view, the subjective experience of memory, that is the consciousness of an episode as past, is the result of a particular type of information processing. In short, there is one memory, but various ways of dealing with the information it contains. Here we find the same problems we found accepting the existence of an episodic trace. Indeed, information processing is in itself present and affects the present. So, either *pastness* is only a present characteristic of information processing, in which case it remains in the present, or else if it is already linked to the past by means of some special form of information processing, which is present, these theories presuppose what they are supposed to explain and the relationship with the past is in this way lost yet again. Besides, information processing, which determines the conscious experience of recollection, for example what Jacoby [2] calls the attributional or inferential process of pastness, is thought to be unconscious. Now, since an episode's being past, namely its pastness is a characteristic of consciousness, it is not at all clear what an unconscious inference of pastness actually is, nor how the result of this inference is supposed to get back to its natural habitat– consciousness.

Tulving evidently realised that in order to explain recollection and knowledge it was not enough to hypothesise a system of episodic memory and one of semantic memory. Relegated down there inside the two memory systems, recollection and knowledge indeed lose any possibility of

---

[1] See the position taken by Jacoby, L.L., Kelley, C.M., & Dywan, J., 1989; Roediger, H.I., & Blaxton, T:A., 1987.
[2] Jacoby, L.L., Kelley, C.M., & Dywan, J., 1989.

becoming conscious. In an attempt to resolve this problem, Tulving associated a particular type of consciousness with each memory system. Thus, episodic memory is associated with *autonoetic* consciousness, and semantic memory with *noetic* consciousness. What Tulving intended to do by associating consciousness to each memory system was to emphasise that episodic recollection is associated with the recollection of yourself in the past, autonoetic consciousness, while semantic knowledge is associated with awareness of knowing, noetic consciousness. However, Tulving's attempt fails. Indeed, it is quite clear that you obtain nothing by *adding* consciousness to episodic and semantic memory. In this way the separation between consciousness and recollection is not eliminated at all but, rather, it is established even more forcefully. For however much they may be associated and for however contiguous they may be, autonoetic consciousness and episodic memory will always remain separated by a void and any attempt at mutual interpenetration is nothing more than a figure of speech. Once their separation is affirmed, the two terms become unintelligible. Indeed, it is impossible to make sense of a consciousness that precedes and is distinct from its being consciousness of the past, nor is it possible to make sense of a past episode that precedes and is distinct from the consciousness of its being past. The same is obviously also true for noetic consciousness and its relationship with semantic memory.

So far we have established the impossibility of considering recollection the result of the preservation of the past in any memory trace whatsoever, be it physiological or psychological. We have also demonstrated that the past can exist only as the past of a present, of the present of a consciousness which transcends its own present to select an event down there, behind itself, where the event took place. You will object that we have got out of it all too easily because we have not taken into consideration the fact that past events always reveal their direct influence on the present. In other words, in order to understand the past it is necessary to start from the present of consciousness, you cannot, however, deny that the past directly exerts its influence on the present, without having to involve a consciousness to select it. If I have a coherent and reproducible idea of "chair" it is because my experience of that object has, so to speak, been condensed into one meaning, that of chair, which now enables me to recognise, name, use correctly, etc., that object which the whole linguistic community to which I belong calls by the same name. And so it seems permissible to assert the persistence and the influence of the past on the present without there being consciousness of that past, as I may not be conscious of any past event when I attribute a meaning to the chair. We will answer this objection, first of all by saying that "chair", as meaning, is devoid of any temporal attribute. As meaning, it does not refer one to the past, nor to the present or the future. Nor, furthermore, does the concept of chair belong to me exclusively, as, on the other hand, does "my" past. Indeed, it is precisely by virtue of its atemporal and impersonal nature that I can communicate this concept to others, regarding which they lay claim to my same rights. Only in the case of recollection, that is when I transcend the present to select "that chair" on which I sat this morning, is the concept of chair temporalised in the past and does it contribute to the fact that the past is not a shapeless mass but a world endowed with meaning. As regards the persistence of the past and its influence on the present, of which meaning can be seen as evidence, we have already seen how misleading it is to consider, other than metaphorically, the present as the effect of the influence of the past which continues. You will allow of course that meaning is in some way the effect of the past, but this does not in any way mean that the cause persists and continues to influence the present.

It is opportune to clarify this point once and for all because the idea that meaning is the result of the permanency of the past is at the base of the problems that current functionalist theories encounter when they attempt to come to terms with knowledge. These theories, in fact, prisoners of the illusion of immanence, consider knowledge, concepts, meanings, as "things" and presuppose that these things are contained in the form of representations of the world, somewhere between the brain and the mind. The quality as much as the quantity of these "things" may increase with experience or diminish to the point of disappearance after brain damage. If, for example, my knowledge of chair was at the beginning of my life limited to a rather simple concept, with time I have learnt to distinguish countless types of chairs, to classify them according to style, to their comfort, to their aesthetic value, to their functionality, etc. However, the knowledge of chair for many people who have undergone brain damage has more or less deteriorated or even disappeared. And so many patients when placed in front of the image of a chair are incapable of producing the name, they no longer seem to know what its use is etc. Is this enough to assert that the meaning of chair is in one's head or somewhere outside of consciousness in the form of representation, that is of a simulacrum of everything I know regarding chair?[1] We will limit ourselves here to only one consideration: in order for it to be true, the hypothesis that knowledge is based on the preservation of concepts and meanings represented within a trace, whether it belongs to the physical or psychological world, must satisfy at least one condition, namely that in the absence of representation no knowledge is possible, just as it is not possible to sell off shares if they have disappeared from the safe where they were kept or as it is not possible to buy beans for dinner if they have disappeared from the shelf of the shop that sold them. It is clear enough that this condition cannot be satisfied. If representation is the necessary condition for knowledge then every possible ontology of knowledge is excluded: knowledge is already given and the possibility of new meanings is excluded a priori. And yet the child grows and learns to attribute meaning to the undefined world which surrounds him at the beginning. And yet the grown man continues to learn new things and to modify the meaning of those that he already knows. You will say that all this takes place starting from simpler representations which experience modifies, sums up, and which become more complex. This resolves nothing if the representation, for however simple you choose to make it, is given at the beginning as a condition for knowledge. And nothing would be resolved by saying that the representation is formed at the first encounter with an unknown object which will be recognised subsequently by virtue of this representation which was formed at the first encounter. Indeed, either the object is *already* given a meaning at the first encounter, at which point representation becomes superfluous, or else, if the object encountered for the first time is not given any meaning, the representation of the object will also be devoid of meaning. It is unclear how, under these conditions, at a later encounter, the object can be recognised. What is ignored is that "knowledge", just like "recollection", does not mean making the object correspond with its simulacrum which represents it somewhere between the brain and the mind, but it means transcending an undefined and indecipherable world in order to give said object a possible meaning.

But it is not only the ontology of knowledge which proves that the notion of representation is superfluous as a theory of knowledge. It is well known, in fact, that patients who seem to have completely lost knowledge of a

---

[1] As it would probably take an entire book, we won't go into the criticism on the concept of representation which is central in a functionalist hypothesis of this kind. Hilary Putnam in *Representation and reality* (1991) gives solid detailed criticism of the functionalist theory of representation.

certain object do, however, under certain conditions, show that said knowledge is not at all lost. Some patients, for example, no longer know what a chair is, they are not able to name the image, indicate its use, recognise that chairs of different shapes have the same name in common and the same function, etc. And yet these same patients in their everyday lives interact absolutely normally with the object of which they are supposed to have lost every notion. They use the chair appropriately just as they use other objects which they also fail to recognise, do not know what to call, etc. Of course you might object that there are multiple representations of "chair" and that the ability to name, to recognise, to define, etc. refer to a different representation of chair from the one necessary to interact with the object "chair" on an everyday basis. In the case of patients who seem to have lost all information regarding chair, but continue to use chairs appropriately in their daily life, the first type of representation has been lost while the second remains. But, yet again, this interpretation does not much help comprehension, nor does it save the notion of representation. Multiplying the possible representations of an object by making each one of these correspond to a certain modality of knowledge is indeed equivalent to undermining the very idea of representation. Representation is by definition *something which stands for or in the place of* an object, be it physical or abstract. Harpagon represents all the salient characteristics of all possible misers and if he is chosen as a protagonist it is precisely because of the way he encompasses these distinctive features. Now, it becomes clear that by attributing a representation to each of the countless modalities through which an object manifests itself in the world, the unique relationship between the representation and the object represented is annulled. That which should be a relationship of many (the various manifestations of objects) to one (their representation), becomes a relationship of one (the object in its fixed manifestation) to one (its representation). But a one to one relationship between an object and its representation is a relationship of identity and not of representation. It is as though in order to describe a miser's traits, Molière had put all the misers of the world on stage. A one to one relationship excludes representation and leaves us facing the object alone and defenceless. Nor, on the other hand, would it help to assert that in patients who no longer know anything about chair, but who continue to use them appropriately, the representation has, so to speak, deteriorated, it continues to exist at a level which enables the use of the concrete object in everyday life, but it prevents symbolic knowledge. But a deteriorated representation is in itself complete representation, whose nature in no way differs from that of the representation which enabled more symbolic knowledge of the object. The additional attribute of deterioration only describes the relationship between two elements of the same nature. Yet again, therefore, in the game of the mirrors of multiple representations, the very idea of representation fades away and with it every possible role it has in knowledge. And yet, though orphan of representation, the object continues to exist *for me*. I can recognise it, play with it, if I close my eyes I can imagine it, I can even remember it in a certain place, I can love it, hate it, etc. In other words, even in the absence of representation, not only is knowledge of the object possible, but knowledge becomes infinite, or infinite ways of knowing the object are possible.

From what has been said so far it is clear that neither recollection nor knowledge can be the outcome of the preservation of the past or of meaning in a trace or in a representation. What conclusion can be drawn from this discussion? First of all that current theories about memory imply an insoluble contradiction which we described under the name of the paradox of the memory trace. However many experimental data may be collected, these theories will never be able to explain recollection as consciousness of the past because from the start they broke off any connection between consciousness and past, consigning the latter to a memory trace, to an episodic memory system or making it the result of an improbable unconscious inference of pastness. Once consciousness of the past has been separated from the past itself, the various theoretical attempts to reunite the past and consciousness are absolutely pointless. What is overlooked is that episodic memory and semantic memory, or the special type of information processing which generates recollection and knowledge, represent the *remembered* and the *known*. Remembered and known imply *he who remembers* and *he who knows*, that is a subject who takes the trouble to address the world in a certain way, that of recollection or that of knowledge. It is by virtue of he who remembers and of he who knows that the remembered and the known acquire meaning. However these theories make exactly the opposite true. In other words, a privileged position is assigned to the remembered and to the known while he who remembers and he who knows are passive and receive "information". We have already emphasised the absurdity of such a vision. If we choose to dwell on it yet again it is because it is so deeply rooted in current thought. Indeed, that of "information", or that of "information processing" is an ulterior paradox of which the paradox of the memory trace is none other than a reflection. Our psychic life, which coincides to a large extent with our conscious life, is thought to be the final result of the brain's information processing. A corollary to the idea is that any machine able to process information according to certain rules, those used by the brain for example, is able to function like a human being. This, then, is responsible for all the so-called research on "artificial intelligence". What is forgotten yet again is that information is such for consciousness, under no circumstances can it precede it as it is the result. When I say that the information "glass-on-the-table" is processed by my cognitive system to produce the perception of "glass-on-the-table", the information "glass-on-the-table" has already been given and the entire processing to which I submit it afterwards is only an act that I offer my consciousness. In other words, the information is such for whoever takes the trouble to consider it "information" and therefore cannot be the cause of anything whatsoever because by definition it is effect, the effect of a consciousness which considers it in its very being. With this it is not at all our intention to place any priority of consciousness over the phenomenon, that is over information. Indeed, we would not gain much by going from a realist's point of view to an idealist's. In both cases, in fact, an abstraction is privileged. Information in itself is an abstraction in as far as it needs consciousness to make it such. Alone it would disappear into nothing. Consciousness in itself is also abstract in as far as its ontological origin tends towards the phenomenon, or towards information if you like. The concrete is given only by the synthetic totality of which consciousness and information are nothing but moments. The concrete is man, or the subject in the concreteness of his existence. And it is from here that we must start to understand recollection, that is the concreteness of a way of being in the world of man. If you privilege information and its processing as the origin of psychic life, as happens in the theories that are based on information processing and relegate consciousness to the position of by-product of information processing, ignoring man *tout court*, you find yourself in another paradox. If information is given originally as *primus movens* of the whole affair, in order to distinguish man from amoeba you have to accept that the processing of the same information is different in man and in amoeba. The latter, faced with a glass of wine will contract or be indifferent while man will recognise it and drink it, if he feels like it, thanks to his special information processing which enables him to recognise the information "glass-of-wine" as such. Now, since neither man nor consciousness are involved in information processing, it is difficult to understand *who* it is that recognises the glass of wine as such and what the difference is between that which takes place in the cognitive system of an amoeba and that of a man. After having ignored man and consciousness, in these theories there is another problem, the problem of *who* is the author of the information processing. In the next chapter, we shall see that these theories, after having refuted consciousness by making recollection and knowledge stem from the memory trace, are forced into a new insoluble contradiction, that of presupposing a kind of *unconscious consciousness*.

CHAPTER 2

THE *HOMUNCULUS* FALLACY

1. MEMORY AND CONTROL SYSTEMS

The assumption that the past is preserved in a memory trace contains, as we have seen, a paradox in that the past is seen to derive from present elements, but how this happens is not explained. The past is thus assumed but not explained, and any possibility of understanding the nature of recollection is therefore lost. But the paradox of the memory trace is not the only problem with current theories on memory. According to these theories, in order for the recollection of a memory or of knowledge to be correct, that is for it to be the recollection of memory or information that we wanted to evoke, certain selection and verification mechanisms of the memory trace must be called into play. Depending on what the subject wants to remember, these mechanisms first make a selection from the various traces stored in the memory systems, and then check whether the result of the selection meets the conditions set by the recollection task. If these conditions are not met, due to contradictions between the selection result and verification criteria, the mechanisms in question continue to make new selections until a satisfactory choice is made, a choice which does not contradict the verification criteria and which also meets the demands of the recollection task. According to these theories, if, for example, I remember eating in a restaurant yesterday evening this is due to the fact that the trace "dinner in restaurant" has been selected from a host of other traces for example, "dinner at home", "dinner at a friend's", in accordance with the criteria and mechanisms which guarantee the selection of the correct memory. The most widespread explanation of confabulatory symptoms provides a good example of an interpretative application of this hypothesis.

Confabulation is a symptom which is sometimes found in amnesic patients and consists in involuntary and unconscious production of "false memories", that is the recollection of episodes which never actually happened, or which occurred in a different temporal-spatial context to that being referred to by the patient. For example, a patient who has been in hospital for several days may have the confabulatory memory of having done the shopping, or of having had dinner with the family the previous day. According to the hypothesis we have described, confabulation is the result of the dysfunctioning of memory monitoring mechanisms, that is of the selection and verification mechanisms of the memory trace[1]. The breakdown of these mechanisms is thought to impede the inhibition of inappropriate answers which are produced as confabulatory answers. If, for example, I want to remember what I did last night, according to the hypothesis in question memory monitoring mechanisms start searching among my memory traces and make a selection, the result of which is, let us suppose, "I had dinner at home". This is then checked in accordance with criteria of plausibility and coherence with other associated memories, for instance "last night I went out", and is then rejected since it does not correspond to these criteria. At this point the same mechanisms begin a new selection and check other possible memories until they find the appropriate memory, "last night I had dinner in a restaurant". If, however, the memory monitoring mechanisms are dysfunctional, "I had dinner at home" is accepted as appropriate and is produced as a confabulatory memory. So according to this reasoning, the possibility of recalling an appropriate episode or meaning requires the preliminary examination of various possible answers, followed by the inhibition of inappropriate answers. Now, this hypothesis has never clarified whether the monitoring processes of the memory act on a conscious, voluntary basis or whether they are outside consciousness and inaccessible to it[2].

Let us look at this problem more closely. Supposing the monitoring processes assigned to the selection and verification of information were conscious and voluntary, in that case their action would be manifest to

---

[1] Baddeley, A. & Wilson, B., 1986; Burgess, P.W., & Shallice, T., 1996; Conway, M.A., & Tacchi, P.C., 1996; Johnson, M.K., 1991; Moscovitch, M., 1989.
[2] Even though it is not explicitly stated, the same memory monitoring mechanisms seem to be considered conscious by Burgess and Shallice and unconscious by Conway and Tacchi.

reflexive analysis since they would be operations of consciousness. The subjective experience of reflection would, then, show me that every time I am engaged in a recollection task, I consciously carry out the operations of selection and verification attributed to monitoring mechanisms. In practice this would mean that while recalling I consciously select a memory, judge whether its contents meet the conditions of the recollection task I have set myself, reject it if they do not and begin a new selection; or accept it as a memory if it meets the conditions of the task. Reflexive analysis, however, demonstrates that this is not at all the case. If, for example, I try to recall what I did last Wednesday at five in the afternoon, what I consciously begin is a search operation of successive approximation. I will remember, for instance, that on Friday morning I gave a talk in such and such a place, that on Thursday afternoon I took the train to get to the city where I was going to give the talk and that on Wednesday afternoon at five o'clock I was trying to prepare the talk for Friday. In other words I operate a reconnaissance in my past, I move from memory to memory until I select one, the one which seems to best answer the question "what was I doing last Wednesday at five in the afternoon?" But each of these recollections *immediately* appears to my consciousness as *real*, that is as a past image of a certain subject in which I recognise myself and to which I am intimately tied by an ontological relationship which does not allow for doubt: I *was* that person who was preparing the talk, taking the train, speaking in public etc. Where I may hesitate is not on the content of my recollections, which can only present themselves apodeictically, but on the date: I may not be sure that it really was Wednesday or that it was five o'clock not six. The process of selection and verification of the memory that best answers the question I ask myself does not concern the veracity of the memory, which is already given and, one could say, emanates from the memory itself; it concerns the possibility of placing it correctly in the sequence of recollections which constitutes my thematized past. But what reflexive analysis shows me above all, is that during recollection I never come up with memories like those produced by patients who confabulate.

One patient of ours, for example, when asked what he had done the previous day would claim to have won a running race for which he was awarded a piece of meat which was placed on his right knee. When asked to give a definition of the word "synagogue" he would reply that it was something to do with physiotherapy[1]. Now according to the hypothesis, which sees memory and knowledge as the result of the verification and inhibition of inappropriate answers by special monitoring mechanisms, in order to be able to attribute the correct meaning to the word "synagogue" one would have to choose from different possible alternatives such as, let us say "a church", "a Jewish place of worship", "a type of fruit" or "something to do with physiotherapy". Only if one manages to inhibit all the inappropriate responses will "Jewish place of worship" be selected otherwise, as in the case of our patient, "something to do with physiotherapy" or any other answer could be given. This reasoning also implies that if, before his amnesia, the patient was asked what he had done the previous day, he would have consciously examined and rejected the possibility of having won a running race and being awarded a piece of meat which had been placed on his right knee, and would instead have produced the correct answer.

You could object that confabulations are often far more plausible than the examples given of the running race and the definition of "synagogue". In fact, most patients who confabulate produce confabulatory memories which cannot be distinguished from "real" memories by an interlocutor who does not know the patient's history and current situation. Here is an example. A patient of ours, MG, in hospital for a brain haemorrhage, while waiting for a CAT scan told the radiologist that he was in hospital because he had come to accompany a friend who had to be admitted to the neurology ward. Once they got to the ward, MG continued, the neurologist who was supposed to take care of his (non-existent) friend realised that there was something wrong with him too and so sent him for a CAT. The radiologist, who knew nothing of the situation, did not even suspect that at that moment MG was confabulating[2]. In this case too, however plausible and indistinguishable from a true memory MG's confabulation was, as demonstrated by the behaviour of the radiologist, one cannot consider it the result of the dysfunctioning of conscious selection and verification mechanisms. It is in fact difficult to imagine that on asking someone in hospital why he is there, this person, when answering, should consciously consider, among others, the possibility of being in hospital to accompany a friend.

---

[1] Dalla Barba, G., 1993.
[2] Dalla Barba, G., Boissé, M.-F., Bartolomeo, P., & Bachoud-Lévi, A.-C., 1997.

But even if that were the case, that is if recalling an episode or a meaning were possible due to conscious and voluntary inhibition of inappropriate answers, something which reflexive analysis leads us to exclude, it remains to be decided on what basis the correct answer is selected. One criterion could be that of plausibility. Less plausible answers are inhibited while the more plausible are accepted. But isn't plausibility itself a meaning which is attributed to a possible answer, in which case shouldn't plausibility also be subject to a process of verification like any other meaning? And shouldn't the criterion which I use to determine plausibility also be verified, and so on endlessly, like in a game of Chinese boxes? It is not worth arguing[1] that in recollection, the correct choice from various alternatives is based on the evaluation of the qualitative characteristics of information, for example, the amount of perceptual detail and the quantity and type of memories associated with the episode we want to recall. In fact, it is a question once again of *quis custodet custodes?* Who can assure me that when I remember meeting Paul the other evening, the bright red of his pullover is a perceptual detail which comes from my memory and not my imagination? Why should I grant these so-called perceptual details the status of veracity which I deny the memory itself? Similarly, who can assure me, for example, that the fact that in my memory Mary is with Paul is an "associated memory" which guarantees the veracity of the main one, that is the meeting with Paul, and not a confabulation? As you can see, there is no way of escaping this circularity.

The subjective experience of reflection thus leads us to exclude the notion that the processes of information selection and verification are voluntary and conscious. Are they then processes which work outside consciousness and which are inaccessible to it? But to accept the hypothesis of unconscious monitoring mechanisms means falling into what we shall call *the homunculus fallacy,* that is the contradiction of postulating the existence of a type of *unconscious consciousness,* that is of unconscious monitoring mechanisms endowed with intentionality which select, evaluate and reject false memories and provide *conscious consciousness* with only real memories. It is unclear on the basis of what theoretic assumption one can attribute intentionality to this kind of process. Since Brentano[2], intentionality has been a characteristic of consciousness and, as Husserl

---

[1]Johnson, M.K., 1988; Johnson, M.K., 1991; Johnson, M.K. & Raye, C.L., 1981.
[2]Brentano, F., 1874.

says[1], represents the need of consciousness to exist as consciousness *of* something. Attributing intentionality to an unconscious process, then, is equivalent to giving unconsciousness the attribute of being *subject*, that is attributing consciousness to the unconscious. Moreover, this unconscious consciousness is inaccessible to the real sense of consciousness. As in a game of Chinese boxes, one man would contain another man, a *homunculus* to be precise, endowed with a shady, inaccessible consciousness which is busy resolving problems like rejecting false memories and is ready to provide conscious consciousness with the result of this detailed selection. But let us examine this problem more closely and see why it is illusory to attribute intentionality to the unconscious.

2. THE HOMUNCULUS FALLACY

Let us first of all clarify what is meant by intentionality. I am conscious of this glass which is on the table. In other words I have perceptual consciousness of glass-on-the-table. I also perceive the glass from a certain angle, not only visual but, let us say, existential: it exists before me, it presents itself to me in a certain perspective and, as an object among other objects, it has a certain relationship with these. Here again, this relationship is not only spatial (proximity, distance, adherence etc.) but also functional, aesthetic etc. In short, the being of the glass-on-the-table is a certain specific and original being which my consciousness is at this moment selecting.

What can be deduced from this? If we were idealists we would say that the glass-on-the-table exists as "content" of my consciousness, which in some way absorbs it. If we were realists we would instead tend to consider the glass-on-the-table as an element of a reality which precedes and transcends consciousness, and to which consciousness can only adhere. And, in his cognitivist diversity, the realist would say that this information, "glass-on-the-table", entered my cognitive system where it underwent a series of computational transformations before becoming perceptual consciousness of the glass-on-the-table. Nevertheless if we free ourselves from what Sartre[2] called alimentary philosophies, that is from realism's

---

[1]Husserl, E., 1950.
[2]Sartre, J. P., 1939.

tendency to make the object "eat" the subject, and idealism's tendency to make the subject "eat" the object, we discover the true relationship between consciousness and world, between subject and object. These are born *together*. They are involved in a relationship where, although they retain their autonomy, neither can exist without the other. The result of this relationship between subject and object, between consciousness and world is intentionality, that is the need of consciousness to always be consciousness *of* something.

Intentionality then, as relationship between consciousness and world, is a basic characteristic of consciousness which has no "inside" but which defines itself by being "outside", intentionally oriented toward things. At this point we must ask whether intentionality can also be attributed by right to the unconscious. Searle[1], while rejecting functionalist positions, draws a distinction between consciousness and intentionality, maintaining that there can be non-intentional conscious states, for instance a sudden feeling of excitement, and unconscious intentional states, for example those beliefs which I am not thinking of at this moment but which determine my behaviour. But why should a sudden feeling of excitement be a state of non-intentional consciousness? Excitement, or its opposite, depression, *are* states of consciousness, as Searle calls them, on the same level as any other consciousness. Like any other state of consciousness, that of excitement or depression does not escape its own law, that is of being destined to come out of itself in order to come to terms with the thing, that world which it is trying to reach and which continues to escape it. Accepting the existence of non-intentional states of consciousness is the same as making consciousness coincide with the thing. Non-intentional consciousness is quite unthinkable because it would be consciousness deprived of its original essence, that is the negation of itself as "thing". One must not fall into the trap of thinking that *first* I am excited and *then* I am conscious of the glass-on-the-table, or that a sudden state of excitement *joins* my perception of the glass-on-the-table *from outside*. What one should say is that *in* a state of excitement I am aware of the glass-on-the-table. Mine is excited consciousness of the glass-on-the-table. Therefore once again there are no exceptions to the law of consciousness: all consciousness is intentional in that it must, by nature, be consciousness *of* something.

---

[1] Searle, J.R., 1983; Dennet, 1978, maintains that intentionality can be not only unconscious but can also be attributed to non-biologic systems such as the computer.

Searle maintains that the idea that consciousness must exist as consciousness *of something* neglects a fundamental distinction: "when I consciously experience anxiety, there is something which my experience is experience of, that is anxiety, but this sense of "of" is radically different from the "of" of Intentionality which appears, for instance, when I affirm that I am consciously afraid of snakes; since, in the case of anxiety, the experience of anxiety and the anxiety itself are identical, while fear of snakes is not identical to snakes"[1]. But in proposing this example Searle confuses the essential structure of a reflexive act with that of a non-reflexive act. He seems to ignore the fact that there are always two possible forms of existence for consciousness; non-reflexive consciousness, that which appears when "I am afraid of snakes" and reflexive consciousness, that is consciousness "of me-as-anxious". These are two different types of consciousness, but both are intentional. The trick Searle uses involves comparing two different degrees of consciousness. In the case of anxiety, he makes the example of reflexive or second degree consciousness; I am aware of being anxious. But first degree or non-reflexive consciousness is only anxiety, anxiety which opens onto the world like any consciousness, and like any consciousness it is intentional in that it is outside itself, as anxiety, towards the world. It is by no means true that "in the case of anxiety, the experience of anxiety and anxiety itself are identical". The anxiety which pervades me in this case is the object of my consciousness, which makes itself conscious *of* anxious consciousness. Without this second-degree reflexive act, which gives me a point of view on my consciousness, my anxiety *is* my consciousness without my being aware of it: I will anxiously drink from the glass-on-the-table without being able to avoid the intentionality of my consciousness which will be *anxious consciousness of the glass-on-the-table*. There is, then, no difference regarding the degree of intentionality between my consciousness of *fear of snakes* and my *consciousness of anxiety*. They are both intentional. The difference is that the former is non-reflexive consciousness while the second is reflexive consciousness, that is consciousness which makes anxious consciousness its intentional object.

If we then analyse the possibility maintained by Searle of unconscious intentional states, that is the so-called beliefs to which we fall victim without being conscious of it, it is clear that these supposed beliefs are not

---

[1] Searle, J.R., 1983. p.16

at all that unconscious background which Searle talks about, but they constitute consciousness itself. Searle says "I believe that my paternal grandfather never once left the American continent, but until now, I had never formulated or clearly examined this belief"[1]. What was this belief of Searle's before it became conscious? Searle maintains that it already existed in his unconscious in its intentional form of "my grandfather never left the American continent". This seems to be a rather rushed interpretation of the facts. Essentially Searle is saying that, in some way, the fact that his grandfather never left the American continent is something that he had always known, even if this thought has only now become conscious. If, then, it has always existed it must have been stored somewhere, and where or what is this place where thoughts are stored before becoming conscious, if not the unconscious? There is almost no need to emphasise the absurdity of such a hypothesis. Even if the unconscious does exist, who will believe that it contains pre-established thoughts and beliefs? This type of explanation, which has a long tradition in psychology, stems from the fact that spontaneity of consciousness is not accepted and thus is traced back to an "elsewhere", the unconscious, the cognitive system etc., where already formulated thoughts are believed to exist in a passive mode, in propositional form, which will then become conscious. What has not been seen is that such a hypothesis, in trying to trace the spontaneity of consciousness to another, unconscious location, only puts off the problem of the existence of beliefs and thought in general, a problem which sooner or later will have to be formulated. An unconscious and intentional thought or belief does not only present the paradox of passivity, that is of the existence of inactive intentional states, but it also implies another question: who, in this unconscious, believes, has believed and will continue to believe that Searle's grandfather never left the American continent? The problem of the existence of an unconscious subject who believes thus arises. We shall come back to this problem shortly. For the moment it is enough to emphasise how even if an unconscious subject were admissible, he or she would in turn have to draw his or her thoughts and beliefs from another "elsewhere", because if the spontaneity of consciousness is not accepted there is no reason to accept spontaneity of the unconscious. The attempt to trace the origins of spontaneity to an unconscious elsewhere is nothing but an absurd, naive attempt to free oneself from the anguish we feel assisting the unceasing *ex nihilo* creation of consciousness which we do not create

---

[1] Searle, J.R., 1983.

ourselves. You could object that consciousness of "grandfather-never-left-the-American-continent", however spontaneous we may consider it, is still coherent with a given fact, that is that Searle's grandfather never actually left the American continent. However we will have to ask ourselves where this consistency between consciousness and reality comes from. There is no need to resort to explanatory idols such as the existence of unconscious beliefs. Consciousness, as intentional consciousness of the world, can only be a perpetual synthesis of past and present consciousness. In short, it is not by resorting to mechanistic determinism, which claims consciousness comes from unconscious intentional states, that we will be able to understand spontaneous, intentional existence. Saying that consciousness is the synthesis of states of past consciousness with present consciousness does not mean tracing its origins to somewhere else, it simply means acknowledging to consciousness an existence *ex novo* in accordance with a certain synthetic form.

As an example of unconscious intentional states, that is of background, Searle gives that of Carter who formulates the intention of presenting himself as a candidate in the presidential elections of the United States. To be more precise, Searle maintains that "an intentional state does not determine its conditions of satisfaction and thus is not the state which is intertwined in a *Network* of other Intentional states and on the *Background* of pre-intentional practices and suppositions which in themselves are neither Intentional states nor parts of conditions of satisfaction of intentional states"[1]. In order to express his intention of presenting himself at the presidential elections, Carter has to know that the United States is a Republic, that there are regular presidential elections where two large parties are rivals in the race for presidency etc. Whoever presents himself as a candidate has to have the backing of his/her party, be actively supported by a large number of people and finally, in order to become president must be voted for by the majority of voters. Well, concludes Searle, even if none of these *states* has a direct link with Carter's intention to candidate himself, he could not form such a plan, that is "the intention of presenting himself for the American presidential elections", without such a *network* of intentional unconscious states. "One could say that his intention *makes reference* to certain other Intentional states, inasmuch as it can only reach the conditions of satisfaction it does, and consequently only be the intention

---

[1] Searle, J.R., 1983.

it is, because it is located in a Network which includes other beliefs and other desires. Besides, in every real life situation, beliefs and desires are only part of an even greater complex of other psychological states: there are subsidiary intentions such as hope, fear, anxiety and expectation, feelings of frustration and satisfaction. In short, what I call 'Network' is nothing other than this holistic network"[1]. What Searle wants to explain is that our acts are not fortuitous but presuppose a 'Network' of meanings which condition their realisation. "We can easily understand what someone's intention to become president is, but we cannot by any means understand the intention of becoming a cup of coffee or a mountain, because - among other reasons - we do not see how such an intention can be consistent with the Network"[2]. What is difficult to understand is how this network can exist and how it can be made up of unconscious intentional states. In fact, if we accept its existence we also have to face the problem of its origins. What is the nature of this unconscious and intentional Network? Even though he vigorously rejects every functionalist hypothesis, Searle seems to make a similar mistake to that which he accuses the functionalists of making. Like them, he resorts to the unconscious in order to explain consciousness. Searle's is not an unconscious made of information processing, but one of beliefs or meanings which condition conscious life as much as the functionalist unconscious does. But Searle's hypothesis is presented with exactly the same problem as is functionalism: that of explaining, once and for all, how man's conscious life can be the result of something which happens in the unconscious in accordance with rules fixed by consciousness, Searle's in this case. We shall come back to the illusiveness of considering consciousness as an "effect". For now it is enough to understand that unless its ontological origin is clarified, Searle's Network is nothing but a figure of speech. Actually there is no apparent reason to make reference to an unconscious intentional Network of meanings to explain the fact that formulating the intention of presenting oneself for presidential elections is plausible and comprehensible, while formulating the intention of becoming a piece of amethyst is not. As we have already said, consciousness cannot but be a perpetual synthesis of earlier states of consciousness.

My present consciousness is new consciousness which is born *ex nihilo* and does not resemble anything before it. But this does not mean that my

---

[1] Searle, J.R., 1983.
[2] Searle, J.R., 1983.

earlier states of consciousness are not synthetically represented in it. Soon I will leave the house to go to the cinema. This will happen, not because I have a sort of redeeming Network which allows me to do this but forbids me to leave the house to hunt a jaguar, but simply because my present consciousness is mundane consciousness of a being which is me, a being which carries around its past without any possibility of getting rid of it. There is, then, no Network of beliefs and meanings on one side *and* a consciousness which is determined by it on the other side. My consciousness *is* the network of the beliefs and meanings of which it is made up. Beliefs and meanings which are not in an unconscious *elsewhere* in a strange state of *active passivity*, that is in an oxymoron - meanings and beliefs whose origin as well as present state need explaining. In fact either they are passive in the unconscious and so have no way of influencing conscious life, or they are active, in which case, where their activity is supposed to stem from needs explaining. Carter's consciousness in formulating his intention of presenting himself at the presidential elections is such as it is, also because at a certain point in his life Carter became conscious of living in a country where there are presidents, presidential elections etc. His present intention is not the result of unconscious intentionality made up of unconscious beliefs, but is the present form of his present consciousness which implies, and is, the synthesis of all his earlier states of consciousness.

If I now take a cigarette to my lips and inhale the smoke, this does not happen as the result of a series of unconscious presuppositions. It is not because I have the unconscious and intentional belief that, for instance, "there are objects called cigarettes of a certain shape which serve a certain purpose, which are bad for your health but also give pleasure, which in order to smoke you must go through a series of movements which involve the contraction of certain arm muscles but not of others, and that each movement consumes a certain amount of energy which is reflected in the consumption of oxygen and carbon compounds etc." This is only one of the countless explanations which I can give for my act of smoking, or to put it another way, one of the possible ways my consciousness thematizes my act of smoking in order to assign it a meaning. Meanings and beliefs do not *precede* consciousness, if anything they *follow* it, that is they are possible thematizations of the world on behalf of consciousness. Consciousness itself has no need for meanings and beliefs which precede it and guide it out of the darkness of the unconscious. Consciousness *is* the synthetic combination of these meanings which, with a secondary operation, can become theses for consciousness which, in this case, ceases to *be them* in order to detach itself from them and make them object of its own thematization. In short, there may be a metaphysical problem in consciousness but there is definitely not an ontological problem: my present consciousness is *made up of* my earlier states of consciousness. We will see later, when our discussion leads us to the problem of temporality, what exactly is meant by this. For now it is enough to have clarified the impossibility of supposing the existence of an unconscious intentional world.

We have just seen that hypothesising the existence of intentional, unconscious beliefs involves the problem of supposing the existence of an unconscious subject who "believes" something (for example that Searle's grandfather never left the American continent). This unconscious subject, then, is supposed to reveal itself just when the conscious subject is ready to thematize this type of pre-packaged thought, stored in the frozen unconscious, together with the unconscious subject, passively waiting for consciousness to defrost it, as if by magic. This type of interpretation, which does not seem to deserve comment, is however worth analysing once and for all.

The first question to be asked clearly concerns the nature of the subject, this unconscious *who* that *believes*. A first objection could be raised at this point, and that is that in reality questioning the nature of an unconscious subject is the same as posing a false problem. In fact there is no need to presuppose an unconscious subjectivity as author of acts like believing or thinking. Beliefs and thoughts could be unconscious without needing to be the beliefs and thoughts *of* someone, that is of an unconscious subject. They would be kinds of pure representations which in themselves were complete and self-sufficient. In other words, that network of meanings which, according to Searle, "are in one's head".

Let us suppose that shortly I leave the office to go and buy cigarettes at the bar on the corner. According to the hypothesis in question, this project of mine is plausible inasmuch as a series of unconscious beliefs make it so. The belief, for instance, that there are shops that sell cigarettes, that these shops have certain opening hours compatible with the time I go to one of these to fulfil my objective, that I am a great consumer of cigarettes, and so on. Good. These beliefs, which make my objective possible, supposedly lie passively in the unconscious, waiting to intervene and guide my behaviour when necessary. Question: who informs them when it is their turn? How do they come out of their passive state to become active? You might say they are *activated*, as functionalist literature does. A group of representations or of neurons are activated in order to attain said goal. But, once again, *who* activates these representations? Certainly not my consciousness. The moment I go to buy my cigarettes my consciousness is pure, non-reflexive consciousness, consciousness without a subject, consciousness of-cigarettes-to-be-bought. They could be said to activate themselves, that is to pass from their passive state to an active one without the intervention of any external factor. But why them in particular? Why should only those beliefs which are useful to one's purpose be activated, and not others? You could object further that it is precisely the need to reach one's goal which activates them. But even if we accept this kind of reverse teleology, which in any case needs clarifying, who is it that goes and tells the beliefs necessary for the purpose that it is they, and not others, that are necessary? There could be said to be a system of beliefs which is in some way always active in the unconscious and ready to face the needs of the moment. But how could a system of beliefs which is in a state of continuous activation, in a sort of erethism work? In a similar condition there would be beliefs in contradiction with each other and in an equivalent state of activation. For example, the beliefs "there are shops that sell cigarettes" and "man has been on the moon" would be activated contemporarily. If both these beliefs are activated at the same time, who can assure me that halfway from the office to the bar I will not decide to go to the moon? This demonstrates, then, that a problem of priority among beliefs arises, dictated by the necessity of the moment. And this priority takes us back to the problem of selecting the appropriate beliefs; since this is not carried out by a conscious "who", the existence of an unconscious "who", author of this choice, must be presupposed.

So here we are, once again, struggling with the nature of a *who*, an unconscious subject who intentionally turns to an unconscious world made up of beliefs, meanings, thoughts, memories and so on. Who is this unconscious subject, this *homunculus* that lives in the shadow of the unconscious, master and origin of conscious life?

First of all it is plain to see that the unconscious *homunculus* is distinct from the object it intentionally addresses, beliefs, memories etc. In a certain sense then, we find the same relationship between the *homunculus* and the object it addresses as that which exists between consciousness and its object. In short, one could say that the *homunculus* is *conscious* of beliefs, of the meanings of the thoughts and memories it has to select, activate etc. But *what is the unconscious homunculus conscious* of? What is the nature of unconscious meanings, memories, beliefs? Let us go back to the case of memory, which is that which interests us most. In its work of selecting and checking memories, the *homunculus* deals with both true and false memories. Its task is that of selecting memories, *sending* the real ones to consciousness and rejecting the false ones. Now, it is obvious that if we accept such a hypothesis, we must also accept that the memories that the *homunculus* examines or, in functionalist terms, the information that the monitoring systems elaborate, must be already specified in syntactic-grammatical terms. Since no active role is attributed to consciousness, all that arrives there must already exist *first,* in the unconscious, in the form that it will have *afterwards* in consciousness. For example, our patient's confabulatory memory of "having won a running race" will be exactly the same in the unconscious, in a sort of state of inactivity, waiting to be evaluated by the *homunculus* as a possible memory. In this way the *homunculus* fallacy not only postulates the existence of an unconscious consciousness, that is, it is based on an oxymoron, but since this unconscious consciousness must have an object to turn to, it also postulates unconscious mnemonic activity already specified in syntactic-grammatical terms. In other words, as in a photocopy of conscious life, memories are found in exactly the same form in the unconscious, ready to be selected by our *homunculus* and *sent* to that kind of passive container which is thought to be consciousness.

It is easy to see how, here too, we fall into the paradox of the trace already discussed at length in the previous chapter. But we find ourselves facing another, equally relevant paradox in this case. That is, the hypothesis that unconscious representations which have already been specified in syntactic-grammatical terms may exist. Some even claim that this syntactic-grammatical specification takes root in the biological structure of the brain in the form of particular cell configurations or groups of nerve cells. It is well known that there is no biological evidence which would lead us to remotely suspect a situation of this sort. But the *passe-partout* answer always given by positivist science is "later on, when we have more data". It is clear, however, that even if perfect technology allowed us to unveil every secret of the brain, what we would find ourselves with would be a series of data declined in terms of cells, molecules, atoms or even subatomic particles, certainly not in terms of grammar and syntax. We may well have nuclear physics of the brain some day, but certainly not neurobiology of syntax. But the absurdity of such a hypothesis lies not so much in the non-demonstrability of its neurobiological aspect as in its seeing consciousness, once again, as originating from a sort of surrogate unconscious.

What has been gained with this operation? Absolutely nothing, since we find ourselves with an unconscious made up of the same elements we left in conscious life: on the one hand a subject with its baggage of intentionality, the *homunculus*, on the other a pre-fabricated unconscious world that the homunculus intentionally addresses. At this point it is clear that what we had invoked to *explain* conscious memory requires an explanation itself. In fact, if the existence of unconscious monitoring mechanisms, the *homunculus*, has been set as a condition to explain the conscious emergence of memory, the criteria in accordance with which these unconscious monitoring mechanisms are supposed to operate also need explaining. In other words, on the basis of what criteria does the *homunculus* distinguish a true memory from a one false? Memories and information that the *homunculus* selects do not come from *its* memory, but from that of the subject which contains them. On the basis of what criterion does it discern a true memory from a false one, or correct information from false information, since these are memories and information which come from *another person's memory*? Certainly the *homunculus* could be seen as accurate witness and infallible annotator of the whole life of the subject it works for. In fact, the life of the subject coincides with its own in a way, since it remains locked in the unconscious of the subject at whose service it is. But if the life of the subject coincides with its own, its memory and that of the conscious subject also coincide. And if these coincide, wouldn't the *homunculus* also need its own unconscious *homunculus* to help it distinguish real memories from false ones? The game of Chinese boxes continues and what we are left with is only a *reductio ad infinitum* clearly of no explanatory value.

3. THE FOUNDATIONS OF CONSCIOUSNESS

a. The problem of the foundations of consciousness

The discussion of the problems we have encountered so far has led us to reject any hypothesis which considers memory as the result of events which take place outside of consciousness. What we have indicated as the paradox of the memory trace has shown us that theories which see memory as stemming from the preservation of events inside physical or functional traces in fact presuppose what they are supposed to explain. The past cannot be contained inside memory traces as they represent only present modifications of a system and their activation cannot, in any way, explain how in the phenomenal experience of memory, the object remembered presents itself to consciousness as past. It is precisely in present consciousness that the past should be looked for as a meaning or as consciousness' original way of addressing the world. Without consciousness, which transcends the present in order to go and look for an event down there in the past where it happened, no memory is possible and the traces which events leave on the physical world, the brain included, remain as signs which no longer send us back to the past, but present signs without any symbolic value.

But the paradox of the memory trace is not the only failure of the attempt to find the origins of conscious memory in the unconscious. What we have described as the *homunculus* fallacy, that is the attribution of intentionality to unconscious processes and therefore the attribution of the capacity of being subject to the unconscious, contains some obstacles which can by no means be considered insignificant. This type of hypothesis is not only absurd in assuming that conscious consciousness is supposedly the result of a sort of unconscious consciousness endowed with intentionality, but also in endlessly deferring the understanding of memory phenomena. We have in fact seen that by accepting the *homunculus* fallacy we are obliged to a *reductio ad infinitum* where every unconscious subject, every *homunculus*, leads to another. The problem of understanding human phenomena is thus deferred to another *anthropos,* to that unconscious *homunculus* of which we have so far seen the logical absurdity. It seems then that memory cannot be seen to originate in the unconscious, and if consciousness is not taken as the point of departure, there is no way that memory can be understood.

Memory, we have said, is a particular type of consciousness, not reducible or deferrable to any elsewhere. It is clear that such an affirmation requires close examination, above all as regards the nature of consciousness. So far we have talked about consciousness without really clarifying what we mean by this term. We shall do so shortly, but not immediately. For now it is enough for us to consider consciousness in the most naive way possible, making it correspond to what direct experience of the world reveals to us. Put in this way, conscious memory is nothing other than the phenomenal experience of remembering, that is of being conscious of something as past. Yesterday's dinner with Anne, my last holidays at the seaside, the unexpected meeting with Paul, all these present themselves to consciousness as past events, and the phenomenal experience which characterises them is a precise experience which cannot be confused with other conscious experiences such as that of imagination or perception.

Before tackling a study of consciousness which will take us beyond the temporary definition we have just given, we should clarify, whatever the nature of consciousness, the problem of its foundations. In other words, can consciousness be based on, that is explained by unconscious structures? On the one hand it is tempting to answer in the affirmative, that is to accept a biological or physical nature of consciousness: after all consciousness is an object of the world and so, like any other object, should not escape explanations of mechanistic determinism. If from the top of a tower I enjoy a view of the spring countryside and the hills over there in the distance, this is because the structure of the tower enables me to do so. Not only, but the view I consciously enjoy is also determined by a series of biological events which go from the projection of the countryside and the hills onto a particular area of my retina and the activation of specific nerve circuits. But such an explanation of consciousness seems not only simplistic but once again, as we shall see, it also contains a paradox, that of the anthropomorphization of the unconscious. In reality, neither analysing the structure of the tower nor that of the retina and the nervous system will lead us to an explanation of my conscious vision of the countryside and the hills in the background. The tower, the retina and the brain are perhaps necessary to enjoy the view, but they are certainly not sufficient or of any use in explaining it. For the tower, the retina, the brain or any other non-conscious element to be able to explain consciousness, it must be assumed that these elements are endowed with an intentional finality which determines conscious vision. But in this way the causal chain is by no means exhausted, rather it becomes stronger and, at this point, where these unconscious elements get their intentional finalising force needs to be explained. As you can see, we find ourselves with the same contradictions we encountered in the *homunculus* fallacy. Once again we are confronted with an unconscious *anthropos* which leads to another *anthropos,* and so on. The anthropomorphization of the unconscious does nothing but delay the problem of consciousness, it does not resolve it. It is not due to the fact that the countryside and the hills are projected onto a particular area of my retina that I can see them distinctly. If anything, you could say that the particular part of the retina which is called macula, is the area where objects perceived in the far distance are most frequently projected[1]. It is not because I am on top of the tower that I can see the countryside, but the tower is the place from which I have the visual experience of the countryside. The study of the structure of the retina and the tower will never explain my visual experience. And it is not because for the moment we do not have sufficient data, though we cannot exclude the fact that one day we might do - as scientists are forever telling us. This type of answer might be appropriate if the problem were, for example, that of building a tank out of tissue paper: for the moment we do not have tissue paper that is strong enough to resist anti-tank bombs but we cannot exclude the fact that one day we might. But accumulating data on the retina, the brain or the tower, however important these operations may be, means investigating *something else*, not consciousness. And for however much data is accumulated, it will then be necessary to explain how these data can explain consciousness. In order to do this there is no other way but subterfuge: the anthropomorphization of these data, that is pretending that consciousness is in reality unconscious, something other than what it really is. This type of subterfuge is somewhat in vogue in present-day thought. We shall look at three examples of this in detail showing how, once the subterfuge is uncovered, the attempts to make consciousness an unconscious entity are bound to fail.

b. The neurobiological anthropomorphization of the unconscious

One of the most characteristic ways of tracing consciousness back to the unconscious is through what we shall call neurobiological substantialism,

---

[1] Merleau-Ponty, M., 1942.

which consists in reducing consciousness to a product of the activity of a part of the nervous system, the brain. The relationship of identity between consciousness and the brain is the thesis of neurobiological substantialism. For the substantialists, consciousness is nothing other than the effect of what a group of specialized cells, neurons, are able to do. In other words, consciousness *is* what the brain does. To understand what consciousness is, it is enough to be able to describe the physiological structure of the brain as exhaustively as possible. When the question is posed in these terms it is not surprising if an optimism bordering on euphoria is rife among scientists regarding the possibility of revealing the *secret* of consciousness which, thus considered, has finally become an approachable problem for positivist science. This unjustified optimism is well described by Crick: "No longer need one spend time attempting to understand the far-fetched speculations of physicists, nor endure the tedium of philosophers perpetually disagreeing with each other. Consciousness is now largely a scientific problem. It is not impossible that, with a little luck, we may glimpse the outline of the solution before the end of the century."[1]. These few words, which so well summarise the intolerance for any reflection that is not purely experimental, would move one if they were merely fruit of ingenuity. But they are words which hide the subterfuge of the anthropomorphization of the brain, that is of the surreptitious identification of the brain with consciousness. Crick is certainly aware that a relationship of identity between brain and consciousness immediately poses the problem of the origin of this relationship and of how it evolves. But like all materialists, Crick is careful to avoid this problem. After all, taking a relationship of identity of this sort literally not only implies that through the brain we will discover consciousness, but also the contrary, that consciousness can explain the brain as much as the brain can explain consciousness since a relationship of identity is, by definition, symmetrical. The dualism between consciousness and brain is not, by any means, resolved in this way, it is only denied on a purely formal level by making one of the two terms coincide with the other. Why on earth consciousness should annul itself in the brain needs to be explained once and for all, or else the great discovery predicted for the end of the century (the twentith), the secret of consciousness, will, at best, reveal the secrets of the brain, but not those of consciousness.

---

[1] Crick, F., 1996. p.486. See also Crick, F., 1993; Crick, F & Koch, C., 1990.

But Crick's integral experimentalism is not the only form of neurobiological substantialism. There are many which support this view on a purely theoretical level. It is hardly worth mentioning that the result is no different. Let us take Searle's[1] position into consideration. According to his thesis, which he called "biologic naturalism", mental states have the same reality as other biological phenomena, such as photosynthesis, cell reproduction or digestion. Mental states are *caused* by operations of the brain and *realised in* the structure of the brain, just as the liquidity of water is caused by its molecular state and realised in its molecular structure. Searle seems to hurriedly maintain a causalism which, however, cannot be taken for granted. The liquidity of water -he maintains-, just like consciousness, digestion, photosynthesis or cell reproduction, is caused by elements which precede it in the causal chain and takes form in the structure which regulates the relationship among these elements. But the molecular structure of water does not, by any means, reveal its *liquidity*. If I look for its chemical structure, what I find is a certain relationship between pieces of matter which are called atoms, and I express this relationship with a conventional symbol: H_2O. In H_2O there is no *liquidity,* just as there is no solidity or gaseous state. In order for H_2O to be liquid, something which has nothing whatsoever to do with its molecular structure is required. That is, H_2O needs to be found at a certain temperature and under certain pressure conditions. But even if the conditions of temperature and pressure are met, we still have not discovered the liquidity of water. In order for water to be liquid, consciousness, above all Searle's, must notice it. Without consciousness bothering to discover water *as liquid*, water, assuming its chemical structure is known, is nothing but H_2O. If its chemical structure is unknown, water is simply *water*, that *thing* we are all familiar with and which we know has certain characteristics, among these liquidity, a term we use to distinguish one state of matter from another. As for temperature and pressure, they only become significant when a consciousness which knows a bit of physics recognises that these two variables are essential in order for water to be liquid. In other words, the molecular structure of water is neither necessary nor sufficient for its liquidity. It is not necessary as water can be considered to be liquid *before,* and quite apart from, any knowledge of its molecular structure. It is not sufficient since even if by some absurdity there were someone in the universe who knew the molecular structure of water *before* knowing that it was liquid, from the former he could never derive the

---

[1] Searle, J.R., 1983. See also Churchland, P.S., 1986;. Churchland, P.S., 1988.

latter. Searle's causality could, in reality, be easily turned upside down. It could be maintained that it is the molecular structure of water that is caused by, and realised in its liquidity. It is because water is liquid that it has a certain molecular structure. But if we decide, once and for all, to leave aside the circularity of causal thought, it is clear that neither the liquidity of water nor its structure can lay claim to priority over the other. They both come into being as meanings, that is as objects which present themselves to consciousness in accordance with different points of view. Water is both liquid and H_2O without one of these being cause of the other, and water cannot be both things contemporaneously in consciousness. The impossibility of contemporaneously determining the position and the speed of a particle, demonstrated by Heisemberg, is not only an abstract, that is mathematical, reality. It is a reality reflected in the concreteness of consciousness which, since it must by nature be consciousness *of* something, cannot be this in the form of number two. But we shall look at this problem later on.

Liquidity like photosynthesis, digestion and cell reproduction (which we shall not discuss here but for which the same arguments used for liquidity stand) are used by Searle as metaphors of consciousness. Like these, consciousness is thought to be *caused* by and realised in an underlying structure, the brain. Let us return to the brain then. Searle maintains, for example, that visual experience is caused by the functioning of the brain, which responds to external optical stimulation of the visual system, and takes form in the structure of the brain. And likewise for all mental states. For Searle, intentional mental states, that is consciousness, are in the brain and will be perfectly explainable when we have a sufficiently perfected science of the brain. A science of the brain which, for Searle, will be radically different from the present one, just as quantum mechanics is different from Newtonian mechanics. Searle's biological naturalism is an attempt to get rid of the mind-body dualism once and for all. However the problem cannot be resolved by forcing consciousness into the brain, as Searle does.

Let us take the example of visual experience once again. Searle maintains that this is nothing but the effect of a sequence of operations carried out in certain structures of the nervous system which start off in the retina and finish up in the cortex of the occipital lobe. If I look at this cup of tea on the table and have a visual experience of cup-of-tea-on-the-table, this happens because a series of events between the retina and occipital cortex take place. We must, then, deduce that every time this sequence of events takes place I will have a visual experience of cup-of-tea-on-the-table. What is more, every time the cup-of-tea-on-the-table enters my visual field, this series of events will take place and produce the same visual experience as an effect. It is plain that this is clearly not the way things work. In fact, the sequence of events which, according to Searle, produce visual experience can take place without producing any visual experience. For example, the cup-of-tea-on-the-table is in my visual field at this present moment but I have no visual experience of it because I am in deep thought about the film I saw last night. In other words, the cup is in my visual field and is producing that whole series of events which Searle talks about, but I do not *see* it, in the sense that at this moment my consciousness is consciousness of film-I-saw-yesterday, not of cup-of-tea-on-the-table. But as well as looking at it without *seeing* it, I can have endless *visual experiences* of that cup: in fact I can see it and hate it, love it, be afraid or fond of it etc. Besides, every vision I have of that cup will be *new* in that it will be radically different from any earlier visual experience of that object. All these possible visual experiences of cup have something in common, that is the activation of visual paths, that is cerebral structures which, according to Searle, cause and contain the visual experience. It is not at all clear how the same sequence of events can *cause* an infinite series of different conscious experiences, and it is pointless affirming a priori that different physical states produce different conscious experiences[1].

You could object that, in reality, the nervous events which bring about the different visual experiences are not identical, but radically different. If they seem identical it is only because we do not yet have a science of the brain capable of revealing the substantial differences which distinguish one state from another. In short, we need that revolution in the neurosciences which should take us from a Newtonian science of the brain to a quantum neuroscience. But what does such an objection mean if not a proposal of *solutio ad infinitum?* In reality it is nothing other than positivism's classic answer: "the solution will come later, when we have more data". The data do not exist, but will in the future, while in the present there is no sign of a science capable of affirming an identity between nervous events and mental events. A substantial part of the cognitive neurosciences has slipped into the

---

[1] Chalmers, D.I., 1995.

cul de sac of believing that the problem of the mind and of the relationship between body and mind is only a question of accumulating data. But accumulating data means "preferring the accidental to the essential, the contingent to the necessary", as Sartre[1] points out. It means not realising that it is "impossible to reach the essential by limiting oneself to accumulating accidental elements, just as it is impossible to reach one by indefinitely adding numbers to the right of 0.99".

Despite the optimism and continual reference to the enormous successes of the neurosciences, in its present state, knowledge about the functioning of the brain is little and fragmentary. But even supposing that one day an infinitely more perfect science of the brain will exist, it is unclear how such a science will ever prove Searle, or anyone who maintains that there is an identity between consciousness and nervous mechanisms, right. The terms in which a hypothetical perfect science of the brain would be declined could effectively only be biological, molecular, atomic, subatomic etc, depending on the degree of power that that science has to analyse the infinitely small. And then? Even when it is discovered that the thirst I feel at this moment corresponds to a certain molecular state of the brain or even a certain state of the subatomic particles of which it is composed, my present thirst is not *explained*. What I observe will be a certain physical-chemical state of the brain, not *my thirst*. In other words, the greatest result we can expect from a hypothetical perfect science of the brain is a relationship of correspondence: a certain "mental state" corresponds to a certain state of the brain. For example my visual experience corresponds, with a certain statistical probability, to a series of physiological phenomena between the retina and the occipital cortex, and that is that. It is clear enough that this relationship of correspondence, far from being an explanation of conscious states, is in itself in need of explanation. In fact, what should be explained is how my consciousness of cup-of-tea-on-the-table is both caused and realised by those same nervous mechanisms which that new science of the brain predicted by the materialists should explain. In short, either the where and how of this miracle, that is the passage from a physical to a mental state, is explained, or else any claim of identity between the physical and mental will remain only a sleight of hand without logic, made up to solve a problem, that of the relationship between mind and body, whose identity is presupposed but certainly not explained.

---

[1] Sartre, J.P., 1938.

What has been ignored is that an *explanation* of mental states, or an explanation of consciousness, cannot in any way go from down to up, from the nerve towards consciousness. The nerve, the neuron and its relations with the other nerves and neurons are substances which must be described in themselves and cannot in any way be the basis of a meaning or any other "mental state" or consciousness. Indeed the opposite is the case. The functioning of the nervous system, or what are considered the psychological or computational conditions on which the historic and ontological development of consciousness is thought to depend, are merely a performance that consciousness offers itself. Consciousness is not an effect of cerebral functioning. The brain, like the body and the soul, is not, in itself, the basis of any meaning and thus has no sense if not in relation to a consciousness which selects it. The claim that everything happens in the brain does not do away with the dualism which neurobiological substantialism wants to get rid of. If anything it reaffirms it, since the passage from neurobiology to the intentional conscious act is not explained. In actual fact, the dualism between mind (soul) and body is both a fact and a false problem. A fact because *de facto* consciousness and body are conceivable only when seen as distinct. But a false problem in that both appear distinct but in the unity of consciousness which perceives them as such, just as an apple and a pear appear as different within the unity of consciousness. In short, there is no doubt that there is a relationship of correspondence between consciousness and the physical world. But this does not mean that consciousness does not distinguish itself, or that it can be explained by physics or biology; in this sense dualism is a fact, and as such cannot be negated. Dualism is the problem of consciousness when it thematizes the body as the probable origin of itself, not of the brain. The performance that consciousness offers itself is none other than the representation of what it is. In short, there is no need to make consciousness the effect of causal processes which occur on a biological level. Nor is it necessary to fall into an animistic dualism which sees body and spirit as separate entities. It is rather a question of inseparable entities, but not because one is based in the other, consciousness in the body or brain, or vice versa, the brain as mere noumenon based in consciousness. Consciousness comes into the world *with* a body and, with it, dies. Its biological basis can go no further. Consciousness does not inhabit the body or brain, which are nothing other than meanings, constructions which consciousness offers itself, just as body and brain are not *causes* of which consciousness is the effect. In other words, consciousness does not correspond to either brain or body, nor does it use them in a sort of inconclusive circularity as instruments in making itself possible. Consciousness simply *is* the body or the brain until these become objects of thematization for consciousness. Consciousness which *looks at* the body or brain is consciousness which ceases to be what it is in order to become conscious of what it is not. It is not a question of maintaining a dualism, but simply of saying that any biological or functional explanation of consciousness is nothing other than a certain form which consciousness itself assumes, but from which it will never be able to draw a relationship of causality. Indeed, consciousness will never be considered the effect of any cause for the simple reason that it is consciousness itself which forms the relationship between cause and effect. But then how can we explain that certain events follow others in accordance with a relationship of causality in which consciousness is implicated as the effect of a definite cause? Indeed what can be said about the alteration or even the loss of consciousness which is found in certain cerebral pathologies? For example, the hallucination which follows the consumption of substances or drugs which act upon the brain, or the loss of consciousness which occurs following a cranial trauma; are these not perhaps proof of the fact that consciousness depends on the brain and that cerebral events in some way determine and thus, in the final analysis, are at the base of it?

It is well known that intense pain, whether physical or psychological, can lead to loss of consciousness. Let us suppose that while I am crossing the road, a six-wheeled lorry drives over my feet and crushes them, and that I lose consciousness as a result of the pain this provokes. Let us also suppose that I do not know about the existence or the functioning of the nervous system. When I regain consciousness, following causal logic I will say that my loss of consciousness was caused by the fact that my feet were crushed by a six-wheeled lorry which drove over them. And, still following the same logic I will conclude that my consciousness is the effect of what happens in my feet. In short, if this course of reasoning is followed, my feet and my brain have exactly the same rights to be seen as the *cause* of my consciousness. Actually, my feet, in the case of the lorry, like the brain in neurobiological substantialism or the cognitive system in functionalism with all its variants, are nothing but meanings which consciousness offers itself and is forced to use to give meaning to itself and the world. A world which is radically distinct from it but of which it can become a part, object among objects, when it steps back to look at itself, to make itself the object of its own knowledge. In short, causal thought, in which consciousness in some of its modes is involved, can lead to the misleading conclusion that it itself is the effect of some cause. What should actually be said is that consciousness is born together with its world, a world of which the brain, seen as meaning, is also a part, just as every other object of the world is meaning for consciousness. Making consciousness or mental states correspond with the brain, as neurobiological substantialism would have it, or with the computational level as the functionalists would, or with any other "thing" means negating consciousness, as we shall see in the next chapter. Indeed consciousness is defined, first of all, as the negation of every identity of its own with any "object" of the world. Being conscious of this chair means first of all being conscious *of-not-being-chair*. Just as being conscious of the brain is in the first place negation of identity with the brain, that is consciousness *of-not-being-brain*.

However, the temptation of resorting to the apodeicticity of the causal schema is quite widespread in scientific thought. One cannot help thinking of that famous anecdote, whose author, like that of all such anecdotes, is unknown. It is about a psychologist who studied the behaviour of fleas. After training one to jump on verbal command, he cut its legs off. After this operation the flea no longer jumped on verbal command. From this experiment the psychologist concluded that the flea's hearing apparatus lay in its feet. Modern cognitive sciences do not seem to have moved an inch from this psychologist's logical paradigm. Anti-Cartesianism is so widespread, explicit and exaggerated that it actually makes one suspect the almost obsessive desire of pineal gland. Descartes' pineal gland in fact serves the same function as other explanatory idols in cognitive science and modern neurobiology. "It is the soul that sees, not the eye", Descartes said[1]. And what is the soul if not the neurobiological substantialists' anthropomorphization of the brain or the functionalists' cognitive processes? Damasio[2], who, after all, dedicated a whole book to "Decartes' Error", seems to be more of a royalist than the king, more Cartesian than Descartes when he maintains that everything lies in the brain. Dennet[3], another anti-Cartesian, writes a voluminous book to explain that consciousness is not in any part of the brain but is everywhere: who could be more Cartesian than him? And who could be more of a Cartesian dualist

---

[1] Descartes, R., 1637.
[2] Damasio, A.R., 1994.
[3] Dennet, D.C., 1991; Dennet, D.C., & Kinsbourne, M., 1992.

than Changeux[1] and his "Neuronal Man", a being without a spirit in which consciousness "emerges" like an iceberg which emerges from the water; or Edelman who sees consciousness as groups of cells, selected by evolution and integrated by reentring circuits[2]? Isn't maintaining that consciousness is somewhere, or everywhere, doing exactly what Descartes did, that is passing from a dualism of fact, that of consciousness when it thematizes the mind-body problem, to a dualism of substances, that is setting the physical world against a part of it, the brain, as seat of consciousness?

However much effort is made to push consciousness into a neurobiological or cognitive elsewhere, it continues to come out of these places, continually negating its being identifiable with anything but itself. All attempts to negate mind-body dualism only serve to re-affirm it with greater vigour. Maintaining identity between consciousness and the brain is not enough, it also needs to be proven. But the more effort is made to prove this identity, the more it recedes, opening a greater and greater void between consciousness and its explanation: the brain. In actual fact, either we give up the misguided attempt of declining consciousness using the rules of a language which is not suitable for describing it, or we will have to resign ourselves to using explanatory idols such as the structure of the brain, a form of anthropomorphization of the unconscious which, far from explaining consciousness, presupposes it. In this way we agree with Merleau-Ponty[3] when he says "since the physical world and an organism cannot be thought of as anything but objects of consciousness or as meanings, the problem of relationship between consciousness and the physical or organic "conditions" exists only on a level of confused thought which grasps onto abstractions, while it would be dissolved into the truth in which, in its original form, only the relationship between the epistemological subject and its object takes place".

The anthropomorphization of the brain in neurobiological substantialism is unintelligible since it starts from a relationship of identity which is affirmed *a priori* but not proved. But even if we were to accept such an identity, ignoring the theoretical paradoxes it contains, we would be faced with still other problems. By choosing the brain as a metaphor, neurobiological substantialism, which attacks consciousness in the name of

---

[1]Changeux, J.P., 1983.
[2]Edelman, G.M.; 1987; Edelman, G.M., 1989; Edelman, G.M., 1992.
[3]Merleau-Ponty, M., 1942.

science, in actual fact contradicts "the Science" of which it is champion. Furthermore, neurobiological substantialism, which proposes to explain consciousness through the study of the brain, places itself directly on an antiscientific level. The brain is only an arbitrarily chosen metaphor of consciousness, lacking in any scientific content. Indeed there is no experiment which proves that the isolated brain is capable of doing anything. Of course an experiment of this sort is unthinkable: separating the brain from the body means decreeing its death. In order for the brain to work it must be able to receive external signals through sensory routes, and in turn be able to transmit signals through the body. If, then, the brain cannot be isolated from the body without the death of both, it is not clear why the brain should be chosen as the Cartesian seat of consciousness. In reality we should give up, once and for all, considering the nervous system, for instance, as inherently "superior" to the sexual system. In the functioning of an organism, it is not possible to separate and therefore to subordinate one with respect to the other. Normal sexual life is integrated in the behavioural whole. The type of cerebral lesions which affect cognitive functions can also bring about profound changes in sexuality, from a drop in sexual love to a purely physical and uninhibited sexuality to its complete abolition. On the other hand extra-cerebral pathologies can, in turn, bring about profound changes in cognitive functions and consciousness. Certain chronic ingravescent diseases, for example, involve quite serious symptoms of depression accompanied by problems in cognitive functions such as memory and attention. The amputation of a limb brings about a radical change in a person's interaction with the world, which is directly reflected in the structure of meaning which the amputated person attributes to his surrounding environment. In short, the biological significance of behaviour is not distinguishable only on the basis of the organs it makes use of, and cannot be expressed in the language of anatomy or physiology. The brain as seat of consciousness is an unusable metaphor since the brain necessarily refers one back to the body, from which it cannot be separated.

But what is the body of which the brain is a part? You could say that the body is characterised by in some way being double. Indeed, on the one hand I *am* my body without being directly aware of it. My body in some way coincides with that being which I am, and which inhabits the world. It is the very meaning of my being in the world which can only come about through this body, of which I have absolutely no possibility of not being. But I am not conscious of this body. When my body moves in space with complex, deliberate movements, as, for instance, when I carry out the necessary motions to send the ball back over the net in a game of tennis, my consciousness is not consciousness of my body which moves in space, but rather of the tennis-ball-which-must-be-hit. In this case my body is outside the thematic field of my consciousness even though I am that body which moves in space to send the ball back over the net. Likewise, when I think or when I talk, I am not aware of being a body which thinks and talks due to the creation of certain conditions in the body itself. I simply think and talk, and my consciousness is totally absorbed by this activity[1]. But if I turn my attention directly to my body, this comes into being as the object of my consciousness[2]. If first I was my body without being conscious of it, now I am conscious of my body while no longer being my body. First I was it, now that my body is thesis for my consciousness, I perceive it with astonishment as something extraneous, an object among objects. First I was my right arm carrying out the motions needed to send the ball back over the net, now that I look at it and ask myself about it, my right arm is mine and that is that, just as that packet of cigarettes on the table is mine. Of course I am linked to my arm by profound solidarity, which does not exist in the case of the packet of cigarettes, and indeed there is a sort of giddiness in consciousness of the body because my body is, at the same time, my being in the world and an object of the world which is outside and extraneous to me, just like all the other objects in the world. In other words, with consciousness of my body I am confronted with the paradox of not being that body which, however, I am, or of being that body which I am not. But once I have overcome the giddiness which this discovery generates in me, the body of which I am conscious remains a body and nothing else, an object of the world, just like the other objects and bodies which populate the world in which I am immersed.

The body, as an object among objects refers one back to the world then, that is to the concrete combination of things which make up the environment that surrounds me. And this reified body is the body which science studies. But the body which science assumes as the object of study, like other objects of the world and which, according to substantialists, is the seat of consciousness, appears as such only to a consciousness which addresses it. In other words the body, like any other object of the world,

---

[1] Wittgenstein, L., 1953.
[2] Merleau-Ponty, M., 1945.

does not exist *per se*, but exists for a consciousness which addresses it. Only when my consciousness is consciousness of body or brain do body and brain come into being as meanings, just as a chair begins to exist only when I bother to select it in some way: by looking at it, thinking of it, imagining it etc. What does this mean? That it is absolutely impossible to establish a priority of the body over consciousness, since the body comes into existence as such only when consciousness notices it. As you can see, neurobiological substantialism, curbed by a causalism which is far too easy to reject, falls into the absurdity of a causal chain of its own creation. Moreover, the starting hypothesis of substantialism, already undermined at its origin by an assertion of identity between consciousness and brain which is not proven, proposes to explain consciousness with the functioning of a small part of the human body, certain areas of the brain. But as we have seen, the brain alone can do nothing since it is not theoretically or experimentally separable from the body. The body, in turn, and in particular the body as the object of science, is nothing other than an object among objects, an element of the world which, just like the liver or atoms, is subject to investigation. The body, like any other object then, refers one back to the world. But the world is nothing other than the combination of relationships introduced by consciousness. It is clear, then, how neurobiological substantialism has locked itself into a vicious circle which starts and ends with consciousness. Once again that consciousness which with a naive subterfuge was confined to the brain, is nothing other than a performance which consciousness offers itself in an attempt to find a meaning for itself outside itself.

c. Psychoanalytic anthropomorphization of the unconscious

The anthropomorphization of the unconscious has a long tradition in psychology and assumes its most complete form in the Freudian unconscious. According to Freud's hypothesis, my conscious life, what I am in current reality, is the result of the action of mechanisms which regulate unconscious forces in accordance with well-known schemes, transfer, movement, condensation, etc. My current behaviour is a symbol of something which precedes it in ontological terms, an unconscious made up of abstract rules which exists before the concreteness of my behaviour. By hypothesis then, the abstract is prior to the concrete, and the concrete is nothing other than an epiphenomenon, the result of the relationship between a certain number of abstract qualities. Furthermore, since these abstract qualities, the rules that govern the unconscious, are seen as universal, the concreteness of individual action is nothing other than the result of a certain combination of universal abstract rules. Apart from the logical absurdity of seeing the concrete as originating from the abstract, even if we accept a deterministic priority of universal, unconscious, abstract rules over the concreteness of conscious life, it is clear that such a hypothesis does not, by any means, achieve its goal; instead of providing answers it raises an infinity of questions. For example, saying that my activity as a scholar is fruit of transfer and of fixation by no means explains my being a scholar of something.

What remains to be explained is why these unconscious support mechanisms, which I call transfer and fixation, have been carried out, and above all, *who* brought them about. Of course, it will be said that everything has its origins in infancy or in the first year of life, or even in your mother's womb when you are still an embryo. But apart from the fact that by tracing everything back to infancy, psychoanalysis ignores the dimension of the future, that is it deprives human reality of one of its fundamental dimensions, as we shall see, once again, infancy is not an explanation, if anything it is precisely what is in need of being explained. I am linked to my earlier being by an ontological relationship, by a profound solidarity which I can neither understand nor deny: I was that child, that infant, and I was also certainly that foetus. But the ontological solidarity which ties me to my infancy by no means implies propaedeutic significance of the latter on my present being. Even if we were to accept such determinism we would then still have to clarify from where infancy draws its determining role on my present being. That is, infancy would have to be explained with something which preceded it, and so inevitably we would fall into a *solutio ad infinitum*. Freudian infancy then, is in itself nothing other than one of those great explanatory idols of our era.

But the need to anthropomorphize the unconscious in psychoanalytic theory becomes even more evident if you consider the notion of censorship. Psychoanalytical interpretation introduces the hypothesis of censorship, conceived of as a real "border" with customs, passport control, currency checks etc. The primitive tendencies, instincts, the complexes which have formed in our individual history, in short our past, are *reality* in the Freudian hypothesis. Conscious symbolizations of this real past are also to be considered as real facts. Assertions of conscious life in all their forms, both normal and pathological, represent facts of concrete consciousness. But the subject finds himself facing facts of concrete consciousness like the deceived facing the deceiver. In other words, facts of concrete consciousness must be interpreted because they hide a truth which lies in the unconscious of one's tendencies, instincts, urges etc. In short, there is both truth of unconscious facts and truth of facts of concrete consciousness, only that the truth of symbolic facts of concrete consciousness is the result of deception. The subject deceives himself about *the meaning* of his behaviour, he grasps it in its concrete existence but not in its *truth*, since he is deprived of the possibility of connecting it to a primitive situation and to a psychic structure which are extraneous to him. The psychoanalyst's task is to make the connection between symbolic acts of concrete consciousness and the unconscious complexes which these express. In doing this Freud has divided the mind into two. On the one hand there is the conscious life which *I am*, on the other an unconscious psychism made up of early phenomena, irreducible forces with which I nevertheless have to come to terms. There seems to be, on the one hand, a priority of conscious over unconscious life. I am the psychic phenomena in that I recognise them in their conscious reality. But in actuality I passively receive these psychic facts from the unconscious and am forced to formulate hypotheses regarding their origin and their real meaning, just like the scientist who formulates hypotheses on the physical nature of a particular observation. For instance, I feel the impulse to steal that enamel ashtray from the shelf in that shop. I fully adhere to this impulse, you could say that I *am* the impulse to commit the theft. If I question myself on the nature of the impulse I find that it is determined, let us say, by the beauty of the object and by a certain desire for that feeling of excitement that transgression produces. The psychoanalytical interpretation of this impulse of mine to commit the theft would say, however, that it represents a desire for self-punishment which is more or less directly linked to the Oedipus complex[1]. Thus there is a *truth* in the impulse to steal which can only be understood through more or less probable hypotheses. The unveiling of such a truth requires the contribution of the psychoanalyst as mediator between my unconscious tendencies and my conscious life. Only someone *other* than myself can carry out a synthesis between conscious thesis and unconscious antithesis. In order to know myself I must have recourse to *others*, which means that I relate to my

---

[1] Example from: Sartre, J.P., 1943.

unconscious as a stranger. If I have some notion of psychoanalysis I will be able to attempt an analysis of myself, always being careful, however, to take the objective stance that I would take with any other object. The result of the analysis, whether carried out by myself or a psychoanalyst, will however always be a probable result, just as the result of scientific hypotheses is always probable. Let us suppose I compare the result with the quantity of conscious phenomena that the analysis has been able to explain, it will however always be a question of a growing probability which certainly does not give the object of investigation that feeling of certainty given by intuition. By postulating the existence of a real unconscious, seat of ultimate truth, and the existence of the true meaning of behaviour, which however eludes consciousness, psychoanalysis in some way presents a sort of lie without a liar. It is not the unconscious which lies, because this is given. However, in my conscious life I am continually *lied to* inasmuch as I never directly grasp the true meaning of my behaviour. But what is it that makes my unconscious continuously lie to me? It certainly is not my unconscious urges or complex tendencies that lie to me since their only interest is to come to light, to express themselves in clear consciousness. In order to explain why unconscious complex tendencies only come to light on certain occasions, Freud was forced to introduce the idea of censorship. In fact it is the censor which notices if my attempt, or that of my psychoanalyst, to unveil unconscious truth is about to be successful, and it is censorship which struggles to reject it because only the censor knows *what* needs to be rejected. In fact, in order to carry out its task successfully, the censor must know what it is rejecting. The censor must *choose* among urges, and in order to choose, it must be able to represent these urges to itself. Otherwise how could it admit licit sexual urges for instance, and allow certain instincts (hunger, thirst, sleepiness) to express themselves in consciousness but not others? But it is not enough that the censor is able to distinguish different urges, it also needs to see negative urges as those *to be rejected*, which implies that the censor must also be able to represent its own activity. In fact how could the censor recognise the urges to be rejected without being conscious of recognising them as those *to be rejected*? It is difficult to conceive of knowledge which is ignorance of itself. Knowledge is knowing that one knows, that is all knowledge is also consciousness of knowing. In short, censorship implies not only conscious representation of the urge which is to be rejected as such, but also consciousness of the operations that the censor must carry out in order to act correctly. But what type of consciousness of self is the censor's consciousness of self? It must be consciousness of being consciousness of the tendency to inhibit unacceptable urges, but for the precise purpose of *not being consciousness of it*. In the psychoanalytic hypothesis of censorship we thus see the reproduction of the *homunculus* fallacy, which we have already described, that is the establishing of an unconscious consciousness which is conscious of itself in order not to be so; a new unconscious *anthropos* to which the same *reductio ad infinitum* applies as is implicit in every theory of the *homunculus*.

d. Functionalist anthropomorphization of the unconscious[1]

The functionalist *homunculus*[2] is a sort of double of the unconscious psychoanalytic anthropos, that *homunculus* which *transfers, condenses, moves, censors,* etc. At least it is in this respect that the weighty psychoanalytic legacy has been fully embraced (unconsciously?) in the functionalist programme. Like the psychoanalysts, the functionalists have a cumbersome anthropos to explain, and as we have seen, not only when explaining memory. Starting from the assumption that the human mind is similar to a type of computer, the functionalist hypothesis reduces it to nothing other than the result of a series of operations carried out by a machine (the brain or any other machine which is able to carry out these operations) on symbolic representations of information which reach it from the outside world. In short, the functionalist hypothesis is based on the idea that a *given* world exists, which is represented in a *given* brain where everything is reduced to computational transformations operated on symbols. The functionalist project has proposed itself as an alternative, superseding behaviourism which rejected every mentalist position, that is every idea which set out to investigate objects which were not directly observable and measurable. The aim of functionalism is to discover what happens in that "black box", that is the human mind; it seeks to describe a

---

[1] Within the cognitive sciences not everyone espouses the cognitivist programme. Some very critical positions on this are expressed, for example by authors such as Dreyfus, Marcel, Varela, Globus, Searle, Putnam (see the Reference section)

[2] Functionalist and cognitivist are used as synonyms here. Within the cognitivist movement there are also positions which are very diverse from one another. However none of these escapes the anthropomorphization of the unconscious which is why my discussion does not require a detailed examination of the different positions.

functional architecture of the mind. But as Searle[1] rightly points out, the functionalist project has repeated the worst mistake of behaviourism by only studying objectively observable phenomena and ignoring consciousness, that is, the main feature of the mind. Thus when the functionalists "opened up the big black box, all they found were a lot of little black boxes inside"[2]. The combination of these black boxes, or modules, to use Fodor's terminology[3], constitutes functionalist man, that is the result of the sum of a certain number of functions which can in turn be dismounted into discreet stages of information processing operated by those small black boxes which Searle talks of. In turn, the functionalist man who is ill and who cannot remember or cannot read because a cerebral lesion has removed his memory or ability to read, is nothing but the result of a subtraction, that is the combination of normal man's black boxes *minus* one or more of these small black boxes whose operations represent the missing function[4]. We shall not discuss here the various logical problems and the poor explanatory value of the functionalist hypothesis. We shall instead show how the same old question reappears with the functionalist hypotheses: *who?* In the functionalists' anthropomorphized unconscious, a number of operations are supposed but their origin is not clarified. In other words, it is not made clear who the author of the computational treatment on the symbolic representations said to populate our mind is. As we shall see, it is a matter which functionalist theory cannot clarify, since it would have to come to terms with an aporia which would falsify the theory itself.

But let us look at the problem more closely through an interpretative example provided by functionalism. Among the various models proposed to describe the different cognitive functions, those regarding reading are generally considered the most complete. It is clear that the description and discussion of the various reading models is not important here. However, despite the differences, radical as they may be, all the models have something in common which is what interests us. They all imply and presuppose *intentional* capacity outside consciousness, and in so doing they anthropomorphize the unconscious. We shall analyse one model for all.

---

[1] Searle, J.R., 1992.
[2] Searle, J.R., 1992, p.XII
[3] Fodor, J.A., 1983.
[4] Caramazza, A., 1984.

Figure 1 shows a diagrammatic representation of a reading model, the so-called two-routes reading model[1]. According to this model, the written word enters the *cognitive system* assigned to reading, in the form of *information*. Here, the information undergoes an initial treatment by the *visual analysis* system, which *identifies* the letters on an abstract level regardless, that is, of their form (capital, small, block, etc.). From here the information proceeds towards the *orthographic input lexicon,* where recognition units for known words, which *recognise* whether certain strings of letters correspond to known words, are thought to be stored. The information is then sent on to the *semantic system* which contains representations of the meanings of words, and *recognises* strings of letters which come from the visual entrance lexicon as having certain meanings.

At the next stage of its tortuous journey, the information reaches the *phonological output lexicon* where phonological representations are stored, that is the sounds of words. The *phonological output lexicon* thus *ascribes* sound to the meaning which it gets from the semantic system. Before arriving at the spoken word, that is the final result of reading, the information has to undergo a final process by a sort of filter, or *phonemic buffer*, which *selects* and *sequences* the sounds necessary to articulate the word.

---

[1] Coltheart, M., 1978; Coltheart, M., 1981.

Fig. 1 Two-routes model of reading

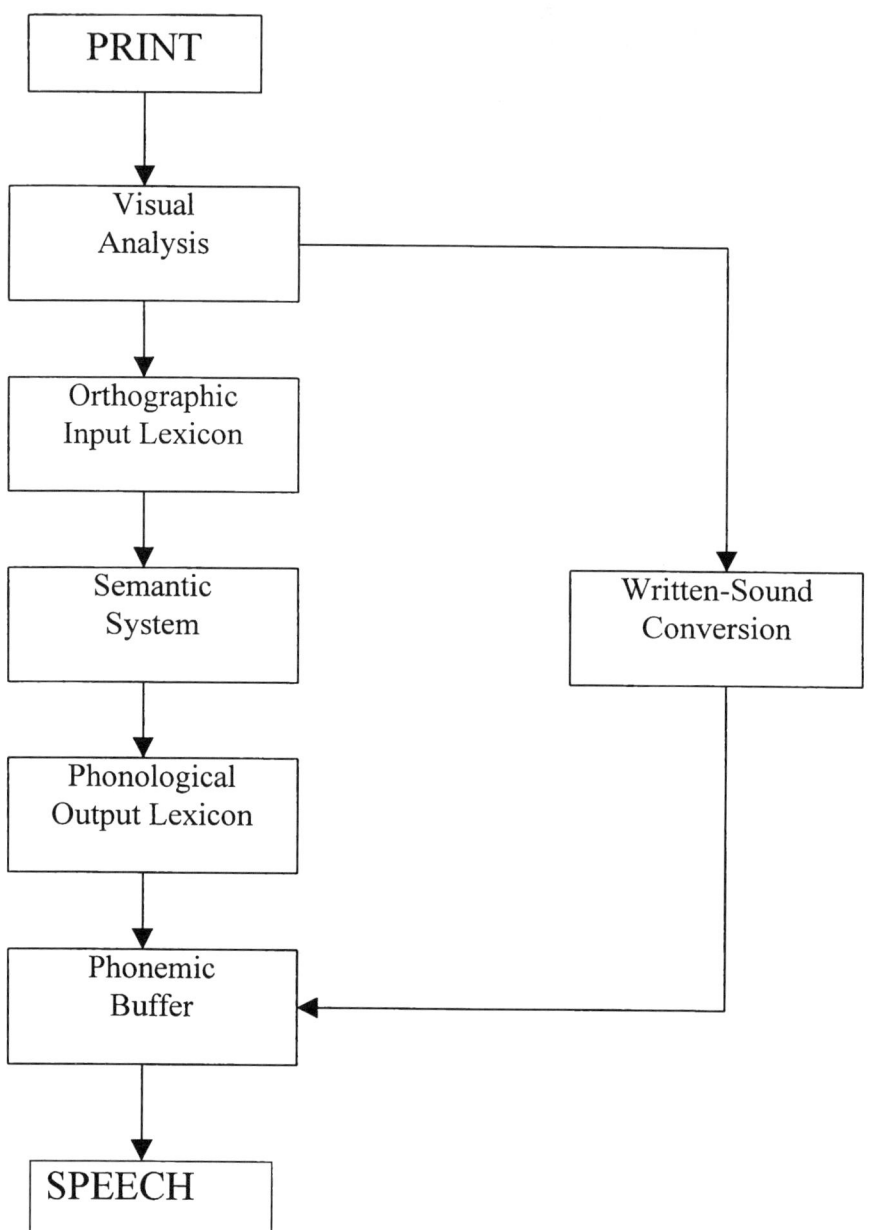

Alternatively, information from the *visual analysis* system may follow a different route to the one described above, it may go directly to the *written-sound conversion* system which *transforms* written information from the visual analysis system into its corresponding sound. From here the information then goes to the phonemic filter, last stop before articulation. This so-called *second route* was postulated to account for the fact that normally we can read words whose meaning we do not know, and also non-words, that is strings of letters which do not represent any known word. This made it necessary to provide a route which does not pass through the semantic system, which allows for the reading of words with no meaning, or words whose meaning is unknown to the reader.

Something is clearly missing from the model we have just described. We deliberately emphasised the operations which should be carried out in the different stages or processes postulated by the model. We thus saw that the visual analyser *identifies* letters, the visual imput lexicon *recognises* strings of letters as words, the semantic system *recognises* certain words as having certain meanings, etc. As you can see, these mechanisms, which are nothing but abstract inferences used to explain the concrete act of reading, carry out *actions*, that is they identify, recognise, etc. In short, each mechanism, each stage of information treatment, is a small *homunculus,* a subject, an *anthropos* endowed with the ability to act. Nevertheless, what these models do not explain is *who* carries out these actions, and *how* these actions are carried out. *Who* analyses the letters? The visual analyser, you will reply. But either the properties which allow the visual analyser to carry out these operations are explained, or the visual analyser remains an abstract entity, magically endowed with the ability of performing actions, that is of being subject; an abstract entity which, moreover, precedes and determines a concrete act, reading. And what does the analysis that the visual analyser is said to perform actually consist in? How does the visual analyser identify the letters and know, for instance, that they are not artichokes? As we have already seen in the case of the psychoanalytic censor, the visual analyser must be able to represent for itself the object that it analyses, that is the letters. It must also know that its action is limited to the letters which will then be sent on to the next stage of information processing, and that this action does not, for instance, include artichokes. The visual analyser then, must also be able to represent its own activity. Indeed, how could the visual analyser recognise artichokes as something *to be rejected*, without being conscious of recognising them as something *to be rejected?* In short, the visual analyser must at the same time be conscious of the object to be analysed and of its own action as analyser. But all this without being conscious. Yet again we find ourselves facing an unconscious consciousness, typical of the *homunculus* fallacy, that is of a consciousness in bad faith. In actual fact, as Tulving[1] pointed out, the various mechanisms postulated in cognitivist models are pure abstractions which could just as well be indicated with letters from the Greek alphabet without changing the models in which they are postulated in the least. Models which, as Marcel emphasised, are not even models "because they seem to do everything but in actual fact do nothing"[2].

And yet, you will ask, what is so strange about postulating the existence of unconscious mechanisms which carry out certain actions? After all, do we not say that thermostats *feel* temperature changes, that photoelectric cells *see* light changes, etc. Apart from the metaphoric use that is made of these terms (nobody really believes that thermostats feel or that photoelectric cells see), there is a substantial difference between thermostats, photoelectric cells and cognitive mechanisms. The former two are instruments created by man for a precise purpose, the latter are said to create man, that is they are said to be the source of his mental acts. If we formulate our question regarding the thermostat as *who* feels the temperature, the answer is "man". It is man who constructed the thermostat in order to feel the temperature better. The thermostat itself is nothing other than the thermoelectric mechanisms of which it is composed. If, on the other hand, we formulate our question with regard to cognitive mechanisms, as *who*, for example, identifies the letters in a reading model, the answer is no longer "man", but an abstract *who* that precedes and determines him.

The reading model we have just described represents an interpretative hypothesis, already somewhat consolidated on the functionalist front. As regards memory, the interpretative models of psychology and cognitivist neuropsychology enjoy a lesser degree of general consensus. We have already seen that in current theories there is great confusion regarding both the nature of the past event which is remembered and the nature of the past itself. We shall deal with this later on. For the moment we are interested in showing how present interpretative models of memory, though not as

---

[1] Tulving, E., 1989.
[2] Marcel, A.J., 1988.

conclusive as that of reading, also fall into the *homunculus* fallacy, that is the anthropomorphization of the unconscious.

From a certain point of view, functionalist interpretations of memory are doubtless more polished than those which have tried to account for other cognitive functions. The most recent attempts to describe and interpret memory reveal the need to account for consciousness as a variable which cannot be neglected in any theory of the mind. Unlike their predecessors, for example the reading model described above, memory models include, more or less explicitly, a small black box which represents consciousness. But the trick does not work all the same. Let us see why.

Consider, for example, the model proposed by Burgess and Shallice[1]. According to this model, the recollection of a personal past episode reflects the activity of a series of distinct components. In the long-term storage system there are memory traces. Memory traces represent both personal events and impersonal knowledge, that is they are both episodic and semantic. Description processes have the function of specifying the type of memory trace which needs to be activated in the process of recollection. If, for instance, the type of recollection I am engaged in is episodic, that is it regards a specific personal episode, the description processes will have the task of selecting an episodic trace, not a semantic one. Once the appropriate trace has been chosen, it is examined by verification processes which establish whether the selected trace is consistent with the memories recalled previously and with the general needs of the recollection task I am engaged in.

Let us suppose, for instance, that I want to remember what I did yesterday evening. In this case, the description processes will select the trace which is appropriate for me to achieve this goal. First of all they will have to search among the episodic traces, not the semantic ones, and they will have to look for something which has to do with the evening and with my recent past. The result of this search could be, for example "yesterday evening I stayed at home to read". At this point the verification processes intervene and establish whether "yesterday evening I stayed at home to read" is a result which satisfies the goal I set myself, what I did yesterday evening, and whether this result contradicts previous memories, for

---

[1] Burgess, P.W., & Shallice, T., 1996.

example, a little earlier I remembered that I had not gone out in the evening for quite some time. Good, in this case I have achieved my aim: I have recalled the type of memory which I intended to recall and it does not contradict other remembered elements or the general goal I set myself. Let us suppose instead that the result achieved does not pass the examination of the verification processes. For example, "yesterday evening I stayed at home to read" is not consistent with the fact that I remember that I have not read a book for several weeks. In this case mediator processes intervene, they mediate between representations in conflict, they judge the plausibility of the result achieved and organise a new search in the long-term store using the description processes. These three processes, description, verification and mediation are, according to the authors of this model, conscious processes. In short, there is believed to be a consciousness which selects memories, one which verifies them and another which mediates between the contradictions which arise between the first two types of consciousness.

It is easy to see that in this way consciousness is fragmented into discreet elements which do not account for the phenomenological reality of recollection. Indeed memory presents itself apodeictically. When I remember "yesterday evening I stayed at home to read", the mnesic experience which accompanies this memory is not split into two or three. It is simply consciousness of-me-reading-yesterday-evening. There is no conscious selection which precedes this consciousness of reading yesterday evening, nor is there any verification which follows it. Let us put the question differently. What type of consciousness is consciousness of description processes? Consciousness of memories to select, evidently. Thus it should be a question of consciousness which is conscious of all memories and, at the same time, consciousness of its own action of selection and of the type of memory to select. Clearly this type of consciousness does not exist inasmuch as concrete consciousness is not, nor could it be, consciousness of all memories and at the same time of some of these memories as those *to be selected*. It is thus a matter of consciousness which is conscious of all memories, but which hides all of them except the one to be selected. And what is consciousness which is conscious of something with the aim of not being so? A consciousness in bad faith, that is, a partly unconscious consciousness. At this point, a consciousness such as this, which is conscious of selecting memories but is actually only conscious of the *already* selected ones, would need another unconscious consciousness which is conscious of all memories, selects some, and then sends to conscious consciousness these selected memories of which it is conscious. But in this way we would fall into the *homunculus* fallacy and into the *reductio ad infinitum* that this involves. The same type of reasoning also applies to the verification processes since these too should be consciousness of the memory to be verified, and at the same time unconscious consciousness of all the memories on which said verification is based. Now, it is not at all clear how the sum of these two distinct, half consciousnesses in bad faith could evoke the conscious memory of a past episode. But, one could say, direct experience actually shows me that in recalling I can make mistakes, and I can notice these mistakes and at times correct them. Certainly, but the memory which I recognise as mistaken does not cease to be consciousness of something remembered, and above all, it has never been, either before or during the description process, or after and during the verification process, consciousness of all the memories amongst which one had, so to speak, a particular saliency which is why it was perceived as that one to be selected or rejected as a mistaken memory. When, for one reason or another, I notice the mistake "yesterday evening I stayed at home to read" and I correct it with "yesterday I went to the cinema", there is no consciousness of anything but these two events, both memories in the same way. I could, if anything, say that the first is mistaken because it is not in agreement with other elements which I can infer from my knowledge, but in itself it is not false, just as it is not true. It is a memory and that is all, a concrete fact, just as this table cannot be true or false but is simply an apodeictic reality.

According to the ideas summarised in Schacter's and Moscovitch's models[1], consciousness is a sort of empty box which can be filled with a quantity of different types of information, i.e. linguistic, conceptual, spatial etc. In other words, the various types of information are found outside consciousness, that is they are unconscious. Information can, therefore, become conscious but it can also be directly expressed without becoming so. When it does become conscious this is because it is passively received by a sort of aspecific consciousness. When it is expressed without becoming conscious, the information passes directly to the response system, that is behaviour, without there being consciousness of it. In addition to these two systems, on the one hand unconscious information, on the other aspecific consciousness which passively receives it, both models provide for a

---

[1] Schacter, D.L. 1989; Mocovitch, M., 1989; Moscovitch, M., 1995.

monitoring system which organises the interaction between consciousness and unconscious information. As you can see, in these models consciousness is a sort of independent entity, aspecific and distinct from the information it passively receives from specific modules of knowledge. In other words, the idea is that consciousness has a content. But maintaining that consciousness has a content means that consciousness and its content are distinct. Now the question is what type of consciousness is consciousness without content?

If we want to separate consciousness from its content we must accept the *Selbständigkeit* of consciousness. But consciousness without content, that is consciousness which is consciousness of nothing, is unintelligible, it ceases to be consciousness. We shall see later that consciousness cannot in any way avoid its fundamental law which is that of being, by nature, consciousness of something. What, then, is consciousness without content, and what is content without consciousness? It is not worth arguing that although consciousness and content are separate, *de facto* consciousness always has a content. Such an assertion would not eliminate the possibility of accepting a consciousness by right which is not consciousness, a sort of consciousness in a state of rest, that is non-consciousness. Besides, the separation of consciousness from its content implies that the latter, that is information which becomes conscious, is already specified in terms of its phenomenic form before becoming conscious. That is to say that, for instance, memories, concepts and, general knowledge, exist outside consciousness in the same form as they have when they become conscious.

It is difficult to understand how this can happen. If we take memory, for example, how can a recollection, whose main feature is that of being consciousness of the pastness of an event, be already determined outside consciousness, and exist independently of this? The same objection clearly holds also for other types of content or information. What is the concept of chair, the map of the city, my friend Peter's face, outside consciousness? Furthermore, if we want content and information which has already been specified to be expressed in behaviour without becoming conscious, what psychologists call the implicit expression of knowledge, we will have to accept that the only difference with respect to conscious expression is the absence of consciousness. In other words, the information expressed inside consciousness or outside it, is the same. But if the information inside and outside consciousness is the same, in that it is already specified in itself, its implicit expression in behaviour should have the same characteristics as its expression in consciousness minus consciousness itself. For example, I am now conscious of this glass on the table in front of me. I am conscious of its position in space, its shape, size, and colour, and of the glass it is made of and its weight. All this information, according to our hypothesis, does not depend on consciousness, it is already specified in the glass. Now, let's suppose that I am no longer conscious of the glass before me. I am engrossed in something completely different so that the glass is, so to speak, outside my field of consciousness. Absorbed in what I am doing, I pick up the glass and bring it to my lips, take a sip from it and put it back in its place. This series of actions reflects the implicit expression of the information "glass". But is the information "glass" which I am implicitly expressing the same as that which not long ago inhabited my consciousness? Let us suppose that there is a witness observing me while I drink from the glass without being conscious of it. Could this witness deduce from my behaviour that I am implicitly using the information that the glass is made of glass, or that it is red? Obviously not. As you can see, the information expressed in consciousness and outside it is clearly not the same. Not because it is different but simply because it cannot exist outside consciousness, before it, already specified in the unconscious, and then come to inhabit consciousness as content.

Having postulated a generic and passive consciousness, whose only role is to receive information which has already been specified in the unconscious, these models are obliged to postulate a sort of control servomechanism to organise the interaction of the other elements. However, yet again, this control mechanism is outside consciousness. Therefore, yet again, we are dealing with a mechanism endowed with unconscious intentionality, that is of being conscious of something so as not to be so. A non-conscious consciousness or, as we have also said, a consciousness in bad faith. This condition has already been described in sufficient detail and shall not be dealt with further.

4. SCIENCE AND MATERIALISM

The various ways of anthropomorphizing the unconscious, in neurobiology, psychoanalysis, and functionalism, reflect various attempts to explain the central aspect of the life of the psychic, consciousness, in the framework of reductionist determinism. Whether the attempt is to reduce consciousness to a series of nervous events which occur in the brain, unconscious psychic forces competing among themselves, or to unconscious computational systems which act on symbols, the result does not much alter the substance: consciousness is the effect of something which happens somewhere else. Neurobiological substantialism takes an openly materialist position, as we have seen in Searle, for instance: consciousness *is* what happens in the brain, that is in matter, and its explanation is to be found in neurophysiology which, in turn, refers us to neurobiology, and this to chemistry and to physics, that is to the elementary structure of matter, since there is only one matter. Psychoanalysis and functionalism are not concerned with basing consciousness in matter, but this does not mean that they are any less reductionist or deterministic than neurobiological substantialism. Consciousness is what happens in the unconscious and this, at least according to the functionalist hypothesis, takes place in a machine, the brain, but not only. My position has already been made quite clear in the previous pages. But to avoid any sort of misunderstanding, let me state that the principles of reductionist determinism, whether in their materialist variety or not, are philosophically false: it is not comprehensible how matter, the Freudian unconscious or the functionalists' computational level can generate the idea of matter, of the unconscious, or of computation. Actually reductionist determinism is the product of the myth of objectivity upon which the idea of science rests. This idea is supposed to be universal but, as we shall see, it is nothing other than a figure of speech. At this point you will expect an idealist conclusion: the idea is self-sufficient, it is the idea which generates matter, the unconscious, the cognitive system. But that is not the case. Our conclusion is not idealistic and science, in order to be science, does not need to resort to reductionist determinism. We will now account for these assertions. We shall examine the strictly materialist variation of reductionist determinism, that is neurobiological substantialism, since it is, in a sense, paradigmatic of every attempt to reduce consciousness to something else.

The materialist perspective aims to reduce the dynamics of the mind to matter, and thus to eliminate subjectivity by reducing the world, man included, to a system of objects in relation to one another in accordance with universal principles. Thus materialism, and with it neurobiological substantialism, is presented as a proper form of metaphysics, since it transcends every perceptible datum so as to bring everything back, *a priori*, to universal matter. But the materialist does not want his ideas to be considered metaphysical. In fact, there is nothing that the materialist hates more in the world than metaphysics, so much so that in his language this word is somewhat of an insult, and is used for whoever strays from the rigorous objectivity of *facts*. The materialist claims to stick exclusively to facts, the observation of which forms the basis of the only legitimate knowledge, scientific knowledge. This point of view has a long tradition and everyone will remember the positivists' antimetaphysical invectives. But they, who were far more coherent, had from the beginning given up questioning themselves on the relationship between mind and body because they thought that no objective truth, in the scientific sense, could arise from an investigation of the sort. The relationship between body and mind is rejected a priori by the positivists since it is far beyond our objective experience of the world. The neurobiological substantialist is much bolder than his positivist fathers, and seeks to solve the mind-body problem by reducing the mind to the brain and its functions. Now, the materialist neurobiologist accuses the idealist of being metaphysical when he reduces matter to the mind. But why should the materialist be excused for being metaphysical when he reduces the mind to matter. The experimental data he has do not, by any means, support his doctrine. Nor, on the other hand, do they support the opposing one. What the *facts* do show is a close relationship between physiological and psychical events, a relationship which can be interpreted in a thousand different ways[1]. When the materialist neurobiologist places psychophysical identity, the relationship of identity, between mind and brain, and particularly between consciousness and the brain, he does not do so by basing himself on the famous *facts* which he claims to keep to, but defines it a priori through intuition or reason. For however much he disguises himself as a positivist, the materialist neurobiologist is a masked metaphysic. And, as if that were not enough, he is a metaphysic who destroys himself with his own weapons, because by rejecting metaphysics he destroys the foundation for his own assertions.

But not only does the materialist destroy the metaphysics upon which his own thought is based, but also the positivism with which he disguises himself. Comte and his followers reduced legitimate thought to scientific knowledge in that they believed that only this, being based on direct

---

[1] Sartre, J.-P., 1946.

experience of the world, could be proved to be effective. For them the success of science was *a fact*. But a fact which belongs to the human world. It is *for man* that science is successful. The positivists were careful not to ask themselves whether scientific rationalism had universal value, that is whether it was valid for the universe in itself, quite apart from man, for the simple reason that in order to do so they would have had to come out of themselves and humanity to compare the universe as it is with the representation that science gives us of it, and thus take God's point of view on man. But the materialist neurobiologist is not so cautious. He arrogates the right to rise above science, subjectivity, and man himself and to take the place of God, which he also denies, to contemplate the spectacle of the universe. But eliminating subjectivity by making it correspond to the physical operations of the brain does not mean you have truly eliminated it and even less that you have managed to explain it. And this, as Nagel[1] rightly points out, is not because there are not yet enough empirical data: the problem is theoretical. Even if we got to the point of finding a miniature of the Gioconda in my brain while I am looking at the painting, my perception of the Gioconda would not be accounted for. The materialist believes he has made subjectivity disappear by suppressing it. But that is not the way things are. In order to suppress subjectivity, the materialist declares himself *object*, that is possible matter for scientific investigation. But having made himself an object, a thing among things, the materialist claims to take an *objective* point of view on things. Thus the materialist is at the same time both object, like other objects of the world, but also outside the object, with an absolute and objective view on things, stripped of all subjectivity. In short, as Nagel[2] says, the view that the materialist has on the world, being free of subjectivity, is a view *from nowhere*. From this universal view the materialist contemplates the world and asserts the rationality of objective reality: everything that is real is rational or capable of being rationalised, he maintains. But in actual fact, without realising it, materialist rationalism destroys itself by moving into irrationalism: if consciousness is conditioned by biology, and this in turn by physics, human consciousness can express the world at most as an effect can express its cause, and not as a thought expresses its object. If everything comes to consciousness from outside, from biological, chemical or physical causes, if it passively receives rationality from the world, how can consciousness express itself on objects,

---

[1] Nagel, T., 1974; Nagel, T., 1986; Nagel, T., 1993.
[2] Nagel, T., 1986.

and believe that its means of expression are the right ones, in this case the means of materialism? In order to judge, it should be, at the same time, both inside and outside itself. Since this is not possible, it must rely on other criteria, criteria which are necessarily internal and subjective. This, then, is how materialist rationalism is forced to resort to idealist subjectivity to found itself, and in so doing destroys its own work. As Sartre[1] notes, "dogmatic when affirming that the universe produces thought, materialism moves straight on to idealist scepticism. With one hand it offers the inexorable rights of Reason, and with the other it takes them away. It destroys positivism with dogmatic rationalism, it destroys both with the metaphysical assertion that man is a material object, and it destroys this assertion with the radical negation of all metaphysics. It sets science up against metaphysics and, unwittingly, metaphysics against science. Only ruins remain".

But then the theoretical problems which hamper scientific materialism stem from a mistaken presumption which is due to irresponsibility, if not to bad faith, and is that of wanting to explain quality with quantity. The universe of science is quantitative, it begins and ends with the analytic measurement of independent, external elements in a relationship of juxtaposition. The very aim of science is to break the complex down into more simple elements to then use the reassembled elements as confirmatory evidence of its own success. Science acts through subtractions and additions of independent elements. In fact, the independence of the elements, just like their exteriority, is a necessary condition for there to be measurement, that is science. Elements that are so influenced by the co-presence of other elements that their very nature changes would make any objective measurement impossible. However a hydrogen atom, in becoming part of a molecule of water, does not change its nature, it simply remains what it was. It is due to this static quality that we can affirm that water is *composed* of two oxygen atoms and one of hydrogen: an addition. But the sum of hydrogen and oxygen begins and ends in what it is, and, as we have seen, it will never explain the liquidity of water. This is a quality which prescinds and in some way precedes hydrogen, oxygen and the sum of the two. In the same way, a neuron remains a neuron, and it is due to this static quality that it can be identified, and its properties, which are revealed when it becomes part of a certain nervous circuit, can be measured. What I measure is its

---

[1] Sartre, J.-P., 1946.

relative state of activation or inhibition with respect to the other neurons in the nervous circuit in which it is inserted. But the fact that it is in relationship with other neurons does not make it disappear into nothing, nor does it transform it into something different from what it has always been. You might say that the circuit in which the neuron in question is inserted represents something new, with characteristics which differ from those of the neuron itself. Certainly, but this does not mean that this new entity represents quality. The visual circuit in which that given neuron of the associative visual cortex is inserted has certain properties which that single neuron does not possess, for example it responds to the stimuli projected onto the retina in a modular way. But what quality does this new combination of properties of the visual circuit express? Certainly not visual perception. Everything that occurs in the visual circuit when it is stimulated can be expressed in terms of statistical probability, thus in quantitative terms. It will never be able to explain the quality of my visual perception of this vase of flowers, of the Gioconda, or of a football match. Let me repeat myself, the very most to which a science of the brain can aspire is to demonstrate, with a certain degree of statistic probability, a correlation between certain physiological, chemical or physical events and certain psychological events. Scientific laws are expressed with quantitative formulae and science has no symbol to express quality as such, and even less so the quality of psychological states.

Counter to every reductionist solution, Thomas Nagel[1] maintains that conscious mental states are as much a part of objective reality as a stone, an oak tree or a brain and thus they can, and must, be studied directly, without the need to reduce them to a physicality which in itself is no more real. What Nagel suggests, in other words, is to make quality the object of scientific study. The aim of a science of consciousness is to clarify the relationship between what things are like *for* the conscious subject, and simply how things *are*, that is to clarify the relationship between the *per se* and the *in se*. One way of setting about the scientific study of consciousness is, according to Nagel, to study mental phenomena which are not too "cognitive", which lend themselves to some kind of measurement in accordance with some quantifiable scale, and which already show some clear connection of order with physical variables. As examples of mental

---

[1] Nagel, T., 1993.

phenomena which are easy to study, Nagel gives those phenomena which vary in intensity, for example the perception of colours, sound tones, temperature or pain. Nagel's antireductionist intentions are no doubt positive and in good faith. However, he does not seem to notice that in proposing to study *intensity* as though it were the key to a science of consciousness, he is not proposing to study the quality of conscious experience which he presents as irreducible, but yet again the quantity which expresses it in a reduced and incomplete way.

Temperature, sound, and colour, as perceived by a conscious subject, are qualities which, if reduced to their intensity, cease to be qualities and become quantities. It is not *warmer* than yesterday, it is warm in a different way to yesterday. The degree of temperature, measured by the cubic dilation of a liquid, is simply a quantity, attached to which there is a vague idea of quality, in a general sense. At the same temperature I might button my coat more tightly because I am cold, while someone else might remove theirs because they are hot. Science reduced this perceptible quality to a quantity when it was agreed to substitute the vague information of our senses with the measure of cubic dilation of a liquid. Likewise, the transformation of water into steam is, for science, a purely quantitative phenomenon, or, if you like, this transformation exists for science only *as* a quantity. It is thus necessary to choose: either we remain on a level of perceptible quality, in which case steam and temperature are qualities, or else we consider temperature as quantity, but then the change from one temperature to another will be scientifically defined as a quantitative change. What science can say is that there is x probability that at a certain temperature, measured with a thermometer, percentage y of subjects will button up their coats, and percentage z will take their coats off, and nothing more.

Where is quality, and in what way could intensity ever express it? The red I can see now is no more intense than the red I saw earlier, it is a different red. If in everyday language this diversity is described by saying that it is more intense, this does not at all mean that the perceptible quality of the two reds can be traced back to an idea of measurable quantity expressed through intensity. In psychology there is a test[1] used to measure colour perception, where the subject has to put a series of different gradations of the same colour in ascending order. You will say, is this not an

---

[1] Farnsworth, D., 1943.

example of how quality can be described in accordance with the rules of more and less, that is according to quantity? Isn't what is measured by means of this test perhaps the visual perception of colours, that is the quality of colour perception? Not at all. What this test *measures* is the ability to perceive different colours *as* different. This blue is different from that one. The fact that this difference is then expressed according to a scale of gradation only proves the ability to judge this diversity according to a definite rule imposed from outside: this blue is *lighter* than that one. In order for this to be possible two blues must be present, and I must compare them according to a rule of gradation of lightness, just as the scientist compares two cells under a microscope and maintains that, according to pre-established rules, one is normal while the other is pathological. This by no means describes the quality of my perception of the two blues, but only my ability to apply a specific rule. Indeed, if my performance in this test is poor, that is if I put the colours in an *arbitrary* order, what could be concluded from this? The psychologist would say that my perception of colours is altered. But that would be an arbitrary conclusion. In fact, my poor performance in the test could merely indicate my inability to apply the rule in accordance with which I was supposed to arrange the different colours because I am no longer able to indicate the type of difference between the various colours, though I continue to perceive them as different. Indeed I could arrange those same colours, whose difference does not escape me, according to other rules: from the one I like most to the one I like least, from the most to the least familiar, from the one most similar to the sky in spring to the least similar, and so on. But these rules which I apply are judgements outside the quality of my perception, they join it but they are not, by any means, a part of it. In short, despite every effort, quality will not be reduced to quantity, not even if we take into consideration those simple mental phenomena that Nagel proposed to start out on a scientific study of consciousness. By this we do not mean that quantity is the negation of quality. Quantity is an attempt to explain quality in a rigorous, that is objective way, just as the equation of a circle rigorously expresses its circular shape[1]. It is merely a reductive attempt, which preserves its *raison d'être* to the extent that it remains coherent to itself and avoids any expression of quality in its very nature.

---

[1] Merleau-Ponty, M., 1942.

According to the reductionists, the irreducibility of the quality of conscious experience is questionable, due to the fact that the progress of science is reducing the *residue* of irreducibility of conscious experience further and further. Dennet, for example[1], affirms that many *facts* regarding "the way things *are* for the subject" are not only explained, but predicted with the development of science. According to Dennet, Ramachandran's experiments are a good example. In these experiments, the paradoxical illusion of motion was predicted by the knowledge of the nervous routes involved in the perception of motor and colour. Since the detection systems of motor and colour are distinct in the brain, when black spots are moved over a drawing where there is a yellow, isoluminescent mark in the background, the yellow mark paradoxically appears to both move and remain still at the same time. From an understanding of the functional separability in the brain of motor, place, colour and luminescence, Ramachandran predicted that this surprising effect would occur. Since, according to theory, these systems were separate in the brain, he predicted that they would also be phenomenologically separate. Dennet sees this as a good example of how phenomenal experience can be predicted and manipulated, starting from knowledge of the subjacent nervous structure. But none of this proves that the quality of the paradoxical phenomenal experience described by Ramachandran is explained by the cerebral mechanisms involved in motor, colour, place and luminescence. Once again, what is demonstrated is only a relationship of correspondence between physiological and mental states. A correspondence which, furthermore, could quite easily be reversed: not recognising the functional separability in the brain of motor, place, colour and luminescence, this separability could be predicted starting from the phenomenon of the paradoxical perception described above. But this relationship of correspondence between physiological and mental states is such and that is that. It by no means explains *how* a mental state is brought about by a physiological state, or vice versa. In short, not only is there no priority by right or *de facto* between the two terms of correspondence, the physiological and the mental, but neither is there anything to indicate that one of the two terms is based on the other, or how the passage from one state to another occurs. However, Ramachandran's theory includes no prediction about the relationship between physiological states and phenomenal experience.

---

[1] Dennet, D. 1993.

We have ascertained the irreducibility of facts of consciousness. The irreducibility of quality to quantity. But where does this irreducibility of consciousness come from? What is the characteristic which makes the quality of phenomenal experience impervious to any analytic-quantitative reduction? The problem of the irreducibility of consciousness lies in the fact that direct experience of the world, what an organism experiences in a given situation, is accessible only from a single point of view, the subject's, what he is experiencing - so to speak - on his own skin. In short, the terrain of consciousness is the terrain of subjectivity, while that of science is that of objectivity. The quality of phenomenal experience can be attributed objectively only according to a nominal scale and by progressive statistic approximation. The nominal value x can be ascribed to my conscious experience of that red vase in the corner, and then we can say that x is more or less the same as another observer's conscious experience of that vase. But these are merely nominal and approximate values which do not in any way describe the subjective experience of seeing that vase. There is no way of objectively establishing that my conscious experience of that vase is similar to that of another observer. That vase is, for instance, a memento of a past love and when I look at it my consciousness addresses it in a certain way: with nostalgia, rancour, love. Together with its shape and colour there is an "additional value" which belongs exclusively to me, and which cannot be predicted on the basis of statistical terms produced by nominal values attributed to "what probably is" the perception of a red vase for a certain number of observers. It is likely that the same physiological events which correspond to any observer's perception of that vase correspond to my perception of it, but then every observer's phenomenal experience is unique and different from anyone else's. The quantity of cells which are activated in the brain is perhaps the same but the meaning of that activation is original and new for each subject who perceives that red vase. Even the paradoxical effect mentioned earlier, where the yellow mark is perceived as being in motion and still at the same time, says nothing about the quality of the subjective experience of that paradox. All subjects who took part in that experiment reported, with a certain degree of probabilistic coherence, having the same paradoxical experience. The experience all subjects probably shared is the paradox of motion and immobility. But who can say whether the subjective experience of that paradox really was exactly the same for all the subjects? In other words, the paradox of motion and immobility is nothing other than the object of phenomenal experience, and not the experience itself. On seeing a red drape, a blind man who has regained his sight, a bull, and a clerk of the land registry office will all experience the red, but what this experience is in the subjective reality of an ex-blind man, a bull and a clerk cannot be objectively known.

The quality of conscious experience is synthetic quality, and as such escapes any analytic break down. Conscious experience is the continual synthesis of the world and of the consciousnesses which have preceded it. Later on, we will examine how consciousness constitutes itself as synthesis. For now we are concerned with what consciousness, as synthesis, cannot be. As synthesis, consciousness escapes scientific investigation, or rather a certain reductionist and materialist science, since this science proceeds mainly analytically. Science dismantles and reassembles, by adding and subtracting discreet elements which are external to one another. But, you might say, science too speaks explicitly of synthesis, for example with regard to chemical combinations. But these are never real syntheses, in Hegel's sense of the word, since each element which combines with other elements preserves all its properties. Whether an oxygen atom combines with hydrogen and sulphuric atoms to make hydrogen sulphide, or with hydrogen alone to make water, it remains as it was. Neither water nor hydrogen sulphide are true syntheses which alter and govern their components; they are simple passive results: static sums, not syntheses. Functionalist models are syntheses to an even lesser degree. Remember the example of the reading model. In it we found a series of discreet elements of information processing, the sum of which constitutes normal reading, while the subtraction of one or more elements constitutes pathological reading which we observe in certain cases of cerebral lesions. Even if we omit all the absurdities of the model which have already been described, the model remains an analytic model which does not explain, nor does it propose to explain, conscious experience of normal reading if the system works, or pathologically if it does not. The conscious experience of reading is much more, and is different from the sum of elements which constitute the model, even if we assume ad absurdum that the model does not reveal the logical absurdities which it, however, does.

But where the confusion of materialist reductionist thought is most evident is in the idea of *cause*. Consciousness, as we have already seen, cannot be considered an effect. Yet materialism considers it so, and could not do otherwise. As a form of *explanatory* metaphysics (it seeks to *explain* psychic phenomena with physiology, the latter with biology, and biology with physico-chemical laws), materialism uses the causal schema on principle. But if we look at science, it is clear that a causal link is not at all scientific. Where is the cause in Archimedes' principle, or in the laws of thermodynamics? Science generally establishes functional relationships among phenomena, and for convenience chooses the independent variable. Besides, it is quite impossible to express causality in mathematical language. Most laws of physics simply have functions in the form of $x = f(y)$. Others establish numerical constants; still others describe the phases of irreversible events but without it being possible to say that one of these phases is *cause* of the following. Could it perhaps be said that karyokinesis is cause of the segmentation of protoplasmic filaments?[1] Materialist causality thus fades into nothing. The metaphysical idea of reducing the psychic to matter, of explaining psychological events with biology or physics, finds no ally in science, where the causal schema is completely alien. Materialist causalism thus remains a practical notion, more suited to common sense than to rigorous theoretical reflection. At best an ingenuous notion, but more likely in bad faith, especially as materialist causalism does not even respect the criteria or internal coherence of the rigorous method it uses. In seeking to make psychic phenomena originate from external causes, materialism chooses the brain *a priori* and appoints it as the cause of psychic phenomena. But who can guarantee that psychic effects are the effect of cerebral activity and not of what happens in the *cauda equina*?, or in the left foot, or of the energy which emanates from that piece of furniture in the corner? If we want to establish a cause-effect relationship, every possible cause should be taken into consideration as possible. But the materialist has already chosen: the brain is his arbitrary cause.

Causalism has also led to the misunderstanding that the causal relationship between brain and consciousness is given but not proven only because there are not yet sufficient experimental data, but sooner or later science will be able to provide this data. But, as we have seen, the problem is theoretical and not experimental. It is not a question of data to be gathered, it is simply not possible to explain consciousness with the brain, just as it is not possible to explain the function of the hammer by studying its molecular structure. To understand how a hammer works all you can do is hammer. Likewise, the only way to understand consciousness is to be conscious. But understanding is still not explaining. Indeed comprehension

---

[1] Example taken from Sartre, J.-P., 1946.

is subjective. I perfectly understand what it means to be conscious of the presence of the keyboard which I am typing on. My experience of keyboard-I-am-typing-on is perfectly clear to me and requires nothing more. Explaining, however, means explaining *to someone*, thus the ground of explanation is that of objectivity. This is where the misunderstanding of reflection on consciousness originates, in seeking to put comprehension and explanation on the same ground. Everyone knows what consciousness is, because subjective experience makes comprehension possible. But when we try to give an explanation of what is already understood, we fall into the temptation of leaving the ground of consciousness and adopting a determinist paradox, that is explaining consciousness with something else, as if we wanted to explain the function of the hammer with its molecular structure. However, consciousness has an advantage over the hammer. While a hammer cannot hammer itself, that is it does not know the reflexive form, consciousness can fall back into itself and make consciousness the object of itself, that is become consciousness of consciousness. A science of consciousness thus remains possible provided that it is conscious of its limits, that it forgoes determinism and addresses consciousness directly in its reflexive form. We shall discuss this later.

5. CONCLUSIONS

What should we conclude from what has been discussed so far? The first obvious conclusion is that the claim of being able to explain consciousness with the unconscious is misleading. As regards memory and its relationship to consciousness, which is the object of this study, we have seen that current theories are limited in explanatory value by at least two problems. These, which we have schematically identified as the paradox of the trace and the homunculus fallacy, have over-shadowed the problem of memory and knowledge, forcing them into a non-conscious mechanism based on terms whose logical absurdity has been demonstrated. Functionalist and substantialist ideas, though often in sharp contrast, actually have much in common. In fact, both see consciousness, intended as direct phenomenal experience, only as an epiphenomenon, as a by-product of computational processes of information processing or of the biological functioning of the nervous system. In this perspective, the main aspect of memory, that is the conscious experience of transcending the present to select an event down there in the past where it took place, is considered to be the final result of a causal chain which functions and exhausts itself outside consciousness. Consciousness itself is thus reduced to a last and irrelevant stage in a causal chain which bases its *primus movens* in cell mechanisms or symbolic representations of the world. The terms of the question are thus reversed: what must necessarily be seen as *a-priori* consciousness, is instead seen as *a posteriori*, that is as something which can be constructed bit by bit in thought, through the collection of external fragments. Vice versa, what by definition must be seen as *a posteriori*, since it is fruit and object of consciousness, (non-conscious mechanisms), is seen as *a priori*, that is as the irreducible origin of consciousness. In short, the mistake of current theories on memory is that of not seeing that what are considered to be physiological, psychological or computational conditions upon which the historic and ontological development of consciousness is thought to depend, are only a performance which consciousness offers itself. In other words, these conditions which have prepared the constitution of consciousness do not come *before* it, but *for* it, that is they are not conditions which constitute consciousness, but conditions which consciousness itself creates. By ignoring this relationship between consciousness and its historic-ontological origin, both the functionalists and the substantialists fall under the illusion of seeing memory as if it were in man as "content" of his consciousness, determined somewhere else. If I remember a house, a glass of water, a woman's body, how could this body, this glass, this building reside in my memory and how could my memory be something different from consciousness of these objects as memorable? Memories are not small psychic entities which inhabit consciousness, but are themselves consciousness in its original form, since this, by principle, is consciousness *of* something[1]. Within this framework, it is clear that neither functionalists nor substantialists were able to say anything of relevance on the nature of memory, nor were they able to give an adequate explanation of so-called cognitive phenomena. Concepts such as that of memory trace, control mechanisms and information processing are only modern explanatory idols which obscure the comprehension of phenomena rather than clarify it. What has not been realised is that consciousness, which is celebrated as an object

---

[1] "The problem is that we have tended to think of memories as unconscious items that one brings to consciousness, not as *part* of consciousness....So we have to understand consciousness before we can assume that memories simply 'rise' to it or are tacked onto it; it must be ascertained whether memory and consciousness are part of the same structure or not." I. Rosenfield, 1992, p.12.

of scientific investigation, cannot be seen to derive from an unconscious elsewhere. Consciousness is not an epiphenomenal by-product of unconscious information processing, or of what neurons do. It represents the main problem and point of departure of any theory of the mind. As is made clear by Marcel[1], psychology without consciousness may be biology or cybernetics, but it is not psychology. In this sense the words of Freud, when he maintained that consciousness *ist eine arme Ding*, seem to resound in the functionalists' and the substantialists' positions.

Our investigation has so far led us to reject any functionalist or substantialist solution to the relationship between memory and consciousness. What has emerged from what has been said so far though is an omission, that is that of not having clarified why an object presents itself to consciousness as *past*. The question we have to ask ourselves at this point then, is the following: what is the nature of consciousness which remembers? A question of this sort obviously refers one to the problem of the description of consciousness, the past and how this in itself constitutes a form of consciousness. Direct reflection, which overcomes the difficulties of the paradox of the preservation of the past in physiological or psychological traces and of the anthropomorphization of unconscious mechanisms, is thus necessary. This is what we shall do in the next chapter.

---

[1] Marcel, A.J., & Bisiach, E., 1988.

CHAPTER 3

VARIETIES OF CONSCIOUSNESS

1. CONSCIOUSNESS CANNOT BUT BE DEFINED AS CONSCIOUSNESS *OF*

If, as Tulving[1] asserts, "consciousness as an object of intellectual curiosity is the philosopher's joy and a scientist's nightmare", this is due to the fact that it does not seem to answer the prerequisites of the Galilean method of scientific research. Indeed it is difficult to find a definition of consciousness which allows us to narrow down the field of inquiry, just as it is difficult to "measure" it and interpret the results of its possible measurement. The fact that consciousness has always more or less implicitly been considered a unitarian entity is largely responsible for most of these problems. From this point of view, the only possibility of defining consciousness lies in distinguishing it from the unconscious: consciousness is that which is not unconscious. This is where all the unresolved and unresolvable questions that have excluded consciousness from any line of inquiry stem from. But a definition of consciousness is in itself impossible, if by definition you mean an arbitrary definition of the meaning of consciousness, or of how the term should be used. It is equally impossible to limit *a priori* the field of concepts which make reference to consciousness. This is not because this type of descriptive process is in itself wrong. Indeed, it is quite easy to define a "glass" either by deciding arbitrarily that it is an object that usually contains liquids and which is used to drink from, or by seeing all or part of a series of concepts which concern the idea of drinking something from an object as leading back to glass. The case of consciousness though is slightly different since the starting point of any

---

[1] Tulving, E., 1993.

descriptive process is consciousness itself, and in defining it you would find yourself in the embarrassing position of having to exclude a part of consciousness in order to reach a definition which was in itself necessarily reductive since the possibility of incorporating consciousness in its entirety is excluded *a priori*. A definition of consciousness is impossible since, as we will soon see, consciousness inevitably escapes everything, especially definition. However, it is possible to describe certain aspects of it, and from these to attempt to get as close as possible to a definition of the essence of consciousness. A paradoxical operation, you could say. Defining consciousness by means of a description of consciousness, that is consciousness that describes itself in order to define itself, is like trying to define a hammer by means of its blows. We are perfectly aware of this paradox and this is why we make no pretence at definition, only at description. It is a hunt in which the prey cannot be caught since it is the prey making up the rules of the hunt. This we know and are therefore content to get as close as possible to it, to at least snatch a whiff of it.

If, therefore, it is a question of hunting consciousness in an attempt to grasp at least a crumb of its essence through description, as far as we are concerned, consciousness under reflexive analysis appears to be irremediably consciousness *of*. This, though, is nothing new. It is confirmation of the work of phenomenologists, Brentano and Husserl in particular, namely that for consciousness to exist and to be conceivable, it must always be consciousness *of* something. In other words, for consciousness to exist it must have an object, or better, consciousness is the quantity of different ways in which an object is seen in the world. This is the first great law of consciousness, the neglect of which has caused, as we shall see, quite a few problems for functionalist theories. But let us see what exactly we mean by saying that consciousness is irremediably consciousness of something.

The need for consciousness to necessarily be consciousness of something implies that consciousness of nothing cannot exist. Consciousness which is not *already* directed towards its object, that is a consciousness which is not already in the ec-static form, outside of itself in the direction of an object, is not intelligible. There is no consciousness *before,* which *then* becomes consciousness of the object of which it is conscious. I am now conscious of this glass in front of me, or you could say that my consciousness is now consciousness-of-glass. What was my consciousness before becoming consciousness-of-glass? It was consciousness of the words that I am writing for example, of my thoughts, of my plans, of the cigarette I have only just lit. In other words, before becoming consciousness of glass, my consciousness was already consciousness of something. And yet, you will object, sometimes consciousness can be consciousness of nothing. Sometimes, for example, you might ask someone, or even yourself, "what are you thinking about?" and the answer is "nothing". Therefore it would seem that there can indeed be consciousness of nothing. But consciousness of nothing is always consciousness of something, that is of that "nothing" of which it is consciousness. And what is that nothing I refer to when I say that I was thinking about nothing? It is all my thoughts together without being any one thought in particular. The succession of a thousand reflections to which my consciousness is forced precisely because it must be consciousness of something. If I say that I was thinking of nothing it is because it is difficult to trace every single thought and because all of my thoughts together do not constitute something which can be reduced to a propositional form, as they do when they revolve around a single theme. And so I can say I was thinking about quantic mechanics or about the last time I made love with that certain woman, but I say "nothing" if my thoughts run together and follow each other aimlessly, in no particular order. The pointless disorder of my thoughts which I describe with the word "nothing" reflects the law of consciousness according to which it must be consciousness of something, of that "nothing" lacking anything better.

2. CONSCIOUSNESS IS NOT PASSIVITY

The first consequence of the need of consciousness to be consciousness of its object is that consciousness cannot be considered a passive being which receives the object of which it becomes conscious. If this were so, you would in fact have to accept the possibility of a consciousness which is first empty and passive, and then becomes consciousness of its object when this is presented from the outside. But we have seen that consciousness which is not consciousness of something is either unintelligible, or else the nothing of which it is consciousness is indeed something. The difficulties met with in the study of cognitive functions by means of Positron Emission

Tomography (PET) are a reflection of this situation. PET allows one to see which regions of the brain increase their blood flow during the performance of cognitive tasks, for example of memory, language tasks etc. In the first studies with this procedure, and still today in some cases, the cerebral blood flow corresponding to the performance of a certain task was compared to the flow corresponding to a so-called condition of "rest" during which the subject was asked to "empty his mind". It soon became evident though that the comparison between the condition during the performance of a cognitive task and that of "rest" produced variable results which were difficult to interpret. This was due to the fact that it is impossible to reach a condition in which the subject really "empties" his mind. This experimental *impasse* could quite easily have been avoided if they had considered the fact that consciousness cannot in any way be passivity, and that for however much you try to establish conditions where consciousness rests, it will never stop being consciousness *of* something. Perhaps consciousness of "emptiness", but still consciousness of something.

Recognising a kind of passive inertia in consciousness, as certain cognitivist models do[1], also means recognising that the object too, or the phenomenon which consciousness passively receives in order to become consciousness of it, may already exist as an object or phenomenon outside of consciousness. Neither is this position comprehensible or acceptable, as we have seen, since the object cannot exist if not by means of consciousness which selects it. In other words, passive existence cannot be attributed to consciousness, an inertia filled with phenomena of which it is simply the spectator. This is one of the reasons why consciousness can neither receive nor be the result of information that comes from the obscurity of information processing or of the physiological. Consciousness is not separable from its object, which is only such in as far as it is selected by consciousness as a spontaneous act directed outside of itself towards the object. And it would be pointless to maintain that consciousness can take on the form of passivity and of inertia but that the flow of information it receives is continuous. If this were so it still would not lose its characteristic of being consciousness *of* something, but it would not have to claim to be active or to have an equal right to the information it receives. But even if we wanted to recognise the possibility for information to exist outside consciousness, in the opaque obscurity of the computational or

---

[1] Moscovitch, M., 1989; Schacter, D.L., 1989.

physiological level, the nature of the continuous flow of information would still have to be explained. That is, from where does information get the strength to leave the passive state, become active, organise itself with other information and become the flow of information which permeates consciousness? We would also have to explain how come this flow includes certain information and not other, and who chooses the information which is part of the flow that goes to consciousness and that which instead remains inactive waiting its turn. It is clear that such a position brings us right back to that series of aporetic problems which have already been described and which are at the basis of the *homunculus* fallacy.

The impossibility of considering consciousness as inactive passivity implies that consciousness cannot but be active. In other words, consciousness cannot but be in action, that is, in continuous apprehension of the world without any possibility of not being such. But if consciousness is necessarily in action, where, you will ask, does this action come from? Where does consciousness find the strength to be always active? The answer is that consciousness' being in action is spontaneous, that is, it does not derive from any cause, there is no strength which, so to speak, pushes consciousness from behind to keep it continuously underway. The activity of consciousness cannot but be spontaneous, because if it were not, if consciousness derived its activity from something else, we would be obliged to admit that something "precedes" consciousness and is in some way its origin. We have already shown, and will demonstrate in more detail further on, how the existence of something outside consciousness is unthinkable and even more so is the thought of something from which consciousness might originate and draw its strength. Certainly, there may be a metaphysical problem in the spontaneity of consciousness, but there is no ontological problem since consciousness comes into the world *already* in action; nothing precedes it, nor does it come from passivity, drawing its strength to do so from something other than itself. The irremediable spontaneity of consciousness generates a certain embarrassment, if not real dismay. It was precisely in seeking to exorcise this limitation in comprehension, this probably unsolvable metaphysical problem posed by consciousness, that an attempt was made to negate its spontaneity by having its activity stem from the computational or physiological unconscious. However, not only was this paralogistic as an operation - that is the concrete, the spontaneous activity of consciousness of which we are all witnesses, was seen to stem from the abstract of the computational or physiological level - but the spontaneous activity which had been denied to consciousness, that is the concrete, was granted to the unconscious, that is to the abstract.

3. BECOMING CONSCIOUS MEANS BECOMING CONSCIOUS OF SOMETHING IN A CERTAIN WAY

So far we have seen that consciousness is described as consciousness *of* something. It is not a question of inert passivity but always consciousness in action, directed towards the world, towards the object to be apprehended. We have also seen that the activity of consciousness is spontaneous since it does not originate from any strength which pushes it or from some place where it is created. But what exactly does being conscious of a definite object mean? And in particular, is there only one way of being so, or are the ways in which an object presents itself to consciousness different? And if they are, where does their diversity come from?

It is clear that to come close to an understanding of consciousness we need to answer these questions. We will answer the first question at once by saying that becoming conscious of something means becoming conscious of something *in a certain way*. The object which manifests itself to consciousness does so in a certain form, or, if you will, from a certain point of view. In other words, the phenomenon of which consciousness is conscious is aimed in a certain direction and has a certain phenomenal form, something like what Searle calls aspectual shape[1]. The word "sense" describes how the object comes into the world both with a meaning and a specific *direction* which connects it to consciousness. Of the tree I see glancing out the window I now am conscious in a certain way. That tree lends itself to my perception at a certain angle which reveals only a part of it to me, that part facing me, while it hides the other, that part facing the building I see in the background. But it is not only the tree's necessarily presenting itself in profile that makes me say that it appears to me under a certain form. Indeed, if I close my eyes, or if I simply take my attention away from the perception of that tree, I can easily imagine its hidden aspect or produce any kind of image of that tree whatsoever. I can imagine it as

---

[1] Searle, J.R., 1990.

seen from above or from below, completely bare as I would see it in autumn, planted in the middle of a field in the country instead of in the middle of buildings as it is now, etc. Furthermore, I can remember having looked at that tree yesterday and many other times before yesterday, I may know it is a beech and not a fir-tree, I may love it, hate it, be afraid of it or be indifferent towards it. Can it be said that it is the same consciousness that becomes conscious of the same object? Apparently not, because it is clear that every way I have of becoming conscious of that tree is original and cannot be easily confused with any other way in which that tree is present to my consciousness, perception, imagination, memory etc. In other words, in its need to become conscious of something, consciousness is also forced to become conscious of that something in a certain way. Just as consciousness that is conscious of nothing is inconceivable, so is consciousness that is conscious of its object in an undefined way.

You will object that when faced with an object or a phenomenon I may feel total indifference, have a kind of neutral attitude. For example, the vase of flowers in the corner of the room means nothing to me, I feel neither pleasure nor hatred, I see it, but I cannot say I perceive it in the true sense since it does not penetrate my consciousness. I glance at it only, without my being in any way altered by its presence. It is clear that an objection of this type actually does nothing but energetically assert that which it is struggling to negate. Indeed what is this indifference of mine towards that vase, this total extraneousness that I have described in such detail if not a precise way in which that vase is present to my consciousness? I don't love it, I don't hate it, I don't like it, it doesn't interest me, it doesn't alter my being: this is the detailed description of my consciousness of that vase at this moment. And this consciousness of vase is completely different, for example, from my consciousness of cigarette that, at this moment, I am lighting for pleasure, whose taste I intensely perceive etc. In other words, there is no neutral consciousness before an object, to which particular modes of perceiving the object are added from the outside. Neutrality before an object is, if anything, already a specific and original way consciousness has of considering it, on a level with imagination, perception, recollection, etc. In short, there are various modes in which the object presents itself to consciousness or, vice versa, consciousness has various modes of considering its object. The description of the various ways in which consciousness is consciousness of *something* is not part of the aim of this work. It is enough for now to have clarified that in addition to consciousness' need to be consciousness of something, there is the need to be so in a certain way and, on reflexive analysis, every way in which consciousness considers its object is original in the sense that it cannot be confused with any other way[1].

4. VARIETIES OF CONSCIOUSNESS

Does the originality of the different modes of consciousness, which makes them at the same time irreducible and unique among themselves, reflect real multiplicity of consciousness or only apparent multiplicity through which a single consciousness manifests itself to the world? On one hand, it is tempting to consider the different modes of consciousness as different, autonomous states of consciousness and therefore to attribute real multiplicity to consciousness. If the phenomenal experience caused by the perception of the glass in front of me is different and not mistakable with the phenomenal experience of the memory of this same glass on this same table yesterday, there would seem to be no reason not to attribute real independence to these two modes of consciousness which are so completely distinct. Neither would there be any reason to maintain that the independence of the modes of consciousness, perception and recollection in this example, is indeed a form of real independence but which arises from a previous level, that of a hypothetical unitary consciousness which multiplies itself when it opens in the world towards the object. In short, perceptual, imaginative consciousness, recollection, etc. are all supposedly different forms through which a single consciousness manifests itself in the world. There would therefore be no need to consider different "varieties of consciousness", each sufficient unto itself and independent of every other. But while on the one hand it is a good idea to attribute to the modes of consciousness the autonomy they have earned in the field by making themselves reciprocally original and unmistakable; on the other, we must accept that the modes of consciousness make sense only as different ways of apprehending the world in the midst of a unifying act which makes said apprehension possible. If I hate that tree out there, my consciousness will be

---

[1] We shall see later how in certain cases mistakes between the perceived and the imagined can be made but how these mistakes do not reflect confusion between perceptive and imaginative consciousness.

without doubt that of the tree inasmuch as it is hated. But in order to hate that tree I must first of all "know" that it is a tree, that is a certain object in the world. If I now remember yesterday's dinner with friends, I will certainly have "recollecting" consciousness of dinner with friends, but this presupposes the probability of having lived that experience, that is, of having had perceptual consciousness of dinner with friends. If the different modes of consciousness were only separate and autonomous, there would be no way of understanding how there could be experience of the world. Indeed, each state of consciousness, isolated from every other, would already be complete, would already have exhausted its task, so to speak. It would be circumscribed in its own world, a world in which the possibility of seeing the new appear would be denied. In other words, it would be the death of consciousness, that is the transformation of consciousness into an *in se* endowed with the same thick inertia of a stone. There is, therefore, need for a unifying act to account for the multiplicity of consciousness, which does exist, so that the different modes of consciousness can find their basic characteristic, namely that of being free and unpredictable flight towards the world.

What is the nature of this unifying act? Let us state at once that a type of unitary consciousness which "is behind" specific types of consciousness, and from which these stem, is inconceivable. If this were the case we would have to accept the existence of an empty consciousness, a type of pre-consciousness from which the specific modes of consciousness derive. We have already amply justified the rejection of such a hypothesis and we shall not go back to it. Is the ego perhaps the origin and author of the unifying act of the modes of consciousness? Many psychologies and *egological* philosophies maintain this. But what is the ego and where is it? If there is a place to look for the ego it certainly is not consciousness. Titchner[1] has already pointed out that the ego is almost always absent from consciousness. In actual fact, consciousness has no need of any ego to unify it, so the latter is neither formally nor materially in consciousness. "When I run to catch a bus, - says Sartre [2] - when I look at the time, when I am absorbed in the contemplation of a portrait, there is no ego. There is the consciousness-of-the-bus-that-must-be-caught, etc.... Indeed at such a time I am immersed in the world of objects, it is they which constitute the unity of my states of

---

[1] Titchener, E.B., 1926.
[2] Sartre, J.P., 1936, p.32.

consciousness and which present themselves with certain values, with attractive or repulsive qualities; but as far as I am concerned, I have disappeared, I have annihilated myself. There is no room for *me* at this level; this is not by chance, or due to a momentary lack of attention, but to the very structure of consciousness." In other words, the ego is not "behind" consciousness but in front as an object for consciousness itself, outside, in the world, an object among objects. The ego, in fact, appears only on one condition, when there is reflexive consciousness. I recollect the tree that I saw yesterday and in this case there is non-reflexive consciousness of tree as recollected, no ego participates in this operation. I can, though, also remember myself while I looked at that tree yesterday. In this case I perform a reflexive act and the ego appears to me as an object of my consciousness. The ego, therefore, cannot be considered a virtual hotbed of unity of consciousness, but on the contrary, it is consciousness which constitutes it as an object when, in its reflexive form, it falls back on itself to become consciousness-of-consciousness.

But where does the unifying act of the various forms of consciousness stem from if not from the ego? From consciousness itself, inasmuch as nothing other than consciousness can be the source of consciousness. For there to be unity in the multiplicity of consciousness, for my consciousness of tree as hated to be possible and for it to have a meaning, the forms of consciousness must be perpetual synthesis of past and present forms of consciousness. My consciousness of tree as hated is the synthesis of everything I have been in the past, including my knowledge of tree. The modes of consciousness, therefore, represent real multiplicity, because each one is original, unmistakable and independent. But it is a multiplicity which is unified in every consciousness as synthesis of preceding states of consciousness. We shall see further on how the explanation of numerous pathological conditions has been prevented because the unifying force of consciousness in the presence of multiplicity has been neglected.

5. WHERE DOES THE ORIGINALITY OF THE MODES OF CONSCIOUSNESS COME FROM?

Where does the originality we have attributed to the different types of consciousness or, as we have also called them, the different modes of consciousness come from? In other words, what makes imaginative consciousness what it is, for example, and what makes it unmistakable from consciousness that recollects or from any other type or mode of consciousness? On one hand, it is tempting to have the originality of the modes of consciousness stem directly from the object. The centaur I am now imagining is imaginative consciousness of centaur inasmuch as it is in the image of the centaur that my imaginative consciousness defines itself. When tomorrow I remember the image of the centaur that I am now imagining, my consciousness will be remembering consciousness of the image of the centaur, that is consciousness of the centaur as past since it is still in the centaur that my remembering consciousness is defined as such. Clearly such a hypothesis is to be rejected. If the definition of my imaginative consciousness depended on the image of the centaur, it would mean that in some way the latter preceded and was independent of consciousness itself. The separation between consciousness of image and the image itself contains a paradox. Indeed, the image would already have to be an image before becoming consciousness of image in order to then become an image imagined by a form of consciousness. But what is this image yet to be imagined which precedes consciousness of image? Nothing. Indeed outside of consciousness, the image fades into nothing, it is no longer image nor anything else. It is in its relationship with consciousness which imagines it, that the image acquires its meaning of image; it is thanks to this ontological relationship that the image comes into the world, emerging out of the nothing that it was before[1]. In the same way consciousness that recollects cannot find its definition in the object because, here too, we would have to accept the pre-existence of the object as past with respect to consciousness that recollects. We have already demonstrated at length how this hypothesis is victim of the paradox of the memory trace, that is of the permanency of the past in objects, and we will not go back over it.

And yet, you might object, experience demonstrates that in actual fact objects indisputably evoke states or modes of consciousness. If I meet a

---

[1] Sartre, J.P., 1940.

tiger on the road I am petrified, if I meet my friend Paul I recognise him, if I smell a particular perfume the last meeting with a woman wearing that perfume will come to mind, etc. In other words, my consciousness of fear of the tiger, that of Paul as a familiar person, that which recollects the woman with that particular perfume, seem to be determined by the tiger, Paul and the perfume. Of course, but this does not prove in the least that there is determinism on my modes of consciousness of the tiger, Paul or the perfume as objects *already* specified as *fearful, familiar* or *past*. The tiger, Paul and the perfume are not frightening, familiar or memories in themselves. If they become so this happens because of me. It is through the being that I am that these three things acquire a meaning. A hunter of tigers who does not know Paul, and who has never smelt that perfume will not have the subjective experiences that I have. His states of consciousness before those three objects will be completely different from mine. Well then, why, if the objects are not specified and do not determine my modes of consciousness, do different objects cause different modes of consciousness? Why, for example, does the tiger cause fear and not recollection, while the perfume I smell generates recollection and not fear? We could join the evolutionists in answering that in any case consciousness has an adaptive role. Phylogenesis has provided man with consciousness to respond suitably to the environment which surrounds him. However the adaptive hypothesis remains a figure of speech without any explicative value if first it is not made clear exactly what is meant by a suitable response. Furthermore, a deterministic perspective of this type deprives consciousness of any freedom and autonomy, reducing it to a stimulus-dependent entity whose background is marked with all of the limitations of behaviourist thought. What has been ignored is that there is no generic environment with a reproducible collection of answers that man or consciousness produce with adaptation in mind; the environment exists first of all *because of me*, because of that concrete being that I am, who reacts to the environment not according to generic adaptive responses, but according to the choice I am condemned to make in the concreteness of the situation in which I find myself. The form consciousness assumes, or the adaptive response before a phenomenon, depends in equal measure on what I have been and on what I intend to be in the future. Here is the tiger in front of me. I am terrified. Why? Because I know that tigers are extremely dangerous animals for man, I also know I am not armed and that I have no means of defending myself. This knowledge of mine, this non-thematized past takes on concrete form in my consciousness of terror of tiger, which is the synthesis of my past and the projection of my probable future, namely the possibility of being killed by the tiger. But here I am in another situation. The tiger is still in front of me, I continue to know that tigers are extremely dangerous, I am completely defenceless but I feel no terror. Why? Because I am depressed and want to die as a release from my present sorrows, or else I am a mystic and am completely indifferent to my body and what could happen to it for better or for worse, or a fearless hero who sacrifices himself to save others. Neither the tiger, what I know about tigers, nor the information-stimulus tiger, have changed with respect to the previous situation, but this time my response is different, my consciousness is no longer that of fear of tigers. My consciousness, in its freedom, has chosen to be *other* and not consciousness of fear of tiger. It is clear from this example that no determinism of the object- phenomenon, stimulus, information- on consciousness can be established. Neither can present consciousness be seen to stem merely from the synthesis of past states of consciousness, which in any case are part of consciousness. In other words, consciousness is free choice of the possible in the concrete form of a definite situation. As a non-being I, with my past, in the concrete present in which the objects, the tiger, Paul, the perfume appear, choose those objects and turn to them in a certain way.

You will say we have got off too lightly because we have freed consciousness from the determinism of the object -phenomenon, stimulus, information- by using extreme examples, the depressed person, the mystic, the hero. In most cases, you cannot deny that meeting a tiger generates consciousness of fear of tiger, and meeting Paul will always correspond to consciousness of a feeling of familiarity in his regards. But, for however extreme, the possibility for consciousness of not being consciousness of fear of tiger is enough to exclude the tiger as the cause of the mode consciousness assumes, and therefore to eliminate any determinist hypothesis of the object on consciousness. As far as we are concerned it is just enough to free consciousness and to place it as a choice among the possible. The second example, that is the hypothesis that my meetings with Paul are invariably accompanied by consciousness of familiarity in his regards, seems to have been proved without exception by experience: it is certain that every time I meet Paul, as long as I have not undergone deep changes in my being such as, for example, those which arise in cases of amnesia, I will recognise him and his recognition will generate consciousness of familiarity in his regards. But let us now suppose that I do not know Paul at all and yet on meeting him I have the same consciousness of familiarity in his regards. This is not at all rare. All of us have certainly found ourselves more than once in a similar situation, that is of thinking we know someone we meet and of therefore having consciousness of familiarity in their regards. If we assumed a determinist perspective, we would have to accept that it is the Paul that I do not know who generates in me consciousness of familiarity in his regards. But if this were the case there would no longer be any difference between the objects -phenomena, stimuli, information- concerning the possibility to generate consciousness of familiarity, since Paul, who I do not know, and Pieres, for example, who I do know, generate the same type of consciousness in me. If there is no difference between objects with respect to the possibility of generating consciousness of familiarity, then every possible determinism of the object on consciousness also disappears. In other words, if every object can determine the same type of consciousness it means that there is nothing specific in a determined object to generate that type of consciousness. In short, it seems quite clear that the originality of the different modes of consciousness is not the passive result of the object -phenomenon, stimulus, information- of which consciousness is conscious.

But is there an opposite form of determinism? Is it consciousness that determines the object? At first this conclusion might seem tempting. Indeed, having recognised freedom of choice in consciousness, and therefore a certain degree of autonomy with respect to its object, you might think that the latter exists in a passive form and is defined only as a result of the form consciousness takes. However, a conclusion of this type is not acceptable because it presupposes priority of consciousness over the object, and said priority implies that consciousness can *first* be consciousness to *then* become consciousness of the object. But we have already seen that consciousness cannot escape its law, that is the necessity to always be consciousness *of* something. Just as an object without a consciousness that selects it vanishes into nothing, so consciousness without an object is an equally unintelligible abstraction. Thus it is not consciousness which determines the object. Consciousness simply turns to the latter in a certain way, but the object remains there, separate from the consciousness to which it appears in all its physicality. However, even though it appears to consciousness, the object never presents itself in its entirety. It remains opaque for consciousness, which cannot cross it but only just distinguish its profile. That which comes towards me and terrifies me is not the essence of tiger but it is "that" tiger which presents itself under a certain form, whose muzzle I can distinguish with its ferocious expression but not its back, its claws but not its tail, that tiger which terrifies me and not that other one which I saw at the zoo and which does not terrify me at all because it is behind bars. The Paul I meet and recognise and who gives me a feeling of familiarity is that Paul who is before me in the flesh, he is not a generic Paul, synthesis of all the past, present and future Pauls. In other words, no determinism exists, no priority of consciousness over the object or vice versa. Consciousness and its object come into the world together and there is no way of conceiving of them separately. Not only but consciousness and the object come into the world "in a certain way", that is in accordance with an ontological relationship which defines both. And it is precisely the specificity of this relationship which sets off the originality of the different modes of consciousness.

6. MEMORY AS A PARTICULAR TYPE OF CONSCIOUSNESS

In the light of what we have seen so far, that is in what we have been able to establish as being some of the characteristics of consciousness, we can now state that memory represents an original mode of consciousness. Indeed, the general characteristics of the modes of consciousness can be applied without any danger of error. There is no doubt that memory is consciousness *of an* object seen *in a certain way*, and that the way in which the object is present to consciousness is unlikely to be confused with any other, for example perception or imagination. We can also state that in one's memory the object presents itself as absent. In other words, consciousness which recollects places its object as absent, both in as far as it is not present and because it is past. Therefore consciousness which remembers, in that it sets the absent object "in the past", sends one back to the past. It is clear that consciousness that remembers, since it is consciousness of the past, incorporates the problem of global temporality as the past in itself is non-existent and always directs one to the present and the future, other temporal spheres.

We have also seen that consciousness is multiplicity under a unifying force, which is reflected in the need every consciousness has for continual synthesis of all previous states of consciousness. What do we find when we apply this unifying synthesis to memory? We find that consciousness that remembers not only remembers the past but, since it is the synthesis of preceding states of consciousness, it *is* the past. What does this mean? It means that memory is built with the bricks of what consciousness was before becoming consciousness that remembers. Therefore, memory presupposes and implies "knowledge", namely the synthesis of the transformations undergone by consciousness in the course of time. When I remember Wednesday night's dinner with friends in a restaurant in the *Quartier Latin*, consciousness presupposes that I "know" what a dinner is, a restaurant, a friend and the *Quartier Latin*. In other words, my memory is made up of meanings that consciousness, through an original and irreducible act, places in the past. But, you may wonder, if memory is made up of meanings "in the past", how is it that I can remember objects without meanings, that abstract painting I saw the other day, for example, that unknown face I saw in the street, that shape I caught a glimpse of without understanding what it was? Certainly the abstract painting, the unknown face, the unrecognised shape do not have precise meanings as do "house", "friend" or "dinner". The abstract painting is an ensemble of signs which do not represent any one precise object, nor do they symbolically refer you to a meaning as do the series of signs "h,o,u,s,e", which refer you to something much more definite. And so the unknown face is none other than what it is, namely something which does not represent anything or refer you to a meaning. This, however, does not mean that the abstract picture or the unknown face are without meaning. The moment in which I perceive them as such, I attribute a meaning to them. Indeed, perception cannot exist without the attribution of meaning, as maintained by certain theories which claim to isolate "pre-semantic" perception from a form of "semantic" perception[1]. The perception of an object means, first of all, its recognition as an object, that is as something distinct from other things, and therefore giving it the meaning of being a specific object. That object may in some cases send me back a meaning, like the tree I see from the window, in other cases no meaning is sent back. But not sending back a meaning is in itself a meaning. The meaning of that picture or of that face is to be found precisely in its being an object which "means nothing specific to me", in its being an object that I do not recognise since it is a symbol of something else[2]. So, perception without the attribution of meaning is absolutely unintelligible. Even the memory of that which in itself does not send me a precise, positive

---

[1] Schacter, D.L., & Tulving, E., 1994.
[2] Merleau-Ponty, M., 1945.

meaning, but a negative one – I don't know what that object is – presupposes and implies a meaning. Without meaning, memory could not exist. Besides, what is so-called infantile amnesia, namely that lapse of memory of the first years of life we all have? Why do I not remember anything that happened in my first few years of life? Because for the child that I was, the world was still a shapeless mass against which objects did not yet stand out, and if they had I would not have been able to attribute any meaning whatsoever to them, not even in the negative, of being an object which means nothing to me. Only when objects have begun to be recognised as such, and to progressively mean something more and more definite, does the possibility of remembering come into play. This is why my past does not appear to stem from my infantile amnesia, rather I feel it progressively diminishing into the obscurity of my early childhood, since I progressively left that obscurity, giving a more and more polished meaning to a world which was originally without meaning.

But if memory as the synthesis of preceding states of consciousness presupposes a meaning, or rather, to use the same expression as earlier, if it is built with the bricks of meaning, what about knowledge? Is it only the collection of meanings of which memory is made, or like memory is it an organised form of consciousness? Let us see. When I say that I know that water in chemical terms is H_2O, that I am Italian, that this pen is blue, what is my consciousness consciousness of? Of water as it is chemically formed, in accordance with certain laws, of hydrogen and oxygen, of myself in as far as I belong to a certain community, of the pen in as far as it is of a certain colour. And so in this case too we can apply the first characteristic of consciousness, that is of being consciousness *of*. We shall also see that my consciousness of knowing what I assert as regards water, myself and the pen is unmistakable with other modes of consciousness: when I assert these things I am certain I am not remembering, imagining etc. Besides, the objects I claim to know something about are present to my consciousness in a certain way, that is precisely as objects over which I affirm knowledge. The characteristics of the modes of consciousness therefore also apply to consciousness of knowing. But, what has consciousness of water as H_2O in common with me as an Italian and the pen as being blue? What makes them a single mode of consciousness? It is precisely their being consciousness of something in the form of knowledge, namely in the affirmation of a state of consciousness. Little does it matter if water, the pen and I are fundamentally different. In reality, before consciousness which selects these objects as something on which to affirm a state of consciousness, water, the pen and I are absolutely the same. Following the same line of inquiry that we followed for consciousness which remembers, we must now establish what consciousness that knows is made of. That is, we should explain what the unifying act of consciousness that knows is synthesis of. In the same way as consciousness that remembers, consciousness that knows cannot but be the synthetic collection of transformations which consciousness has undergone in time. Therefore also consciousness that knows is made up of bricks of meaning and of the past, namely of all that it was before becoming here and now consciousness of water, the pen and me in a certain way. In this sense therefore, consciousness that knows is as temporal as consciousness that remembers, but unlike the latter it is not consciousness of time. It is evident that the structure of consciousness that remembers and of that which knows, as organised forms of consciousness, both containing the past, require clarification regarding the past and its relationship with the other dimensions of time. In the following chapter, the study of temporality, which we have put off until now, will show us what the conditions are that make memory and consciousness possible.

CHAPTER 4

TEMPORALITY

1. PHENOMENOLOGY OF TEMPORALITY

A recollection could be said to be the result of an act which aims at representing an absent object. Yet the *absence* of an object is not in itself enough to connote it as a remembered object. Indeed, if absence were sufficient as a characteristic, there would be no way of distinguishing a remembered object from an imagined one, for instance, or a memory from a symbolic representation of an object. The centaur that I imagine on closing my eyes or the word "chair" that I read represent, that is they stand in-the-stead-of, absent objects. In the case of the centaur it is the representation of an imaginary object, in that of the chair the representation of a real object. Both these objects are absent in the sense that their presence in consciousness is mediated, by an image in the first case, and by a sequence of signs to which I can attribute sound and meaning in the second. But though absent, neither the centaur nor the chair are "remembered". Thus in order to understand the nature of a remembered object we must ask ourselves what type of absence, or *non-presence,* it is a question of.

The remembered object's particular, original way of being absent inevitably leads back to the problem of the past, inasmuch as the object which presents itself in memory is, by nature and by definition, an object "in the past". In short, recollection aims at representing, and making present in consciousness, an absent object which is characterised by being both absent and past. Without contradicting ourselves we could say that a remembered object is defined as a "presence in the past". Indeed it is present in consciousness while continually laying claim to being past.

It is clear at this point that an investigation into the nature and essence of the past is a necessary preliminary condition for any study on the nature of memory, and this is what we are about to do. Our investigation into the nature of the past will inevitably lead to the study of other temporal dimensions since past, present and future are not isolated, independent elements, the sum of which determines temporality. In other words, the past will have to be considered, from the start, as a subordinate structure of global temporality, which in turn is seen as the synthesis which gives meaning to the single subordinate elements, past, present and future. In fact, if we were to consider the past and the other subordinate structures of temporality as isolated elements, independent from one another, we would find ourselves confronted with the paradox already emphasised by the phenomenological tradition: the past is no longer, the future is not yet, and as for the present, it is nothing other than the result of an infinite division, a limit with no dimension of its own. The study of the past will thus lead us to the study of the other temporal dimensions as well as of global temporality.

a. The past

Although a presupposition about the nature of the past is necessarily implicit in any theory of memory, this presupposition has never been clarified. The being of the past is somehow negated in these theories, in the sense that the past is considered as what *is no longer*. This assumption has produced, as we have seen, the theory of memory traces: if something is no longer present but continues to exist in the form of memory, it must be preserved in the form of a more or less stable modification in the organism which remembers. As we have clearly seen, the theory of memory traces contains a paradox, that is it derives the past from the present in an arbitrary way. If, then, every theory of memory which is based on the preservation of the past is to be rejected, in order to understand the nature of memory we must come to terms with the problem of the nature of the past.

In his theory of memory, while acknowledging that the past has a right to exist, Bergson[1] has sought, in vain, to relate it to the present. The past, he

---

[1] Bergson, H., 1896.

maintains, does not cease to be but simply ceases to act in the present, and stays there, set at its date, for ever. Its relation to the present comes from duration, which is multiplicity of interpenetration through which the past continuously binds itself to the present. Bergson's is a vain attempt because it does not clarify the origin of the act which links the past to the present. In other words, for want of clarification of the origin of this act, the terms duration and multiplicity of interpenetration remain empty. Husserl's position presents similar problems. He sees a game of "retentions" in present consciousness, which fix past states of consciousness, keeping them at their date of occurrence. However for Husserl consciousness is always present, or rather instantaneous. What is not clear is how the past emerges through a series of instantaneous states of consciousness. The game of retention he talks about remains meaningless if its perpetrator is not identified. Thus acknowledging the past's right to exist does not get us anywhere. If the instantaneous present is given priority, any links with the past are automatically broken: for however much the past may exist or "be", it will never reach either Bergson's or Husserl's present.

The common mistake which prevents these theoretical attempts from linking the past to the present is that they only consider the past as an isolated *in se* rather than as a subordinate structure of temporality. If the past were considered within temporal dynamics as a whole, it would be easy to see that "my" past is above all *mine*, that it exists in function of a certain being which *is* me. Furthermore, my past is the past of a certain present which, once again, is *my* present. In other words the past cannot exist but as the past of a present. Its belonging to me, or its *meeness* which Claparède[1] talks of, is not only a subjective nuance which I ascribe to memory, but rather the result of an ontological relationship which links the past to the present, the founding element of their relationship. My past never appears in splendid isolation. It could not even be thought of as such. It is originally past of *this present* which I am. Let us clarify this point.

The other evening while I was having an argument with Mark I saw him as being rather unreasonable. And yet today I consider him a reasonable person. Where does this contradiction stem from? You could simply say that the Mark of then was another Mark, completely different from the present one. But what is meant here by "another"? Where does the difference

---

[1] Claparède, E., 1911.

between that Mark and this one lie? If we were to limit ourselves to considering the question from a static temporal perspective we would resolve nothing: Mark was as present then, when he was arguing with me, as he is now when I say he is reasonable. In other words, Mark's irrationality is a present characteristic inasmuch as I considered him irrational in the present. Where does the diversity between the Mark of then and the one of now come from, if in both situations it is a question of a present Mark? And why do I now say: that evening Mark *said* irrational things? Is there a third Mark then, who is characterised by being irrational and past? If there were, if the discriminating characteristic of this third Mark were merely that of being "past", then every link with the present would, by definition, be negated. The possibility of bringing him back to the present of consciousness would be lost for ever. It would be a question of a man lost in the past with his attribute of irrationality, and every attempt to bring him back to the present would be destined to fail. But under what kind of magic can I think of Mark as a past Mark? If there is no way of preserving his past irrationality somewhere, where should the attempt to lead that irrational, past Mark to his natural place in time, the present of consciousness that remembers him, start? In other words, if it is absurd to think that the past exists as such, isolated from the present, how can we wrench it from its splendid isolation and reconstruct the links which join it to the present? I say that the other evening Mark was irrational. Who is it that *was*, in this case? Mark, of course. But which Mark are we talking about, the one that was arguing with me? Absolutely not: we would have to say that that Mark *is*, not *was*. For the whole time in which he said irrational things we must say of him that he *is* irrational. If, on the other hand, we are talking about a Mark who became past, every connection with the present is lost and that Mark remains isolated down there with his attribute of irrationality. "If we want a memory to remain possible - Sartre says - we must allow for a synthesis of reconnaissance which from the present arrives at preserving its link with the past - a synthesis which is impossible to conceive of, if not as an original way of being ."[1] If I say that Mark *was* irrational, I say it of this present Mark, of whom I can also say, without contradicting myself, that he is a reasonable person. It is not the irrational Mark that *was*. Of that person we must say he *is*. It is the present one who *was* irrational. But what is this synthesis of recognition, this original way of being that Sartre talks of, for want of which the past is abandoned to its isolation? This Mark who I say

---

[1] Sartre, J.-P., 1943.

was irrational is not past *in se* just as in no case can he be present *in se*. Being present or being past means being such for someone, for a consciousness. The Mark that was irrational that evening is not past *tout court*, but is first of all past *for me*. That is, he is *my* past and he is the past of a certain present which is *my* current present. It is thanks to me that that Mark has not faded into nothingness but has become past. "The dead who could not be saved and transported onto the concrete past of a survivor" says Sartre [1] "are not *past*; they and their past are annulled". If we want to find the past we must thus look for it in the concrete present of a consciousness which transcends its own present to select an event down there where it was.

On the other hand if no past is possible without the present of a consciousness to select it, the opposite is also true: I can have a present *because* I have a past which gives meaning to this present. My present is soaked in my past and acquires significance only as present of that past. But we must be careful not to think that the past is in some way possessed by the subject or by consciousness. The relationship between my present and my past is not a relationship between elements which remain external to one another. The external relationship between possessor and possessed would relegate the past, once again, to its unattainable isolation and would create an insuperable abyss between past and present. Actually rather than have a past we should say *be* our own past. In short, there is no past but for a present, which to exist must be its own past. This is what we should mean when, like Merleau-Ponty[2], we say that the past makes sense to us only inasmuch as *we are it* or that *wesen ist was gewesen ist,* as Hegel says. But what does *being* one's past mean, and how can the present *be* the past?

I *am* my past in that nothing of that past is extraneous to me. When I say that the other day I *was* happy or that I *was* a medical student, I am totally responsible for those events in the entirety of my present being. And it is because I was a medical student that I now am what I am. But having been a medical student is not meant here to have a propaedeutic value with respect to my concrete present. In fact I could just as well say that having been happy the other day is part of what I am now. The present which I am, is the condensation of what I have been, for better and for worse. You could object that we are not always responsible for our past. For example, for acts committed in a state of altered consciousness, as in the case of certain

---

[1] Sartre, J.-P., 1943.
[2] Merleau-Ponty, M., 1945.

pathologies, the present of a subject is not held either morally or juridically responsible. Or rather, much more simply, I can demand not to be reproached for a past state inasmuch as *now* that state no longer exists. I may have been a revolutionary fanatic but am so no longer, and today I no longer feel responsible for that revolutionary being. Even juridically I am no longer held responsible once I have served the sentence for the consequences of my past being. Of course. But for however much I may seek to distance my past from myself, this will never change its nature. It will continue to be *my* past and I will continue to be my past in the present which I am. I can deny and reject it as much as I like but I will never be able to cease to be it, I will never be able to make it an impersonal past. And besides, what is the point of regret? It is a desperate attempt to distance our past from ourselves. But not desperate in the sense that we should be for ever condemned to our past. We are only so in death which, as Malraux said, by transforming life into destiny, makes being coincide with having been. But it is still a desperate attempt because at the very moment in which I deny my past, I do nothing but affirm it and show even more clearly its solidarity of being with my present. In this sense I cannot but be responsible for my past, and my present cannot but be my past.

But tracing the past back to the present of a consciousness does not mean, as it may seem, falling back into the error of the theory of the trace which claimed to recreate the past from elements borrowed from the present. We must not fall under the substantialist illusion, that is, into the temptation of considering the past and memory as "things" inside consciousness and the object as a "thing" inside memory. There is no "general" consciousness which can be filled at will with this or that object, as a warehouse is filled with stock. There are no objects inside consciousness, consciousness and its object are born together. This pen which is in front of me is already consciousness-of-pen-as-present. Likewise, Mark arguing with me on a certain evening is already consciousness-of-Mark-as-past. The present of consciousness has nothing to do with the present of an object except in one particular case, that is in reflection, when consciousness objectifies itself. In all other cases we cannot say that consciousness is present as we would say of any object because, while an object can only be present to a consciousness, the present is the place of consciousness or, to use Merleau-Ponty's[1] words, the area in which

---

[1]Merleau-Ponty, M., 1945.

being and consciousness coincide. It is from this present of consciousness, which is completely different from an object's present, that the recognising synthesis, which re-establishes the links between past and present, departs. When we said that there was no contradiction in saying that if I remember an object or an event, these are "present in the past", this is exactly what we meant. That is, that memory is an original way that consciousness has of transcending the present to select an event down there, where it was. But transcending the present does not mean it attaches itself to the past. If that were the case it would be a matter of a past consciousness, which is unthinkable. Transcending the present means rather giving a temporal dimension to the object that consciousness takes into consideration. And this temporal dimension is consciousness itself which, as we shall see later on, cannot but be in the *ek-static* form, that is outside itself in the present, extended towards the object whose present it is, in the past from which it flees, in the future towards which it runs.

We have seen that the past as such cannot but be thought of as the past of a consciousness' present. The moment has therefore come to question ourselves on the nature of the present.

b. The present

What is the nature of the present? On one hand it is tempting to define the present for what it is, in contrast to the past which is no longer, and the future which is not yet. But on the other hand, as Husserl[1] notes, if we were to free the present of all that it is not, that is of the past and the future, we would, in reality, find ourselves with an infinitesimal instant, the ideal end of an infinite division, a nothing lacking any dimension of its own. But the present is not an instant, but a dimension which distinguishes itself from all the others with its characteristic of *presence*. Yet presence must not be interpreted here as Bergson's[2] duration, and even less so as a series of separate static instants. Bergson explained the unity of time with duration, which is continuity that comes about through imperceptible transitions from one instant to another. But that is like muddling together past, present and future, and, in short, negating time. And yet if the present is considered to

---

[1] Husserl, E., 1893-1917.
[2] Bergson, H., 1896.

be a combination of separate instants, it is not clear how one instant passes onto another. In the absence of a subject which is responsible for a unifying synthesis, every instant remains isolated and lacks any possibility of linking itself to the previous instant or to the next. Present is as much in opposition to past as it is to absent. "Present" answers the pupil during roll-call, meaning *I am here*. Present thus first of all means *present to....* But who is present and to whom are we present?

I am present to the objects that surround me, to the world in which I am immersed. But can I say that the objects, the world, are present to me and to one another? If that were the case, the present would be reduced to a reciprocal relationship of presences regulated by a simple external relationship of contiguity. Clearly this is not how things work. Presence to... describes an internal relationship between the being which is present and the beings to which it is present. In short, presence to... requires a consciousness. It is consciousness which is present to the chair, to the table, to the world. In order to be present to this chair I must be linked to it by a relationship which makes me select the being of this chair from where it is, which in some way unites me to it but without making my being correspond to the being of the chair. Objects, beings which are isolated *en-soi*, are neither present nor absent, just as they cannot be past or future. This chair can be present to this table only on condition that there is also a being present which has in itself the possibility of presence, that is a consciousness. To be able to come into the world as objects of a subject which is present to them there needs to be a consciousness which selects them and which selects itself as present to them.

But what is the relationship between present consciousness and that to which it is present? In other words, *to whom* is consciousness present? Consciousness is present to everything which it is not. Rather, the presence of consciousness makes everything which it is not acquire unitary significance. I am simultaneously present to this chair, to this table, to the room, the city, my body, other bodies, to the whole world. In short, it is thanks to consciousness that the beings of the world become present. Beings manifest themselves as co-present in a world in which consciousness, as Sartre says, "unites them with its blood, through that total *ek-static* sacrifice of itself which is called presence"[1]. Before the sacrifice of consciousness,

---

[1] Sartre, J.-P., 1943.

beings were neither united nor separate. It is with consciousness that the present enters the world and beings of the world are co-present, inasmuch as the same consciousness is present to all of them together. We have clarified *what* present is, and *to whom* the present is present. We now have to clarify what presence is.

We have seen that presence cannot be defined as the simple co-existence of two beings outside one another, because a witness is required to ascertain their co-existence. This witness is consciousness, which establishes the co-existence of all beings inasmuch as it makes itself present to all beings contemporaneously. But what happens when consciousness is present to a being in itself, to this chair, for instance? In this case there cannot be a witness, a third element which establishes presence. It is consciousness, which in order to be present to ... must *already* be witness to its own presence. In other words, the relationship between consciousness and the being to which it is present is an internal relationship, an internal bond, not an external relationship of contiguity. Consciousness attaches itself to the being to which it is present. This close attachment of consciousness to the being, however, passes through the negation of its identification with the object to which it makes itself present. I am present to this chair, I am profoundly attached to its being and yet I am not this chair, I do not identify myself with it. Rather, presence is the very recognition of the impossibility of identification with the object. Consciousness' presence to the object implies that consciousness is witness to itself as not being that object. In this sense the present *is not* inasmuch as it is negation of identification with the object. And this is how the present assumes its own dimension which is that of evasion, of continuous flight from the being which is *there*. In other words, the basic structure of the present is negation as internal relationship between consciousness and an object. The idea of the present seen as an instant derives from an operation of reification of the present which leads to making the present correspond to what the subject is present to, for example the time on that clock. When I say *it is seven o'clock*, I do not select the present instant but the object to which I am present and from which I am separated by an inestimable void.

If presence is the negation of the identification of consciousness with an object, could we say that non-presence is the opposite, that is affirmation of identification between consciousness and an object? In everyday language we often say that someone "is not present": for instance I could say that

Mark, who did not understand what I was saying because he was thinking about something else, was not present, just as I can justify someone's inappropriate gesture by saying "he was not himself". What do I mean by this? That when I was talking to Mark and he was not listening to me because he was absorbed in his thoughts, he was like an object as far as I was concerned. In other words, at that moment Mark had the same consistency for me as this chair, this table, or the wall facing me. Why wasn't Mark *present* when I was talking to him? Because at that moment he was not performing any *act of presence* which is the opposite of what is commonly done. Performing an act of presence means negating that I belong to the world which I have before me and affirming my consciousness as bitter condemnation to the separation of the world. Non-presence annuls this separation, but in so doing it does not by any means establish identification between consciousness and object because, as we have seen, consciousness can only be consciousness *of...*, that is witness to a separation. What non-presence actually indicates is the absence of consciousness, although that does not mean that consciousness annuls itself in non-presence. When Mark was not listening to me he had the same consistency as the chair and he himself was not present to that chair. In other words, his consciousness was absent. Does this mean it was annulled? Not at all. Mark absorbed in his thoughts was present to these. His consciousness was, so to speak, "elsewhere" and was making itself present to other beings which were neither the chair nor my person.

The present is thus flight from the being which is *there*. On the other hand, the present is also flight from the being which was, that is the past. Where does the present run to if not towards the being which it will be?

c. The future

We have seen that the past is inconceivable if not as the past of the present of a consciousness which, in the act of remembering, transcends the present in order to select an event from down there, where it occurred. Similarly, the future cannot be thought of if not as the future of the present of a consciousness which transcends the present to select an event from over there where it will take place. In other words, not even the future can be considered an isolated *in se*. A full moon is not the future when I see a waxing moon. A waxing moon is, in itself, nothing other than what it is, and it contains no future element or anything which predicts a future event[1]. There is nothing potential about it. If a quarter moon heralds the next full moon, this only happens through a consciousness which, on observing the quarter moon selects the full moon as the future of its own concrete present. It is only through human reality that the future comes into the world and takes on meaning. Just as an impression left on the sofa would not refer one back to the thousand times that someone has sat on it were it not for a consciousness which is capable of selecting it as a sign of past events; a waxing moon would not refer to a full moon were it not for a consciousness which sees it as the omen of a future event. If the future exists, this is only by means of a consciousness which *is* also its own future.

But what does *being one's own future* mean? As in the case of the past, we must once again reject the idea that the future exists in the form of representation. Just as in the case of the memory trace which was supposed to represent the past but always remain only present, so, even if we wanted to accept the idea of representation, the represented future would remain in the present and we would once again need some strong magic to see it represented *in the future tout court*. Yet again, if we want to understand the being of the future we have to start from the present and select in the present the act of consciousness which transcends its present, that is its being, to project itself *there where it will be*.

The relationship between present and future is a relationship of finality, which could be defined as an overturned causality, that is the effect of a future state on a present state. For example: the actions I perform when I make a cup of coffee only make sense for the end that will be achieved, drinking the coffee. It is the future act, drinking the coffee, which determines the actions I am performing now, it links them to one another and makes them significant. It is this overturned causality which links the future to the present and rejects it as a simple "now" which is not yet. If it were merely a question of a "now" to come, we would find it isolated once again, and with no chance of linking itself to the present again. The future is what I must be in the continuous possibility of not being it.

---

[1] Example taken from Sartre, ,J.-P., 1943.

Earlier we said that presence is flight. This flight is double, because in escaping the being that it was, consciousness flees towards the being that it will be. What is the other meaning of the flight of consciousness towards the being that it will be if not that of filling a void, a lack, an incompleteness of which the present is made. The being of the present flees its own incompleteness towards its complete being, that is towards the connection with all that it is lacking. In this sense the future is that very lack which snatches the present being, seen as lacking, from inert presence. If nothing were missing, the present being would lose its characteristic of presence. It would be a pure, inert, atemporal being, lost in the isolation of complete identification, something like the state of a meditating Buddhist monk. It is thus the lack, the future, which permits the being of consciousness to be present, because it is outside itself, drawn towards a lack. In this sense the present being must be its own future, because the foundations of what it is, are in front of it and are always a future form.

But the flight of the present from its own incompleteness, this reaching out in order to compensate for a lack, reflects consciousness' desperate attempt to link up with what it is not, to complete itself by acquiring what it will be. It is a desperate attempt because the future never allows itself to be reached, it slips into the past as the ex-future of a certain present, that is it becomes a future in the past. Even if my present is completely identical to what I anticipated for myself, for example, after having performed the necessary motions I finally drink the coffee I prepared, I will always have another future in front of me, another gap to fill. The coffee I drink is not the future I have reached, but the present of my being now from which something is still missing. Drinking my coffee as future is now part of my past in the form of the future in the past, that is of the future of that being that I was. From the unattainability of the future, which translates itself into a continuous separation from my possible being, derives the anxiety which accompanies the present. I am the anxiety of not sufficiently being that future which I must be and which gives meaning to my present. The future is the continual possibilization of the possibles which give direction to the present but which cannot be reached.

It is clear that the future thus described has nothing to do with a homogenous and chronologically organised series of instants to come, just as the past is not the discrete organisation of instants which have been. What remains to be clarified is the relationship between the temporal dimensions

2. Ontology of Temporality

a. The before-after relationship

If temporality is seen as a comprehensive structure, it is clear that this is the result of a relationship which is perpetuated, the *before-after* relationship. The basic characteristic of the before-after relationship is its irreversibility. If I say that A comes before B, it means that A will *always* come before B. Furthermore, in order to be joined by a relationship of succession, A and B must be separate elements in such a relationship. What is it that separates them? Time, you might say. Indeed, is it not time which separates me from my after, that is from my future and from my past? Without time I would *now* be both the dreams I hope to fulfil and the suffering I want to be cured of. Thus time is the measure between two elements, the distance which separates them: two cities are separated by an hour's train journey, a student has three months to go before graduation. But from a similar view of time, what Merleau-Ponty calls time-space in contrast with real time, it is easy to ascertain that temporality is reducible to an infinite succession of befores and afters and, like a point on a straight line, the indivisible element of temporality is the *instant* which is located before certain instants and after others, but which in itself is neither before nor after but merely an indivisible, atemporal element. In this way the world is fragmented into an infinity of instants, which are juxtaposed but separate, and thus it becomes difficult to understand how one instant passes to the next. The problem thus becomes that of explaining how a world, that is a series of connected instants and of changes in time, can exist. You might say that the separation between before and after is a special form of separation, that is, it is a separation which reunites. Certainly, but if the relationship between before and after is an external relationship between atemporal elements, where can such a unifying force come from? You will say that the before-after relationship is such for a witness. But either the witness is a temporal being, and then the same problem holds for him too, or, if it is an extra-temporal subject, the I-think in Descartes, God in Kant, one expects to construct temporality as an external relationship between atemporal substances. One wonders how the before-after relationship and temporality itself can exist under these conditions. Either one implicitly and surreptitiously temporalizes the atemporal or, if its atemporality is left intact, time will become a purely human illusion, a dream.

Bergson certainly did not solve the problem by introducing the concept of duration. Of course, Bergson's duration breaks up Descartes' instant into a multiplicity of interpenetration, but Bergson seems to forget that duration conceived of in this way is a synthesis which requires an organising act. Who is responsible for such an act, Bergson does not say. However the difficulties which Bergson found in his theory of memory reflect this state of affairs. Saying that the past attaches itself to the present and penetrates it is merely a figure of speech. If the past, as he maintains, is an inactive *in se,* it will never go so far as penetrating the present in the form of memory, it will quietly stay down there, without having any effect on the present at all. Duration could be said to make the past join the present, but if who is responsible for this unifying act which I call duration is not clarified, we are back where we started from.

What has been ignored is that the before-after relationship is not an external relationship between atemporal elements, but an internal relationship between elements which are temporalized with this relationship. If I say that A comes before B, the priority of A presupposes in the nature of A what Sartre calls "an incompleteness of A (instant or state) which aims at B. If A precedes B, it is in *B* that A can receive this determination. Otherwise neither the rising nor the annulling of B, isolated in its instant, could confer upon A, isolated in its own, the slightest particular quality". Similarly, in order to be after A, B must somehow be in A in order to guarantee for itself the characteristic of posterity. Every element of the sequence is in a condition of *ek-static* unity. Thus every element will in some way always be out of itself in order to be before or after the other. Right, you might say, but how can a state be *out of itself?* Why is the division which emerges in the *ek-static* elements never realised? Who is responsible for this *ek-stasis*?

Sartre says that temporality is a dissolving force within a unifying act and that succession, rather than being a true multiplicity, is a quasi-multiplicity, an attempt at dissociation within unity. In short there is apparently no priority of unity over multiplicity, or vice-versa: temporality is unity which multiplies itself. This contradiction, multiplicity which unifies and unity which multiplies itself, is only apparent. In reality the internal relationship between before and after, which unites and separates, is only possible inasmuch as a consciousness establishes it. Indeed consciousness can only be temporal. It is thanks to consciousness that the before-after relationship exists, it is thanks to human reality that multiplicity acquires meaning as the union of elements in a reciprocal relationship. But, you might object, are we not perhaps assuming what we intended to explain? If consciousness is *already* a temporal being, doesn't the same contradiction apply here too? The only possible existence for consciousness is, as we have already seen, the *ek-static* form. This implies that consciousness is temporal *per se,* and does not need a witness to record its being temporal. A consciousness with no past, present or future would be a collapsed consciousness, stripped of its very nature, which is that of transcending itself in order to open itself to the temporality of which it is made. Later we shall see how this actually happens in pathological cases.

The almost irresistible tendency to consider time as *content* in objects has also led to a faulty interpretation of the results of certain neurophysiological experiments. Libet's experiments constitute one example [1]. Since Penfield's experiences we know that electric stimulation of the somatosensory cortex during a neurosurgical operation produces a sensation in the corresponding part of the patient's body. For instance, the stimulation of a point on the left somatosensory cortex produces a brief tingling sensation in the patient's right hand. In his experiments, Libet compared the time necessary to produce the tingling effect in the hand after stimulation of the cortex and after direct stimulation of the hand itself. Since both the stimulus applied to the hand and that applied to the somatosensory cortex are "analysed" by the cortex, Libet expected that when both stimuli were applied simultaneously to the hand and the cortex, the "cortical" stimulus would be felt by the patient before the one applied to the hand, which has a greater distance to cover in order to reach the cortex. But what he found was that the stimulus applied to the hand was felt by the patient *before* the one applied to the cortex and this happened even when, instead of being simultaneous the stimulus to the cortex preceded the one applied to the hand. This phenomenon has given rise to endless dispute between

---

[1] Libet, B., 1965; Libet, B., 1981; Libet, B., 1982; Libet, B., 1985;
Libet, b., Wright, E.W., Feinstein, B., & Pearl, D.K., 1979.

materialists and dualists. The former[1] consider the experience of the sequence of stimuli reported by patients as a *temporal illusion*, the others[2] see this phenomenon as proof that what happens in consciousness has nothing to do with what happens in the brain.

Let us examine this phenomenon more closely. In one case, stimulus A (the one applied to the hand) precedes stimulus B (the one applied to the cortex), in another case the same two stimuli are simultaneous. But are the successive and the simultaneous stimuli really the same? In other words, is A which precedes B the same as A simultaneous to B? On one hand it is tempting to accept such identification: we are dealing with the same electric discharge applied to the same place, at the same instant. This is how the protagonists of the dispute see it. What they do not realise is that yes, the stimuli are the same, but they are *pour-soi* instantaneous and atemporal. There is nothing, nor could there ever be anything in A which specifies its simultaneity with, or its priority over B, unless there is a consciousness which takes the trouble to attribute the meaning of simultaneity or of sequence to the two stimuli. Without a consciousness, the two are not linked by any temporal relationship. The contradiction of the possibility of both simultaneity and succession disappears if you consider that they appear to two different states of consciousness in different conditions. On one hand the consciousness of the patient who perceives a succession, on the other that of the experimenter who perceives a simultaneity. Both simultaneity and succession are the result of the temporalization of two events by two different states of consciousness. There is no priority of one over the other, nor can we get away with saying that the simultaneity perceived by the experimenter is "real" while that perceived by the patient is illusory. Both are equally real. You will object that the simultaneity of the stimuli observed by the experimenter is, however, guaranteed by experimental rigour because both stimuli are administered by a machine which is programmed to apply them to the hand and to the cortex of the patient simultaneously. But, either by some magic we make the machine which administers the stimuli a temporal being, or you will agree that, once again, the presumed simultaneity with which the machine releases the stimuli is

---

[1] See, for instance: Churchland, P.S., 1981; Churchland, P.S., 1981.
Churchland, P.S. (1981). The timing of sensation: reply to Libet. Philosophy of Science, 48, 492-497.
[2] Libet, B., Wright, E.W., Feinstein, B., & Pearl, D.K., 1979.
Popper, K.R., & Eccles, J.C., 1977.

nothing other than the simultaneity with which the experimenter who programs the machine wants the stimuli to be released. Without the experimenter, the electric shocks released by the machine are neither simultaneous nor in succession. In short, what is being confused here is the discrepancy between an improbable "objective time", that of the experimenter, and the time experienced by the patient. Again, there is no priority of the first over the second since both are of the same nature. As for the machine, it is merely the guarantee of the simultaneity wanted by the experimenter.

But then, you could say, why do two states of consciousness, that of the experimenter and that of the patient, perceive time so differently, and why is the stimulus applied to the hand, which has a greater distance to cover to reach the brain, perceived before the one applied directly to the point of arrival? There does not appear to be any metaphysical problem with the fact that two states of consciousness perceive the same event in different ways. Once again, if you see a problem here it is only because we forget that an event in itself is nothing, but only acquires significance when a consciousness takes the trouble to select it. And in order to select an event, consciousness must become aware of it from a certain point of view. Making sense of something does not merely mean giving it a meaning, but it also means addressing it in a certain way, from a determined direction, so to speak, from the angle at which the thing presents itself. Of this vase which is in front of me and which I perceive as whole, I do not select the crack which is on the other side of it and which would make whoever looks at the vase from another point of view perceive it as broken. The sense of simultaneity with which the experimenter attributes the two stimuli is determined by the particular point of observation which he assumes, just as the sense of succession perceived by the patient is determined by his position with respect to the stimuli. As regards the fact that the more distant stimulus is perceived by the patient as prior to the one applied directly to the cortex, this presents, if anything, a methodological problem, certainly not a metaphysical one. This phenomenon only tells us that measuring the length of time taken by two stimuli to reach the somatosensorial cortex is certainly not a good way of measuring temporal consciousness. But this is certainly not enough to conclude, as Libet does, that consciousness has nothing to do with the brain, nor to affirm, as Churchland[1] does, for example, that the

---

[1] Churchland, P.S., 1981; Churchland, P.S., 1981.

sequence experienced by the patient is illusory. In this sense Dennet is right in affirming that consciousness does not have a place in the brain. In any case, granted that temporal consciousness can be "measured" in neurophysiological terms (though we have already seen the problems that such a hypothesis presents), the somatosensorial cortex is certainly not a good candidate for becoming the place where such a measurement should take place.

What can be concluded from what has been said so far? First of all this: if consciousness cannot originally be but temporal, that is in the unity of its three *ek-static* forms, this implies that there cannot be a consciousness which does not already have a relationship with its own past. I have already mentioned that consciousness is overcoming and flight. What does consciousness escape from? From everything, you might say. From itself, from the world, from the present and the past. However, what consciousness flees from, what it overcomes, is not given. The world, presence, the past, are not *in se* which lie patiently waiting for a consciousness to select them. Without a consciousness they simply do not exist. The past is thus a basic structure of consciousness because the latter can only exist by overcoming, and overcoming implies something to overcome. Thus, however we may want to consider it, consciousness is born to a relationship with its own past. In other words, at the beginning there is not a consciousness of the present which then becomes consciousness of the past because consciousness, since it must be its own past, comes into being *with* a past. In light of these observations, the problem of birth also assumes a different form. In fact it seems somewhat strange that, at a certain point consciousness comes to inhabit the embryo, and thus there is first a living being in formation without a consciousness and then, all of a sudden, a moment in which a consciousness without a past comes to inhabit this being. But this is not so strange if we bear in mind that there cannot be a consciousness without a past. Consciousness is born as annulment, overcoming and negation of the *in se,* that *in se* which I was and to which I am tied by a relationship which is characterised by the word *before.* An embryo is what I was before without ever having been so in the form of consciousness. This is how we understand that the past does not appear to us as something definite, clearly marked out in the background of our existence. That is how it would be if a consciousness without a past were born and could be conscious witness of every present which would then become past. But the past appears indefinite, and jagged, and the further back I go, the more it gets lost in the dark until it reaches the pitch black of that foetus which, nevertheless, I was. And it is precisely because that is what I was, just as I was that new-born baby, that I am tied to it by profound solidarity which I can neither understand nor negate. Because if that foetus or that new-born represent the *de facto* limit of my memory, they do not represent the limit by rights of my past. There is perhaps an unsolvable metaphysical problem in birth (how is it that I come from that embryo?) but there is no ontological problem. In fact we do not need to ask ourselves why there is birth of consciousness because consciousness, as overcoming and negation of the *in se*, cannot but present itself as *already born*. The original existence of universal time, in which a consciousness without a past suddenly appears, is incomprehensible. It is from consciousness as already born that a world appears with universal time in which a moment can be distinguished when consciousness did not yet exist, as can beings from which it was not born and a being from which it was born. In short, consciousness comes into the world as the relationship with the past which it must be without any possibility of not being it.

But this *ek-static* relationship that consciousness has with its past which it must be, by no means implies that consciousness is necessarily consciousness *of* the past, that is that the past is a thesis for consciousness which thematizes it. Being the past of consciousness is not, as for example in the case of perceptive consciousness, thematization and negation of identification with an object. Of this cup which is before me, I, as not-being-cup am conscious. In other words, thematized consciousness is negation and detachment from an object inasmuch as I am not it. In the case of the past, however, I am it and cannot but be it. The past is behind consciousness, unnoticed and omnipresent travelling companion, outside its thematic field. Of course this does not mean that the past cannot be thematized. If I turn around, my travelling companion who was silently following in my shadow appears in front of me and talks to me. Now I am conscious of my past and being conscious of that past I negate myself as *being* that past or, if you prefer, I assert myself as *not-being* that past. Of course it does not cease to be past, by any means, but I cease to *be it*. Hence before, when the past remained behind me without being thematized, I was my past without knowing it, now that it is in front of me, I *know* it without being it. How is it possible, you will object, that consciousness is its own past without being conscious of it, without thematizing it? And yet the past is my consciousness, continually, without my being able to escape from it. It is the very sense of the words I use, the faces I recognise, the gestures I make, the decisions I take, in short it is my very link with the world as combination of meanings. The past which I am is that which, as we have seen, psychologists call knowledge or semantic memory. And what is knowledge, what is semantic memory if not the past that consciousness is without thematizing it? And what is that which psychologists call episodic memory if not the thematization of the past, that is the past which becomes thesis for consciousness which, as such, negates its earlier being as present?

Our investigation has led us to clarify an ontological presupposition which has been totally ignored by current theories of memory, and that is that consciousness, as temporal consciousness, comes into being already with a past. Furthermore, it has been seen that the three dimensions of time are unintelligible if they are not considered as the basic structures of consciousness. Locking up the past in a memory trace and making memory the result of the reactivation of a trace in which the past is apparently locked, means obfuscating the problem of memory and denying oneself the chance of a scientific theory of memory. But is a scientific theory of memory possible? And if so, under what conditions? We shall see.

CHAPTER 5

KNOWING AND REMEMBERING

1. ONTOLOGY OF KNOWLEDGE

So far we have seen that the fundamental characteristic of consciousness is that it must, by nature, be consciousness *of* something. We have thus formed a dyad: on the one hand there is consciousness, on the other there is that *something* - object, thing, phenomenon - of which consciousness is conscious. But we have also seen that consciousness, when considered in isolation, is nothing but an abstraction, as is the phenomenon - the object, the thing - since it cannot exist as such without *appearing* to a consciousness. Concrete existence manifests itself as a synthetic whole in which consciousness and phenomenon, in taking shape, acquire that concreteness they were lacking when considered in isolation. The relationship between the two is thus constitutive of the elements themselves as they relate to one another. However this does not mean that the origin of this relationship can be indistinctly sought in either consciousness or in the phenomenon. It is only in consciousness that it can be found; it is only in consciousness that that particular relationship known as knowledge is defined. Consciousness is responsible for this relationship in that it originally comes into being through its relationship with an object. It is now time to further clarify the relationship between consciousness and object and, more generally, to pose the problem of the origin of knowledge.

First of all knowledge, seen as the relationship between consciousness and a phenomenon, is immediate in that there is no mediator between the two. The reflection of the immediacy of knowledge is intuition. You could object that immediacy and intuition are merely aspects, particular cases of knowledge which, more often than not, are anything but immediate and intuitive but quite the contrary are the result of deduction, reasoning and *logos*. But deduction, reasoning and *logos* are merely instruments which lead to intuition, that is to the very origin of knowledge. If intuition is attained, the instruments used to reach it disappear in the face of the apodeictic fullness of intuition, they appear irredeemably incomplete and rudimental in front of knowledge. If intuition is not attained, the instruments of logic which were used are just signposts that indicate intuition which is off course. But what is intuition produced by the immediacy of the relationship between consciousness and a phenomenon? Husserl, like most philosophers, says that it is the presence of the "thing" *in persona* to one's consciousness. This is supposed to describe the apodeictic fullness of intuitive knowledge. But the elements of the relationship of presence should be overturned. In the previous chapter we saw that *presence* cannot at any time be associated with a thing or a phenomenon. Presence is a means by which consciousness extends itself towards a thing. This glass on the table is not present to me, but rather as a glass *it is*, and that is that. It is I who am present to the glass when I turn to it to pick it up. As far as intuition is concerned, we can say that this reflects the presence of consciousness to the thing. But what does this mean?

The need for consciousness to be consciousness *of* something has been emphasised throughout this work. It is now time to be more precise and examine the significance of this need for consciousness to be consciousness *of* something. The presence of consciousness to an object takes place by means of radical negation; it is the presence of consciousness to that which consciousness *is not*. I am present to this glass in as far as I radically negate any identification between the glass and myself. In other words, I am present to that which I *am not*. This type of negative relationship is implied *a priori* in every theory of consciousness. It is impossible to see an object for what it is unless a relationship of negation which identifies the object as that which consciousness *is not* has first been established. The object is first of all, before any construction or conceptualisation, what appears to consciousness as *not being* consciousness. Before being made of glass and being used to drink from, the glass on the table is an object which is distinct from my consciousness since they are separated by an inestimable void described as an ontological relationship between consciousness and the glass, and which is realised in the existential concreteness which determines the relationship between these two elements. The relationship of presence on which knowledge is based is therefore a negative one, and its negativeness is to be found at the very heart of consciousness since this is the way in which consciousness establishes itself as such. In other words, the relationship of negation is not established by consciousness as an external judgement on an object: there is no thematized consciousness of not being that glass, unless this thesis is explicitly drawn up. But consciousness is, by its very nature, consciousness of not being that glass since, if it were not, consciousness would acquire the opacity of the object, that is, it would cease to be consciousness. Knowledge therefore initially establishes itself as the negative way of being consciousness has before an object. Knowing does not mean establishing a relationship *a posteriori* between two elements, nor does it represent an operation or special virtue of consciousness. It is consciousness as present to... and its negation of being the object to which it is present, which constitute knowledge. And this negative need consciousness has before an object reflects its need to be irremediably consciousness *of* something.

The presence of consciousness to an object as *not being* that object does not imply any form of *pre-consciousness* of the object but it establishes itself primarily as knowledge. That is, you must not think that in order to deny being an object consciousness need first have, in some way or another, knowledge of the object's being because otherwise it could not deny being that of which it knows nothing. It is true that concrete experience might lead you to the following conclusion: if I deny being that glass it is because I already in some way have a notion of a glass, which allows me to see myself as being different from one. But it is clear that this type of conclusion precludes any ontological possibility of knowledge. The ontological relationship between consciousness and an object to which it is present must allow *every* type of experience and knowledge. Therefore it is impossible for me to *already* have knowledge of an object that I am not, before establishing it as an object. If it were possible, that is, if a certain type of knowledge, for however vague and incomplete, preceded the presence of consciousness to an object, no knowledge would be possible since knowledge of an object which precedes the presence of consciousness to that object would in turn need an origin and this would lead to an infinite series, a *solutio ad infinitum*. What on the other hand makes knowledge possible, *every* form of knowledge, not only that of the already known, is the *a priori* birth of an object in the world, that is of an object for a subject. And since the birth of an object in the world originates in consciousness, it becomes the birth of consciousness as presence to the object that it is not. In other words, the basic relationship which determines that consciousness is not the object to which it is present is the foundation of every form of knowledge of that object. Let us examine this relationship in more detail.

First of all, the object to which consciousness is present in the form of not being that object is not isolated, entirely cut off from me. Indeed it would be impossible to deny being that object if this were separate from the being of my consciousness. I cannot negate identification with the glass in front of me if I am not tied to it by a certain type of ontological relationship which makes the existence of myself and of the glass possible. Where does this relationship originate? It is tempting to seek its origin in consciousness, since it is consciousness which is present to the object as not being that object. And this is certainly true. But there is more. The origin of the ontological relationship of knowledge is definitely to be sought in consciousness, but in a form of consciousness which comes out of itself to go towards an object and eventually attach itself to it. And this consciousness which is outside itself, that is in an ek-static form, is defined as consciousness by the very object to which it attaches itself, that is by that which it is not. My consciousness of not being a glass finds its definition *in the* glass, at the absolute fullness of the *in se* with regard to which consciousness represents nothingness, an absence which comes into existence from that fullness. And so in that ontological relationship between consciousness and object which we will call knowledge, the only recognisable element which is always *there* is the *known*. The knower, as determined by the known, is not perceptible, fades into nothingness. The knower is only that which allows there to be a known, a presence to the known object, because this, in turn, is neither present nor absent, but simply *is*.

But if the only element found in knowledge is the known, does this mean that every possible existence of the *to be known* must be negated? Certainly not. It is just that what has still to be known, namely the unknown, can be a part of the ontological relationship between consciousness and object only as that which *will be* known. At present the unknown is nothing if not my future, part of that project that I am. But, as we have already seen, when the unknown becomes known it will lose its characteristic of future and will simply be known, as *to be known* slides into the past as future in the past. The fact, then, that in knowledge only the known is met with, does not in any way exclude the possibility of knowing what is presently unknown, nor does it contradict what empirical existence shows us, namely the continual possibility of new knowledge. It is only that knowledge comes into the world as objects to which consciousness is present in the form of the known.

But in the object which presents itself to consciousness as known there is nothing already given, past or to be taken for granted by consciousness. On the contrary, the known object or the experience of knowing is absolutely new for consciousness, which is continually discovering itself as consciousness before that object which it is not. Besides, what is the meaning of surprise if not the discovery or the reassertion of the existence of consciousness? And what is habit if not a certain form of collapse of consciousness? I am, so to speak, used to this glass in front of me since I have seen it, touched it and used it a hundred thousand times. Of course, my consciousness continues to be present to the glass as not being that glass. But its strength is somehow weakened in that the glass is not only known but is *recognised* since it no longer demands, with the same strength as on their first meeting, that consciousness assert itself as not being that glass. In other words, getting used to objects, their recognition, always implies a consciousness which recognises and which establishes itself as not being the recognised object. But the negation of consciousness before the object has, so to speak, faded, it is consciousness which tends towards non-consciousness, that is, towards the death of consciousness. While on the other hand, surprise before a new object is the affirmation of full consciousness. In front of a picture, a person or a landscape which I have never seen, I rediscover my existence as not being that picture, that person or that landscape. In the face of novelty consciousness is reborn to new life, rediscovering and reaffirming itself as not being that new object to which it is present. It is from novelty that consciousness draws the lymph on which it is nourished, and it is through novelty that consciousness constantly flees from the death to which habit would force it. It is thanks to this kind of vital instinct that consciousness seeks novelty, the meeting with that which *is still unknown,* to have proof of its existence. So here then is the meaning of knowledge, continual proof of the existence of consciousness: I am not that object in front of me, therefore, I am.

The object, therefore, appears to the world as not being consciousness, or rather consciousness is defined as not being the object to which it is present. The object, however, manifests itself to consciousness *in a certain way*, and this way is generally seen as the quality of the object. The cigarette to which my consciousness is present now manifests itself through its cylindrical shape, its white colour, the smoke it emits, the taste that I am enjoying, etc. Where does this way the cigarette has of manifesting itself, namely its qualities which I call shape, colour, smell, taste originate? In the past the subjective origin of quality was insisted upon. If the cigarette appears to me in a certain way it is because *I* perceive it in that way in the depths of my being. For however impossible it is to deny a certain subjectivity to quality since no one besides myself will ever be able to state what the *cylindrical shape* through which the cigarette appears to me is *for me*, neither can it be denied that the cigarette's cylindrical shape is not only a subjective way of knowing the cigarette but *is* the cigarette. In short, the object does not appear to consciousness as an empty entity which combines various qualities which are, so to speak, stuck to it from the outside. The cigarette is entirely determined by each of its qualities and each of its qualities runs into each of the others. "It is the sourness of a lemon that is yellow", says Sartre[1], "it is the yellow of a lemon that is sour; you eat the colour of a cake, and its taste reveals its shape and colour to what we may call our nutritional intuition; while if I plunge my finger into a jar of jam, the sticky coldness of that jam is for my fingers the manifestation of its sugary taste. The fluidity, the warmth, the bluish colour, the wavy movement of the water in a swimming pool, each of these qualities manifests itself to me through the others". And it is this total interpenetration of qualities which constitutes an object. If I distinguish the qualities of an object, if verbally I can *break* the swimming pool *down* into fluidity, warmth, bluish colour, wavy movement of water, it does not mean that the swimming pool is the *sum* of these qualities, but simply that I am verbally describing what appears to my consciousness as a single object. Of course, I may dwell upon the colour of the water, but then the swimming pool will no longer be the object to which my consciousness appears by negating itself, but the colour in itself and nothing more. In short, qualities send you from one to the other and together they constitute the being of an object which never appears as an empty being to which various qualities have been added from the outside.

In modern psychological and neuropsychological theories, the problem of knowledge and its pathology has, to a great extent, been complicated by qualities having been considered as separable and as *additions* to the object from the outside. In particular, the idea that an object in itself is

---

[1] Sartre, J.-P., 1943.

characterised by belonging to various qualitative categories –shape, colour, function, etc., has generated a conception of the organisation of the semantic system, that is of knowledge, which by preferring the abstract, the category to which the object is believed to belong, to the concrete, the object itself and its announcing itself to consciousness, encounters insoluble difficulties in accounting for the so-called pathology of knowledge. What has not been understood is that the object is not a synthetic unity of the qualities of which it is composed, and even less so the simple sum of these. But an object *is* the very qualities which consciousness perceives when it places itself in front of said object as not being that object. Each quality of the object *is* the entire object. If any of its qualities is varied, the others too are varied and the result is not the object *minus* or *plus* a certain quality, but a different object. A blue lemon is not a lemon whose *yellowness* has been taken away and *blueness* added. It is a blue lemon *tout court*. It manifests itself to consciousness as "other" with respect to a yellow lemon. In the same way, the patient who does not recognise a cherry as red is not missing the "redness" of a cherry. This lack can only be seen from the outside, that is it needs a witness to notice it and to declare it. For the patient the cherry is as it appears, as he imagines it, blue, white or green and that is that; he does not notice any absence, any missing "redness" of the cherry. Besides, the idea of an object seen as the sum of its discrete qualities presupposes a world fragmented into an infinity of abstract qualities of which the object is only a synthesis, in turn abstract, since it would be a synthesis created from abstract elements. In short, a lemon as the sum of yellow, sourness, roughness and ellipsoidal shape with protrusions at the poles is unintelligible. This is not a lemon, it is nothing but a sum of abstractions. Besides, such a hypothesis would mean that, when I actually perceive, imagine or remember a lemon, *first* the yellow, sourness, roughness and shape of a lemon appear to my consciousness, and *then* from the synthesis of these I create a lemon. This is clearly false. As for the possibility of a lemon being created by consciousness thanks to a preliminary unconscious synthesis of its various qualities, we have already seen that this would only lead to the aporia described earlier. In short, the object presents itself at once through its qualities and it is *only* conceivable through the qualities it expresses. What is a lemon that is not yellow, sour, rough-skinned and of a certain shape? Nothing but an abstraction. A quality is an ontological relationship between consciousness and an object. Consciousness turns to an object as not being that object which, in turn, is its qualities. I am not that lemon in as far as I am not its yellowness, its sourness, its roughness, etc. In this sense, quality has nothing to do with the exterior appearance of an object because an object has neither "inside" nor "outside". For there to be qualities there has to be an object which presents itself to a consciousness, which by its very nature cannot be that object.

In this sense, then, quality is anything but the "filling" of something, but rather it is the determination of a void, the void of consciousness aiming at a quality without being able to reach it. Knowing (a quality) does not mean, as has often been claimed, taking possession of an object, eating and assimilating it, nor does it mean making it coincide with some mental representation. If anything it means establishing a void, the void which separates us from quality. Indeed on one hand quality maintains a relationship of absolute closeness to us, on the other it is out of reach, unattainable, that which by definition shows us to ourselves as not being that quality. Quality is the indication of what we are not, of the way of being which we are denied. The perception of the smell of a rose is, for consciousness, consciousness of the impossibility of existing as a perfume. In this sense not only does an object not distinguish itself from its qualities, but any knowledge of a quality is knowledge of a definite object, that is, of a *this*. A quality, whatever it be, manifests itself as an object for consciousness. The music I hear, without yet being able to associate it to the instrument it is coming from, is already fully an object for my consciousness. The perfume I smell, the colour I see are already fully objects for my consciousness and not subjective impressions. In other words a quality may appear to subjectivity but it does not correspond to subjectivity itself. If I now perceive this glass as being transparent, its transparency is not a subjective nuance of my perception of that object but belongs to the glass itself. It is the glass which reveals itself to my consciousness *as* being transparent, not my consciousness of transparency which is attributed from outside to a glass which in itself is neither transparent nor opaque. You may wonder how the glass manages to be transparent in itself? The glass, like any other object, reveals itself to the world as a unity. But its revealing itself to the world means nothing other than revealing itself to a consciousness which in turn negates itself as *this* object. In negating itself, consciousness is able to adopt various points of view, or rather, it is from various points of view, as we have already demonstrated, that consciousness comes into the world, negating itself before a *this*. To every negation of consciousness before an object there is a corresponding total unveiling of said object "from a certain point of view".

And the object's way of revealing itself from a particular point of view is precisely what we call its quality, namely the ontological relationship between consciousness and *this* object before it. A quality, in short, is an expression of consciousness, which in its freedom selects an aspect of this object. Besides, empirical experience demonstrates how the unveiling of *one* quality of an object always seems unmotivated, as though it were gratuitous *de facto*, fruit of the freedom of consciousness; certainly I cannot deny that the pack of cigarettes in front of me is red and angular, but I can choose to see it as angular-red or as red-angularity. In short, this object in front of me presents itself to my consciousness through a free act on the part of consciousness, thanks to which it is quality which constitutes *this* object.

And so quality, in as far as it reveals an object, establishes itself as an ontological relationship between consciousness and the object to which consciousness is present. Quality manifests itself and reveals *this* object in front of me. But this object in front of me, which expresses itself through its quality which my consciousness aims at by internally negating itself as being that quality, is not the world nor does it represent it. The world is a totality made up of many *this*, or if you prefer a totality which breaks down into innumerable *this* which arise from the totality whenever consciousness bothers to consider them. But what is the relationship between the various objects, or if you will, between the various *this*, or better still between *this* and *that*? To establish any sort of relationship between a *this* and another *this*, the second *this* must first of all come to consciousness, that is detach itself from the totality of the world, or from the background according to *Gestalt* psychology, in order to be defined as another *this*. Obviously this can only happen thanks to another negation on the part of consciousness which declares itself as not being the new *this*. But it is also necessary to keep every new *this* at a distance from the other because it is not the other. And so another act of negation to separate *this* from *that* is necessary. It is a matter of external negation which is added to that carried out by consciousness which negates itself both as *this* and as *that*. It is a negation *between* objects by means of which each one denies being the other, or affirms itself as not being the other. This glass *is not* that pack of cigarettes and I am neither of the two. If there were not the internal negation of consciousness which denies being both the pack of cigarettes and the glass, there could be no perception of either the glass or the pack of cigarettes. But if there were this internal negation of consciousness, but no external negation of the pack of cigarettes as glass or vice versa, there could be no perception of the pack of cigarettes or of the glass as distinct objects. This external negation between this and that is expressed by means of the word "and". This *and* that means precisely this *is not* that. The word *and* therefore reveals the relationship of exteriority between two objects which remain indifferent to one another, the essence of which does not vary an iota because of the negative relationship which joins them, since it is a purely external relationship. When I say this glass *and* that bottle, nothing in the glass is changed by the presence of the bottle or vice versa. This conjunction, which expresses the relationship of exteriority and indifference of objects, represents a void, the nothingness which separates objects as finite beings from one another. And this void, this nothingness of separation is *quantity*. Indeed, quantity is pure exteriority; it does not in any way depend on added elements and it is nothing other than the affirmation of their independence and reciprocal indifference. Counting means breaking down a totality which presents itself as a whole which ideally can be broken down. The result of an addition is not part of any one of the counted elements, nor of the totality in itself. I do not count twenty objects on my desk since these initially present themselves as a "collection of objects on the desk". Counting twenty objects leaves both the essence of each and the concrete unity of the collection perfectly intact. In short, that there are twenty objects is neither a property of the collection of objects on the desk, nor a property of each of them. None of these objects is in itself twenty or the twentieth object because the attribution of *twentieth* is only the reflection of consciousness which counts, which perceives the void, that nothingness of separation among the objects. The relationship of quantity is therefore a purely negative relationship of exteriority. And this exterior nothingness which belongs to neither the things nor to their totality is the *space* which unites and divides elements which are independent and indifferent to one another. And so quantity and space are one and the same type of negation. Space and quantity come into the world as a consequence of the fact that *this* and *that* have no relationship to one another. When I say this bottle is bigger than that glass, oil is lighter than water, when I count these three pencils, when I point to the third street on the left, when I say in the city, at the side of the bell-tower, I create categories, artificial groups of things which leave them utterly intact without enriching or impoverishing them by one *iota*; all it shows is the infinite diversity of the ways in which consciousness is able to perceive the reciprocal indifference of objects. What does this mean? That knowledge of an object does not in any way imply knowledge of quantity or space, and vice versa, that is knowing quantity and space does not mean knowing an object. I may no longer know that this is a glass and that is a bottle, but I can continue to count *two* objects which no longer send me the qualities they did when I perceived them as glass and bottle. Vice versa I may recognise the glass and the bottle but no longer know that there are two objects and that one is in front of the other. In other words, there is a substantial ontological difference between quantity-space, which is a pure relationship of exteriority between objects, and quality, which is an internal relationship between an object and the consciousness which selects it.

So far we have dealt with the problem of the relationship between consciousness and an object by indicating the structures through which this relationship is realised. But what we have indicated as the structures by means of which an object appears to consciousness represent only some aspects of the relationship and should not be given precedence. Out of necessity we have considered how an object appears to a consciousness which is present, or rather instantaneous. But consciousness, as we have emphasised, is not instantaneous but always ek-static flight from a past which it is, without being able to be it, towards a future which it is, without yet being able to be it. This way consciousness has of being ek-static is reflected in the relationship between consciousness and an object, namely in that ontological relationship which we have called knowledge. Indeed, an object comes into the world for consciousness not only *as it is* but also as it *will be*. In other words, within the known there is always the possibility of an object not being what it is in order to be what it is not. An object's continuous possibility of being *other* than what it is now, is the capacity of the object as a reflection of the object-consciousness relationship in which consciousness projects its ek-static flight from the present towards the future onto the object itself. And so this glass is not only transparent, heavy, cylindrical but it also manifests itself in the whole, in the possibility of not being any of these things. It may fall and break, for example, and become a collection of pieces in which the qualities of a whole glass are no longer recognisable. There is therefore a certain precariousness about an object which is always ready to make itself *other* following the path of consciousness which projects itself onto it as the perpetual possibility of not being what it is. The object's potentiality therefore contains a negation: the negation of consciousness which not only instantaneously denies being the object before it, but also negates the object as being what it is or, if you wish, affirms it as being what it is not in the future mode. But potentiality is not all that ek-static consciousness projects onto an object as other than what it is. Indeed an object comes into the world with a *function*, it is seen by consciousness as a tool. Its being a tool is also in the future and so in a certain sense its nature is a part of its potentiality. But the object's being a tool is distinct from its potentiality in as far as it is an external relationship between various objects. This glass is distinct from that bottle *because* it is used to drink from while the bottle is used to pour the water that will be drunk. But you may object, what difference is there between the quality of the object which we described earlier and its function which we are describing now? Basically the glass distinguishes itself from the bottle as much for its so-called qualities as for its function. Certainly, qualities distinguish objects just as much as functions do. This pen is different from this sheet of paper both for how it appears to me, that is of a certain shape and colour, and for its function. But the qualities of the pen describe an internal relationship between consciousness and the pen. The pen *immediately* appears to me as having a certain form and a certain colour, that is it appears to me, as we have already said, *in a certain way*. Its function, on the other hand, does not present itself immediately to my perception of pen but, so to speak, it *announces* itself as possible. We do not want to assert that the thing reveals itself *first* as a thing and *then* as a tool. It appears, without a doubt, at once as a tool-thing. But in its being a tool its function is not revealed but only announced as possible, while in its being blue the quality *blue* is revealed immediately. In other words, I never identify a pen as *object to write with*. Even when I see one in action under the guide of my hand it does not appear to me *in function of*, but as tool-thing, having, therefore, a function which has still not been revealed to me. What I identify is not the function of the pen, if anything it is its movement on the sheet. For the pen and sheet of paper to acquire a function, there needs to be an act which transcends the apodeictic presence of the sheet and the pen and sees them not as isolated objects which reveal themselves in a certain way, but as objects in the *future*, in the background of the world, that is of other objects. Then, and only then, thanks to an act of consciousness that transcends the apodeicticity of the full presence of the object, will the pen which appeared to me as blue become an object *to write with* and the blank sheet become something to write on. Thanks to this new act of consciousness, the object ceases to be absolute presence but appears as having a certain function and as such refers to the infinite series of objects in the world. And this act of consciousness, thanks to which the object appears in the background of other objects, describes that relationship of exteriority between objects which we have called function. Function, therefore, because of its characteristic as external relationship between objects, is distinct both from quality and from potentiality, which are internal relationships between consciousness and an object.

The examples considered so far in the description of tool-thing and its function have dealt only with man-made objects. You may feel that the characteristic of being a tool and of function is applicable only to this category of objects or to a part of it and that it is not applicable to *all* the objects of the world. What is the function of a penguin, of a sunset or of the Gioconda? It is true that certain objects are made by man *for* a certain function while others are not, and in this sense it is certainly difficult to find a specific function for a penguin, but not for scissors or a hammer. But this empirical distinction does not clarify in the least how things are seen by consciousness. The distinction between quality and function, as a distinction between an internal relationship between consciousness and an object and an external relationship among objects, remains beyond empirical distinction, which tends to negate it. As far as consciousness is concerned, the penguin, a sunset and the Gioconda have as much of a function as do a hammer and a saw. As objects of the world, all objects have a function, quite beyond quality which reveals the presence of the object in question. In reality, the empirical distinction is to be found between what is useful and what is not, and not between what has a function and what has none. And so we recognise the gratuity of the function of objects which are not made *for*, but this does not mean denying their being tools or their function. The penguin has the function of swimming, of drinking, of catching fish, the sunset that of taking place at a certain time of day, the Gioconda of being observed by millions of people. It is of little importance whether I am a useless spectator of something useless, it is of little importance if I will never be able *to use* the penguin, the sunset or the Gioconda. They remain where they are, with their quality and function, objects among the objects in a world scattered with objects in external relationships with each other. In other words, objects do not come into the world only as *possibles* of mine, that is as the concrete possibility of carrying out my task by means of them, as Sartre maintains, they come into the world *also* as possibles *of the world*, that is as possibilities of which I am a useless spectator.

In this brief description we have seen that knowledge manifests itself as definition of consciousness which negates itself as object or which affirms itself as not being that object. In this sense knowledge implies the whole of temporality as a totalizing structure by means of which that ontological relationship between consciousness and an object that we have called knowledge comes into being. Being temporal by nature, as we have already seen, consciousness places itself in relationship with an object in a temporal mode: before this vase I continue to negate myself as being what I was in the need to be so and project myself in what I am not yet. This temporal dynamism of flight on the part of consciousness is reflected in the object itself. The temporality of consciousness is not consciousness *of* temporality but it is *objective* temporality, which is determined from the outside, onto the object. But consciousness can be consciousness *of* temporality, it can thematize time by making memory and the future arise in the world as projects of which consciousness is conscious. This is what will now be dealt with.

2. ONTOLOGY OF MEMORY

We have said that consciousness in its reflexive form can thematize time and therefore reveal itself to be a certain present consciousness which has a past and a future. But what exactly does to thematize time mean, and what is consciousness which reveals itself to be temporal consciousness? It means that the object which presents itself to consciousness with its qualities appears to the former in a temporal mode, that is past, present or future. The vase of flowers appears to me as being of a certain shape and colour, but it can also appear to me as *now present*, as an element of the world which is my world at this moment of my existence. In the same way the vase may appear to me as an element of a past world which I was, or of a future one which I will be. In other words, this vase appears in the background of my temporal existence, of which I become aware through a reflexive act. First, in pure knowledge, my consciousness was temporal without being conscious of being so and the object appeared to me in all its opacity as a pure atemporal *being*. Now, my consciousness which thematizes time becomes aware of being temporal and the object appears to me as being *in a certain time mode*, that is past, present or future. But what is the origin of the thematization of time or of the temporal thematization of an object? Why does an object at a certain point appear to me in the past, present or future? We must not make the mistake here of thinking that thematized temporality is in any way *something* which is added to an object *from the outside*, a type of external addition that follows the object's qualities which have a type of ontological priority over temporality. There is no priority among what we have called the qualities of an object and the object's being temporal. This vase is not *first* red and *then* past but gives itself to consciousness as red *in the* past. In this sense the object is to the same extent red and past, or present or future. In short, for consciousness that thematizes time, the object is a temporal object.

And so temporality is temporality of an object which appears in the world in a certain temporal perspective. But the attribution of temporality to an object does not mean that it has the properties of an object, the properties of being in itself, isolated from consciousness. For there to be temporality in an object there must be a relationship of temporality between consciousness and the object. That is, there must be a consciousness which sees the object as temporal. In the absence of a consciousness which bothers to consider this red vase as past, this vase is neither red nor past, it is nothing. For there to be thematization of an object as temporal there must therefore be a consciousness which transcends its own worldly concreteness to create itself as consciousness *of* time, that is, as present consciousness, conscious of its own present, of the past from which it flees and of the future towards which it runs.

But what type of consciousness is it and what distinguishes it from consciousness that knows described earlier? When I say that I am now writing, earlier I was at the café, later I am going for a walk, my consciousness is no longer pure *presence to the object*, it transcends the pure relationship of diversity with the object to place itself in a dimension which transcends both the object and consciousness that knows, which is seen as pure presence to a being that it is not. And this new dimension of consciousness is characterised by intuition of the present as element of an existential structure which provides a *before* and an *after*. Here we need to clarify that in reality, inside consciousness which thematizes time, two different moments or two distinct forms of consciousness must be distinguished: consciousness of the object as temporal, and consciousness of consciousness as temporal. I may realise that the pen I am holding is present, that is an element of that *now* which is my present now. I may remember having used the same pen this morning and foresee using it tomorrow. What is my consciousness consciousness of in these examples? It is without a doubt consciousness of pen as present here between my fingers, past when I used it this morning and future when I will use it tomorrow. In this case it is the pen which presents itself as a temporal being, that is as present, past or future. The pen itself appears to me, to use Husserl's words, *in the flesh* in the present, past or future. But this is not the only possibility consciousness has of thematizing time. Indeed, I can *see myself*, through a reflexive act, while I am using the pen now in this present of mine. That is, I can be conscious of myself as that being which is using a pen in this present. In the same way not only can I remember having used the pen this morning, but I can *see myself* while I was using it this morning or while I am using it tomorrow. I can be conscious of what I was, of what I am and of what I will be with regard to the pen. In this case that which appears to me in the flesh is not the pen in the past, in the present or in the future, but it is me, it is my present, past and future consciousness of pen which is the temporalized object of my consciousness, which through a reflexive act places itself where it is, where it has been and where it will be.

There is no point in emphasising the importance of this difference between these two ways consciousness has of thematizing time which implies different types of relationships between consciousness and its object. The first type of relationship, the condition in which consciousness temporalizes an object, is an internal relationship between consciousness and the object which does not differ much from what we described with regard to the act of knowing. Indeed, in the object which presents itself to consciousness as temporal, that ontological relationship of negation which we have already described is re-established. The difference is that in this case, consciousness not only denies being the object, but it denies being that object *in a certain mode* of time. I am not this pen but neither am I the present of this pen, nor its past or future. If I were, the being of my consciousness and that of the pen would move in synchrony and what we would have would no longer be the temporality of an object but the atemporality of pure presence, namely of knowledge. In order for there to be temporality of an object, a new act of negation needs to be inserted in the relationship of negation which separates and unites consciousness and an object, namely the negation of being temporal on the part of the object. I am not this landscape that I see from the window but neither am I the present of this landscape, nor the past of the landscape that I saw yesterday or of the one I will see tomorrow. But this new negation, this ontological relationship which gives rise to a present, past and future of the object, exhausts itself, so to speak, in an internal relationship between consciousness and the object without either element being able to claim priority over the other. When on the other hand consciousness has itself as object in the temporal mode, what is established between consciousness and its object, namely consciousness itself, is an internal relationship but one which encloses within itself another relationship which is external, namely that between the consciousness of which I am conscious and its object. This point needs to be clarified. When I am conscious of my consciousness looking at the landscape from the window, when I discover myself as onlooker of that landscape, of what is my consciousness consciousness? Of consciousness that is looking at the landscape, without a doubt. Things do not change when instead of present consciousness looking at the landscape, past consciousness or future consciousness are considered; my consciousness will always be consciousness of consciousness looking at the landscape in the present, past or in the future. The relationship which is established between consciousness and its object is therefore still an internal one. But what, for my consciousness, is the relationship between consciousness that looks at the landscape and its object, namely the landscape itself? Evidently, for my consciousness it is a matter of an external relationship between objects of the world: my consciousness and the landscape. My consciousness denies being that consciousness which is looking at the landscape, be this a past, present or future consciousness. But inasmuch as its not being that consciousness, the relationship between that consciousness and its object, the landscape, is of no concern to me, it is a question which is resolved between that consciousness and its object. As we have seen, for that consciousness the relationship with its object is an internal relationship, but for me, useless spectator, it is an external relationship between objects. It is of little consequence that in one of those objects I *recognise* myself, that that consciousness of which I am conscious is what I was, I am or will be. It is of little consequence if I am tied to that consciousness by a deep feeling of solidarity of being. The reflexive act reduces it to object without exceptions. Between my consciousness and the consciousness of which I am conscious in the present, past or future there is a void, an inevitable distance which I am continually trying to fill, without success. My present, past or future consciousness is there, with its landscape, and nothing will allow me to interpose myself in their relationship which remains an external relationship between objects of the world, just like that between this glass and that bottle.

The thematization of time can therefore take place in two different modes of consciousness: consciousness which turns directly to its object as temporal and consciousness which turns reflexively to itself as temporal consciousness. What is the ontological significance of this difference? What changes when consciousness turns to its object in the temporal mode and when it turns to itself and sees itself immersed in a dimension of time? First of all we must clarify, or rather remember, that time is not presupposed in the relationship consciousness has with its object but it comes into being as the ontological reality of this relationship. The past, present and the future come into the world as a project of consciousness which not only is temporal but which chooses itself as temporal at the moment in which it turns to its object in the temporal mode. This choice has different effects depending on the temporalized object that consciousness chooses. The internal relationship which belongs to the relationship between consciousness and the temporalized *in ser*, that is, the object which makes itself present, past or future, reflects consciousness of pure temporality, namely the possibility of a being to be in the form of time. This vase of flowers, this landscape, this glass, this feeling of love, do not just exist, but are present before me, or down there in the past, or else projected into the future to come. Therefore in this case it is a question of consciousness of time seen as a possible dimension of the existence of the world and of the objects that compose it. While the relationship between consciousness and temporalized consciousness, thematized *in* time, of which consciousness is consciousness, reflects the discovery of one's personal ontology: I was that someone looking at that landscape, I am the person using the pen, I will be that person going on holiday after he has finished this book. It is only in this mode of consciousness that I *discover* I have a past, a present and a future; it is only thanks to this reflexive act that my existence appears to me as dilated in time and that I realise that my present image is nothing but a moment of the whole temporal being that I am and that I cannot help but be. And so being there, memory, the future, birth, death come to the world as possibilities that I am, but that I continually try not to be, without any possibility of not being them. I am everything I flee from and it is because I am that I flee from it, because my consciousness to be such must continually negate being what it is.

We have described the temporal thematization of an object and that of consciousness. But what is the relationship between these two ways consciousness has of making its object temporal? Can temporal thematization of an object, that which we will shortly be able to call direct temporality, and temporal thematization of consciousness, namely indirect temporality, have the same ontological status or can one claim priority over the other? Even though strictly speaking ontological priority does not seem to be applicable, on examination, direct temporality seems to have some right to it. Where does this right to precedence come from? It comes from the type of object of which consciousness is conscious in the temporal mode. Direct temporality is temporal thematization of objects of the world, it is consciousness of this vase, of this pen, of this room as present, past and future objects. In indirect temporality, on the other hand, the object of consciousness is consciousness itself in the temporal mode. We have already seen that for consciousness to exist it must be consciousness *of* something and this something is first of all an object, not consciousness itself. If there were no ontological priority between direct and indirect temporality we would be faced with consciousness which became at the same time consciousness of an object and consciousness of itself. But consciousness of this type is inconceivable since consciousness is defined by its ontological relationship with the object of which it is conscious by negating itself as being that object. Consciousness must therefore first affirm itself in its ontological relationship with an object to then be able to carry out that reflexive act which allows it to become conscious of itself in the temporal mode. After all, first the child recognises an object as past and then recognises himself as a being who carried out certain acts in the past. First the child says "I have already seen that" and then "I remember having seen...". The amnesic is able to recognise, to have a sense of familiarity with objects which have previously been presented to him, but he does not know what he did the day before or even a few minutes earlier; he recognises an object as past but does not recognise *himself* as a being with a past. There is therefore an ontological hierarchy between direct and indirect temporality: direct temporality first comes about in consciousness which is forming and later disappears in consciousness which is disintegrating. The importance of this ontological hierarchy is found in the act of *recognising oneself* as a being of this world who is here-and-now but who is also down there in the past, and beyond in the future. An act which transcends simple recognition of time as such, that is of the possibility an object has to be present, past or future, and which is realised in the recognition of the temporal being of consciousness, namely of that ontological reality which enables my being not to be limited to seeing itself through the formula "I am" but also to inevitably define itself by means of "I have been" and "I will be".

The thematization of time comes into the world as transcendence, that is as negation of the present instant. It is thanks to the act of transcendence that Cartesian *cogito* is transformed and the "I am" becomes "I was" and "I will be". It is thanks to indirect temporality that I can see myself down there where I was in the past and can project myself over there where I will be in the future. Indirect temporality puts me in touch with what I was, with what I am and with what I will be. It is only then that existence becomes fully meaningful, because my consciousness is no longer isolated and defenceless before an object but is consciousness of a consciousness which is temporal. Heidegger's *dasein* is enriched by the possibility, which is not guaranteed, for consciousness to be indirect thematization of time. "I was" and "I will be" are possibilities which permeate the *dasein*, opening up a possibility which can be ignored but not denied. In short, consciousness is not only temporal but it can be consciousness *of* time and thus consciousness of its own existence as temporal consciousness. Discussion on the ethical implications of indirect temporality is obviously important but goes beyond the scope of this work.

Direct and indirect temporality reflect an act of transcendence from the mere presence of an object, and as such they go beyond direct experience of an object. Temporality is established as an act of freedom on the part of consciousness which places its object, be it an object of the world or consciousness itself, where it pleases in time. As an act of transcendence, consciousness which thematizes time goes beyond direct experience of an object even if, as we shall see, it presupposes it. In other words, thematization of the present, past and of the future does not imply or demand objectivity, namely the determination of subjective experience on the part of the object. The past that I remember has only a probable link to what happened in the past and it is certainly not the events that I have lived through that determine what I now remember. Memory is nothing other than a form of temporal consciousness which thematizes its object in the past, nothing more, nothing less. This takes place as the realisation of a free act of consciousness which can remember what it wants to without what took place having any hold on the memory. What took place, namely my past life, does not exist nor could it exist without the temporal act of consciousness which thematizes a certain event in the past. We demonstrated this when we described the paradox of the memory trace: if an event becomes past this is because a present consciousness selects that event *in the* past. Before and outside this act of consciousness, the event never *happened*, if anything it *happens*, that is it establishes itself as a certain present of the being that I am. In the total freedom of my temporal choice, I can easily remember this pen between my fingers yesterday even if yesterday I never picked it up. It would be pointless to tell me I am wrong, that what I remember is false. From my point of view the memory of the pen between my fingers yesterday is neither true nor false: it simply *is*, that is it presents itself to my consciousness apodeictically without the possibility of doubt or hesitation. But, you will object, in most cases my memory does not fail: when I remember having had breakfast this morning I remember what is *true*, that is I really did have breakfast this morning with coffee, milk, etc. Most of the time my memory coincides with what *actually* happened. Certainly, no one can deny that there is a correspondence between what you remember and what happens, but this does not mean leaving the probabilistic level or being able to deny consciousness the freedom to negate this correspondence, namely to remember what probabilistically is not among the events that the being that I am has lived. Later we shall see in more detail the nature of the relationship between memory and the remembered event. At the moment we just want to emphasise that the act of remembering is a free act of consciousness and as such may freely go beyond the empirical reality of the remembered event.

There is no particular difficulty in considering memory as a free act of consciousness which thematizes its object in the past without there being any need for solidarity between what is remembered and the empirical reality of the remembered event. But the matter seems to become more complex when the present is considered. Indeed, in the case of the present, the apodeicticity of phenomenal experience seems to derive not so much from the freedom of consciousness but from the very *presence* of the object before me in the flesh. In other words, in the case of present thematization of an object, consciousness seems unable to escape objectivity, namely that fatal attraction which the present object exerts on it. This glass is present and I am present to this glass: there does not seem to be much room here for a free act of consciousness which can transcend such a clear link. But being present in the temporal mode means transcending the object's attraction, namely that relationship between consciousness and the object which we described with regard to knowledge. Thematizing time in the present mode means establishing a present as negation of the past and of the future, that is affirming and thematizing a subordinate structure of temporality in the background of the others which have been denied it. I am present to this glass and this glass is present to me in as far as the relationship which links us is a relationship *in the* present, and not in the past or in the future. In this sense the relationship of pure knowledge is transcended since within this relationship a new form of negation comes into being, the negation of consciousness which negates its object as past or as future. Right, but how does this new form of negation prescind empirical reality, how can it transcend it, the glass is still there. Yes, the glass is still there, as are this table, this room, this city, this world. But the question I answer when I thematize the world in the present implies the assumption of temporality which goes beyond the mere presence of the thematized object as *something* known. This glass is there, with its shape and colour, the water it contains *and* it is present. To become aware of its being present, not past, not future, there needs to be that act which transcends the *presence* in itself to then perceive that presence as *present*. In the same way, when I realise I am present as consciousness present to a world, there needs to be an act which transcends my attachment to an object, that fatal attraction mentioned earlier, in order to see me as here and now, a here and now which is not exhausted in itself but which, in the dynamics of temporality, sends me back to the negation described earlier, namely to not being down here *first* or down there *later*. And, according to our study, the later, the future, is seen yet again as the result of a free act of consciousness which chooses its own object according to that subordinate structure of temporality known as the future. Tomorrow I will use this pen, I am certain, but the fact that I will really use it is only probable. Even so I am certain that I will. Certainly, in the future there is, by definition, a greater dimension of probability than in the past or in the present, but this is not what determines the relationship between my being now and my thematization in the future of my experience. The thematization of the future presents itself as an apodeictic form of being, independently of the empirical probability of the planned event.

However, the freedom of consciousness to thematize an object in the temporal mode is in some way conditioned freedom. The temporal object of which consciousness is conscious is always a *certain* object, an object which presents itself to consciousness as a certain temporalized known. The temporalizing act may go beyond empirical experience, but it cannot prescind the ontological reality of the negative relationship consciousness has with its object, what we have called knowledge. If I remember this pen on the table yesterday, it is still *this* pen that I remember. And this pen is on the table at a certain past time that I call *yesterday*. The temporalizing act I carry out is seen as the temporalization *of* something. And I am linked to this something that I temporalize by a certain relationship of knowledge. In other words, in order to remember the pen on the table yesterday as I am now remembering it I must at the same time *know* what the pen, the table and yesterday are. These three objects present themselves to my consciousness in a certain way and I recognise them in that way. If the pen, the table and yesterday were for me other known things with respect to what they are, the possibility of remembering would not be annulled, but the memory would assume another form. It would become, for example, the memory of a cylindrical object on a surface at an indefinite past time. If I didn't know what a pen, a table and yesterday were, these three objects would appear to me in memory as three totally different objects from those that appear to me if my knowledge is maintained. And it is not a question of forcing memory into a sort of rigid stability of meanings. Even though I know what a pen, table and that certain time I call yesterday are, I can still remember these three objects without their having to present themselves in my memory as pen, table and yesterday. In short, as free choice memory can turn to the remembered object with different levels of consciousness. I can remember this pen as a pen but also as a cylindrical object or as a black shape. But even though it is a free act, memory and temporal thematization of an object are conditioned by the quality of knowledge: I cannot remember what I do not know. If I do not know what a chair is I cannot remember this chair as a chair, if I do not know what a train is I cannot project myself as taking a train tomorrow. In this sense, though within the freedom of a temporalizing act, deep solidarity links temporalization and knowledge, since the temporalized object gives itself to consciousness as known, and the quality of a memory is therefore conditioned by the possible quality of the known. The temporalizing act, of which memory is a subordinate element, is therefore a free act in as far as it does not presuppose empirical experience but produces it, but its freedom is a function of the quality of the known, namely of the ontological relationship that consciousness establishes with its object. In other words, I can remember what never actually happened, but the quality of my memory depends on the quality of the known which presents itself to consciousness as memory.

This brief description of the ontological structures of knowledge and of memory shows how knowledge and memory take form as free and united acts which realise the relationship between consciousness and its object. To which interpretative hypothesis does what has been established so far lead? And how does the relationship between consciousness and its object come about in concrete existence – both normal and pathological? This is what we shall see in the last part of this work.

CHAPTER 6

MEMORY AND CONSCIOUSNESS

1. IS A SCIENTIFIC THEORY OF CONSCIOUSNESS POSSIBLE?

Before going any further, it is worth summarising the points established so far. First of all we saw that current theories of memory are based on a paradox: that the past is passively preserved in memory traces. We then demonstrated how these theories are based on a fallacy, the *homunculus* fallacy, that is on the assumption that there is a sort of unconscious consciousness which, however, cannot be accounted for if not with a *solutio ad infinitum*. Then in our description we established certain characteristics of consciousness, most importantly that of having to be consciousness *of* something. A study of temporality allowed us to identify the conditions under which the past comes into being and establishes itself as an organised form of consciousness. Finally, we established the ontological conditions under which knowing and remembering come into being and present themselves as distinct acts of man's concrete existence.

At this point it remains to be seen whether, in the light of the results of our investigation, it is possible to outline a scientific theory of consciousness, and in particular a theory which can account for the difference between the temporal being of consciousness which manifests itself in knowledge, and the thematization of time which is reflected in consciousness of the past, present and future. In other words, is a scientific theory of consciousness possible and under what conditions?

The aim of science, and thus of any theory which claims to be scientific, is to be *objective,* that is to consider the object of its investigation from outside, in a neutral way, attempting to establish the laws which govern the object's existence. The laws that science establishes are objective in the sense that they are confined to the object and are independent of both the observer and the observation point. The law of gravity establishes that, in the absence of friction, a free body moves downwards at a uniform rate of acceleration represented by the constant g. The uniform acceleration of that body is independent of the observer and will repeat itself every time it encounters the necessary conditions for the transformation of its potential energy into dynamic energy. In short, science describes a relationship between consciousness, that of the experimenter, and the object of the experiment, in which consciousness is annihilated by the centrality of its object, which permits nothing apart from itself. The measure of quantity is the method that science uses, and quantity is a characteristic confined to the object studied. Consciousness is relegated to the role of inert, superfluous spectator. This building is twenty metres high, this book weighs a kilo, that isotope is emitting a hundred millicuries: these are objective facts to which consciousness is irrelevant. Of course what we have described is a rather cut-and-dry view of science. In reality, excluding consciousness, that is the experimenter, from an experiment is artificial and naive, and in certain spheres it has been acknowledged that it is impossible to truly exclude the experimenter's consciousness. But for however much effort is made to include the experimenter among the variables, consciousness will never be given its due ontological role, that of placing itself in a relationship with the object *in a certain mode*. Indeed, recognising the role of consciousness and admitting the ontological relationship which is established between consciousness and an object, a relationship through which both come into being, means excluding *de facto* any possibility of science, which is based on the priority of the object, celibate prince who has no relationships if not with himself. In short, science is in a paradoxical situation: in order to be science it must simultaneously admit and deny consciousness. First of all t must admit it because it is from consciousness that scientific laws are born. The constant of gravity, g, exists because a consciousness has taken the trouble to establish it. Straight after, this consciousness has to deny its role, because its presence, by relativizing the object within an ontological relationship, would revoke the ultimate aim of science, namely objectivity. There is thus an ambiguity in science which, on the one hand presupposes consciousness and on the other denies it as a relevant variable. The result of this is a science without consciousness, in which the object stands on its own without needing anything which is not already registered in its own being. But a science of this sort, that is a science which negates consciousness, still has a reason for existing because despite the ambiguity on which it is based, it allows that furtive objectivity to be established, without which technical innovation would perhaps be impossible. In fact, science is based on theoretical ambiguity, the source of its success. Excluding *de facto* the experimenter from the experiment and granting every right to the object of the experiment means creating the possibility of establishing universal rules which transcend the relationship between consciousness and an object, and which merely set themselves as rules which govern the relationship *between* objects. The consequence of this exclusion of consciousness is reflected in technological development. The extent to which this development is synonymous with "progress" would be worth discussing but this is not the place.

If the aim of science is objectivity, that is adherence to the object, and its method is that of measuring, that is establishing quantitative relations, it follows that the aim of a scientific theory of consciousness is necessarily the objectivation of consciousness and the determination of quantitative relations to describe it. In other words, for a science of consciousness to be possible, consciousness has to be a measurable object, independent of the observer and the observation point. Clearly, then, a scientific theory of consciousness has to be based on a subterfuge which generates a significant anomaly. Indeed, objectivising consciousness, that is considering it as an object means transforming consciousness into what it is not. Consciousness, by definition, is pure subjectivity which describes itself according to rules of quality, not of quantity. This vase of flowers before me, the memory of meeting Paul last night, the blue I am now imagining are present to my consciousness, establishing that subjectivity which I am. And I alone am responsible for this subjectivity, that particular way through which I am conscious of the objects which surround me. Of course, at the same time that entirely subjective being which I am is not only a being for itself because that subjectivity is also an object *for others*. I am continuously observed, object for other consciousnesses, just as others are objects for my consciousness. But my being object is completely different to my being *for myself*. Objectivity, as we have already seen, requires and is based on negation. The object is what my consciousness is not and so cannot have the characteristics of consciousness. The only being which for me has the characteristics of consciousness is *my* consciousness. And even when my consciousness becomes object not for others but for myself, that is when, with a reflexive act, I become conscious of my consciousness, the consciousness of which I am conscious is a me which is *not me*, which does not have the characteristics of consciousness. The objectivation of consciousness thus reflects a radical metamorphosis. Even if I could *see myself* distinctly as object, what I would see would not be an adequate representation of what I am, but only the perception of the distance which separates me from myself, that is the objective perception of my being *other* which is radically different from my being for me, that is from that being which I am in the non-reflexive mode. My seeing myself as *kind*, for example, by no means describes what I am for myself, because I cannot be kind for myself, that is in the non-reflexive mode of consciousness. The qualification of kind characterises me as object: it is that being of which my consciousness is conscious which is kind, not what I am in the non-reflexive mode, namely my consciousness.

Even considering my consciousness as object for the consciousness of others, it is plain that this does not establish me as object for myself, that is as I am, but *for it*, namely the way I am in the mode of the object. In other words, what I am for others does not in any way reveal what I am for myself, even if I am tied to that objective me by a profound solidarity and I am separated from it by an inestimable void. When someone describes my character saying that I am "jealous", "nice" or "irascible", I do not "recognise" myself at all in this description and yet I know that "it is me", an object-me which I cannot deny being and yet which does not describe what I am for myself at all. In this way the object-me, or object-consciousness, constitutes a form of knowledge which does not refer to the essence of consciousness, that is to what I am concretely as subject, but to a metamorphosed consciousness, a consciousness which has made itself object. And this is the metamorphosis that science requires to be able to make consciousness the object of its investigation. Therefore any scientific theory of consciousness can clearly only be a theory which concerns object-consciousness, that is a degraded form of consciousness and has to renounce, by definition, the possibility of having "fresh" information on consciousness because this, in its complete form, defines itself as what is not object. Bearing these limits in mind, a theory of consciousness must be able to 1) propose models which account for the interaction of the different modes of consciousness, and in particular, for the purposes of this work, models which describe the difference between the temporal being of consciousness, which manifests itself in knowledge and the thematization of time which is reflected in consciousness of the past, present and future; 2) account for present knowledge; 3) describe a method for the verification of the theory.

2. A HYPOTHESIS ON THE RELATIONSHIP BETWEEN MEMORY AND CONSCIOUSNESS

Throughout this work we have emphasised that consciousness cannot be considered an empty dimension, a sort of box which is filled and becomes consciousness of what comes to it from an elsewhere, from the physiological, psychoanalytical or functionalist unconscious. Consciousness, as we have seen, is activity not passivity, it is intentional extension towards ..., it is not the last passive stage of processes which occur outside of it, as some functionalist[1] models would have. Consciousness is becoming intentionally conscious of something *in a certain way*. The first consequence of our assertions is that different *modes* of consciousness exist and each of these represents an original, irreducible way of addressing the world. In other words, consciousness is a free act which sees the world from a certain point of view, and every look consciousness takes at the world represents an original mode of consciousness which cannot be confused with other modes. This is not the place to draw up a taxonomy of the different modes of consciousness. Besides, it would be a pointless task in that it would be endless. Indeed, the acts of consciousness being unique are infinite. But our aim is to make certain distinctions that will allow us to see, even if at a rather general level of description, the differences between certain modes of consciousness. The working distinction proposed within the framework of a hypothesis which should enable an attempt at scientific investigation of consciousness regards three modes of consciousness which we have called *knowing* consciousness, *imaginative* consciousness and *temporal* consciousness.

The term knowing consciousness summarises what was said in the previous chapter about knowledge and its ontology and refers, in a certain sense, to what psychologists call semantic memory, though a substantial difference distinguishes knowing consciousness from what is presupposed in the idea of semantic memory. Unlike semantic memory, knowing

---

[1] Moscovitch, M., 1989; Moscovitch, M., 1995; Moscovitch, M., 1995; Schacter, D.L., 1989.

consciousness is not based on the idea of unconscious mental representation. Knowing consciousness has nothing behind it if not itself. We have already discussed the idea of mental representation at length, and rejected it. We shall not come back to it. Knowing consciousness is knowledge *of the object*, it is already *outside itself* and directed towards the object to be known. It is knowledge of the object *in a certain mode*, a mode which makes it unmistakable and original, a mode which makes it impossible for what I know, for example, to be confused with what I remember or imagine. But, you might say, how can I recognise this pack of cigarettes as *red* if I do not *already* have, somewhere between my mind and my brain, an *idea of red*? We have already demonstrated how this sort of hypothesis is unintelligible since it presupposes the existence of *unconscious ideas*. If I recognise the pack of cigarettes as red, it is not because I operate a sort of correspondence between the pack I perceive and a mental image which I carry inside me. Rather I *am conscious* of the pack of cigarettes as red because my present consciousness, being a synthesis of all my past consciousnesses, is also consciousness of red. But I can also see this pack of cigarettes as ugly, dangerous, attractive, almost finished. In short, the meanings I attribute to the pack of cigarettes are concretely infinite and depend on my conscious being here and now as synthesis of what I have been before and elsewhere. And in this sense knowing consciousness is temporal inasmuch as it is a synthesis of what I have been, for better or for worse. But, at the same time, this knowing consciousness which is temporal is also atemporal, in the sense that the time it is made of is not present to it, it is not recognisable. Knowing consciousness *is* the past but it is not consciousness *of* the past, or of the present or the future. There is no time in the pack of cigarettes in front of me even if it is thanks to time, that is to the past which I am, that I can see the pack as red, ugly, dangerous etc.

Of course, knowing consciousness is a rather generic term which includes distinct phenomena that psychologists prefer to keep separate, such as perception, language, knowledge of the world, etc. We have chosen to group such diverse phenomena under a single category, which may seem somewhat arbitrary, in order to emphasise the difference between knowing consciousness and other types of consciousness. Unlike other modes of consciousness, in knowing consciousness the object appears as immediate presence. Furthermore, in knowing consciousness the object is present but lacking in temporal connotation and this distinguishes it from temporal consciousness. However, the distinction between the various phenomena grouped under knowing consciousness does indeed exist. A profound nothingness, for example, separates language from perception. Through perception alone I can *know* that pack of cigarettes without having to resort to language. In other words, there is knowledge of knowing consciousness which precedes and is independent of the linguistic act. Before what Malraux calls the drama of denomination, there is already knowing consciousness. This pack of cigarettes is here, in front of me and I look at it, I see it as being of a certain colour, a certain shape etc. In short, I already know it, without having to give it a name, without having to say *red, angular,* etc. When I use language to describe it I perform a supplementary act which roughly describes my perception and is anyway completely distinct from it. But isn't it rather dangerous to consider the linguistic act a form of knowing consciousness? Indeed you could object that when I talk, when I write, I am not conscious *of* language. Of course, but *through* language I become conscious of the world, just as when I perceive something I am not conscious of my perception but of what is perceived. When I use language I discover the world through language. I give objects names, I set them in relation to one another according to linguistic rules, I affirm, deny, etc. In other words, when I use language I become conscious of the world, I know it, in a certain mode, which is the mode of language. As an act of knowing through which the world presents itself to me in an immediate, atemporal relationship of presence, language is truly part of what we have called knowing consciousness.

Like knowing consciousness, imaginative consciousness is an organised, irreducible form of consciousness. Imaginative consciousness reflects a particular way of addressing the world. The object of my perception and that of my imagination are identical: this pack of cigarettes, for example. But consciousness places itself in a relationship with the object in two different modes. The image which is present to consciousness is not a faded reproduction of a real object, as has long been thought, but the reflection of an original relationship between consciousness and the object. Imaginative consciousness and knowing consciousness are different by nature. Imagination is an activity of consciousness which has completely different aims to those of perceptual consciousness. The latter gives partial, progressive representations of the object while in the imagination the object is present in its entirety. Furthermore, while perception, language, what we have called knowing consciousness, clearly aim at knowing, the aim of imaginative consciousness is not to know, and so it is totally indifferent to the values of certainty and truth. Clearly knowing and imagining are completely different functions and this diversity reflects different relationships with the world. The relationship that knowing consciousness has with its object is "realising", it is a relationship which tends to see the object as real. The imagination, on the other hand, far from serves this function. The relationship that imaginative consciousness has with its object is one of "non-realising", in the sense that the aim of the imagination is precisely that of seeing its object as not belonging to objective reality.

And the unreal object which is present to imaginative consciousness is completely different from that which is present to knowing consciousness. The object of knowing consciousness continually reveals and hides itself. The more I observe this pack of cigarettes the more I notice details which escaped me before. On the other hand, the image which is present to consciousness reveals nothing, it is in some way *already revealed*. "I can keep looking at an image for as long as I wish: I will never find anything but what I put there" Sartre[1] says. In other words, in knowing consciousness, the object constantly goes beyond consciousness, while in the imagination the object is nothing but consciousness. So, for example, my perceptual consciousness may betray me while my imaginative consciousness won't. I can perceive this pack of cigarettes as a box of sweets and thus be mistaken. In the imagination however, the image is all there, no mistake can be made: if I imagine a box of sweets, it is the box of sweets that I imagine and not a pack of cigarettes which erroneously appears to me as a box of sweets. Sartre[2] called this *quasi-observation* our disposition towards the imagined object. Indeed in imaginative consciousness we observe, but it is an observation which teaches us nothing, it adds nothing to what is already there. The world of images is a world where nothing *happens*. "I can make one or other object evolve into an image as I wish, I can make a cube rotate, make a plant grow, a horse run, there will never be the slightest difference between the object and consciousness. Not an instant of surprise".[3]

We have seen that in being intentional, that is in having to be consciousness *of,* consciousness sees its object in a certain mode. It follows that every consciousness sees its object in its own mode. In perception, for example, it is seen as something which really exists. This pack of cigarettes

---

[1] Sartre, J.-P., 1949.
[2] Sartre, J.-P., 1949.
[3] Sartre, J.-P., 1949, p.29.

is here in front of me and my perceptual consciousness of pack of cigarettes is both negation of myself as being that object and affirmation of that object as real presence to what it is not. Imaginative consciousness sees the object in a completely different way, the object is actually seen as *non-existent*, or, if you choose, as not real. For however many different forms it may have, imaginative consciousness emphasises the characteristic of non-presence and unrealness of its object. Whether you imagine a Chimera or whether you imagine where my friend Paul is at this moment, the imagined object is seen as something unreal which transcends reality. It is of little consequence that the Chimera is, in itself, an unreal being, while my friend Paul is a being which does exist. When I imagine them, both present themselves as non-existent, that is as beyond the concrete existence of objective reality. For however vivid, strong, or striking an image is, it is present to consciousness as something which does not exist.

We have seen that the aim of imaginative consciousness is not to know, it is not the basis of any knowledge, inasmuch as the object is seen in its entirety. However imaginative consciousness could not exist if it were not established by knowledge. While knowing consciousness establishes itself as consciousness by itself, imaginative consciousness requires knowledge to establish it as such. In other words, in imaginative consciousness, knowledge is constitutive of consciousness itself. How could it be otherwise? If I imagine a centaur, a sunny day, a woman, this happens because *I know* what a centaur, a sunny day, and a woman are. Establishing itself as images, knowledge undergoes a radical metamorphosis, transforming itself into something non-existent, that is into the opposite of what it is, assertion of reality. This somehow degraded knowledge is the very structure of imaginative consciousness.

The third type of consciousness we mentioned is temporal consciousness. We have already seen that knowing consciousness is temporal consciousness inasmuch as it is the present synthesis of all the consciousnesses that preceded it. However, in the being temporal of knowing consciousness there is no thematization of time. In other words, knowing consciousness is temporal but it is not consciousness *of* time. Consciousness of time, that is the thematization of the object in the temporal mode is what we have called temporal consciousness. Temporal consciousness, inasmuch as it sees its object according to the subordinate structures of time, that is the past, the present and the future, is an organised form of consciousness, original and irreducible mode of addressing the world. Unlike knowing consciousness, temporal consciousness transcends objective reality, the mere presence of the object in order to set it in time. When I say that I remember yesterday's dinner, that now I am in my office and that later I will go out to buy some cigarettes, knowledge is presupposed, as we will see later, but it is not the aim of the temporalizing act that I am accomplishing. In order to remember yesterday's dinner, to affirm that I am *now* in my office and to plan the act of buying cigarettes, I have to *know* what a dinner, an office, and cigarettes are. But this knowledge is only the structure on which my act is based, the aim of my act is to select the object in the temporal dimension. It is *through* knowledge that the temporalizing act is realised but it is not *to acquire* knowledge that it is realised. Although temporal consciousness is an organised structure because past, present, and future, as we have said, are not isolated dimensions but continuously refer to one another, consciousness of the past, present and future are nevertheless subordinate structures of temporal consciousness and for the sake of clarity we will describe them separately.

Consciousness of the past is an act through which the object of consciousness is seen as absent, or as not present. But unlike imaginative consciousness, which sees the absent object as non-existent, for consciousness of the past the object is absent *in* the past, or if you prefer appears to consciousness as present in the past. It is this consciousness of the past that we call memory, Tulving's episodic memory. But memories which appear in consciousness of the past are not memories of a generic and impersonal past. When I say that I remember that Kennedy was killed in 1963 in Dallas or that Dante wrote the *Divine Comedy*, I am not conscious of the past but of a past episode. In this case the episode's being past is merely a notion, a quality that joins other qualities to form a certain type of knowledge. Kennedy is president of the United States *and* past, Dante is a poet, Italian *and* past. In other words, it is a generic and impersonal past, not *my* past. For there to be a consciousness of the past, that is memory in the mode of temporal consciousness, there has to be a strong link between the being I am now and the being I was before. It is to that past being of mine that consciousness of the past refers, and it is that past being that the memory represents.

Consciousness of the past, that is memory, can have two forms: it can be reflexive or non-reflexive. In reflexive memory the object seen in the past is myself, or rather the consciousness that I was. I can remember myself when I was having dinner with friends last night, I can *see myself* while making certain gestures, saying certain things and thinking of others. But I can also have a representation in the immediate past of these gestures, of what I said, of my friends in the restaurant. That is a representation which does not imply the presence of *me in the past* to consciousness, but just my past in itself. This is what we call non-reflexive memory or non-reflexive consciousness of the past.

In order for consciousness of the past, that is memory to exist there needs to be a present of which the past is past. It is present consciousness that is consciousness of the past. But present consciousness can also be consciousness *of* the present, that is it can see its object in the temporal form of the present. Consciousness of the present is an act that temporalizes the world in the present and is quite different from perception which is purely presence of consciousness to the object. There is no temporal dimension in my perception of this chair. It is only when I feel contemporary to this chair, to this table, to the city, to the world, that the present comes into being as consciousness of something in the present mode. So consciousness of the present, far from corresponding to perception, represents thematization of perception in the present.

Consciousness of the present, like that of the past, can also be reflexive or non-reflexive. In the reflexive form I am conscious of my consciousness as present. In the non-reflexive form I see the world as present, that is as contemporary with that being which I am now.

The third subordinate structure of temporal consciousness is consciousness of the future, which sees its object in the future. It is thematization of my probable possibles in the future. By probable possibles we mean what is based on knowledge, and this radically distinguishes consciousness of the future from wishes. Tomorrow I will be in Paris and I will continue working on this book. This is one of my probable possibles, a thematization in the future of my being which is based on and is synthesis of knowing consciousness of my being in the world: I know I live in Paris, that I am writing this book and that tomorrow is not Sunday. When instead I say "I would like to be an astronaut" I am not expressing a probable possible, but something that transcends the knowledge of the mundane being that I am. Consciousness of the future also has a reflexive and a non-reflexive form.

The great law of consciousness according to which it has to be consciousness *of* something obviously implies the existence of something that consciousness is not, that which we have called the object of consciousness. The object, in our hypothesis, can be seen by consciousness in at least three different modes which we have called knowing, imaginative and temporal consciousness. We have also seen that imaginative and temporal consciousness are based on a structure of knowledge, that is knowing consciousness. Earlier our investigation led us to reject any priority of consciousness over the object or of the object over consciousness, that is it led us away from both the idealist and the materialist perspective. Indeed, we saw that consciousness and its object are born together through an ontological relationship which defines them both. Furthermore, we rejected the idea that the object could passively exist in the functional or physiological unconscious in the form of trace or physical or virtual representation, to then become active at the moment in which it becomes conscious object. However, though united by an ontological relationship which defines them both, consciousness and its object remain, by definition, distinct entities. Indeed consciousness is consciousness inasmuch as *it is not* the object, and to be consciousness it has to perform an act of negation, that is it has to deny being the object and assert itself as not being that object. Equally, the object is that which consciousness is not, and it asserts itself as being what consciousness is not. We have described the three modes in which consciousness sees its object according to our hypothesis. We now have to question the nature and origin of the object since it is linked to but distinct from consciousness. First of all, the object of which consciousness is conscious can only be the synthesis of what consciousness *has been before* and of what consciousness *is no longer*. This point needs to be clarified. When I have perceptual consciousness, that is I already have knowing consciousness of this book which is in front of me, and I recognise it as "book", the object I recognise represents the synthesis of my past experience of book and of my present experience of the object in front of me. That object is what my consciousness is not, namely object, but it is so in the mode of "book", that is as the reflection of what my consciousness has been and what I call previous experience of book. In this sense it is in the object itself that my past consciousnesses are represented. But, you might object, I can also have perceptual consciousness, and thus knowledge, of objects I have not had previous experience of. Of course, how else could new knowledge exist? Now there is a picture in front of me which I have never seen, an object whose function I do not know, an animal I did not know existed, do I still have a right to assert that these objects are a synthesis of what my consciousness has been and of what it is not yet? Certainly, because if these objects did not somehow represent what my consciousness has been, every time I came across a new object it would appear to me as new, whereas I perceive objects that I recognise and objects that I see for the first time. And these represent what my consciousness has been, precisely because my consciousness has never been consciousness of those objects. The object to be known represents what my consciousness has been to the mode of negation, it is a synthesis of what my present consciousness is not, and of what my past consciousness has not been.

Does this description of the origin of an object as synthesis also hold for the other modes of consciousness? Can I say that when I imagine a centaur it is synthesis of my past consciousness and of what my present consciousness is not? Of course, inasmuch as the difference between imaginative consciousness and knowing consciousness is not the object but the way in which consciousness sees the object. In other words the object is always the same permanent synthesis of what I have been and what I am not. When I remember this book on my desk yesterday it is the same object that I now perceive and remember. The same object that with an original act of consciousness I dig out from down there, in my past. Even if I consider the reflexive form of memory, the question does not change. When I remember myself in the past, for example when I was talking to friends last night at dinner, that object-me of which my consciousness is consciousness, is a synthesis of what my consciousness is not now (indeed I am not that me of yesterday) and of what my consciousness has been (I was my consciousness of yesterday, which was a synthesis of all previous consciousnesses). The same description also holds for the other subordinate structures of temporal consciousness, that is for consciousness of the present and of the future.

Clearly, the conclusion to be drawn from our description of the origin of the object as synthesis of what consciousness has been and of what consciousness is not now, is a far cry from the idea of representation and of traces, in fact it is the exact opposite. Being conscious of an object in the various modes of consciousness does not mean making it correspond to an internal representation or to a trace hidden in the depths of the psychological or physiological unconscious. Quite the contrary, representation is *outside*, it is in the object. It is the object which represents me, and not I who represent the object to myself. It is the object that is the reflection of what I have been and synthesis of what I have been and what I am not.

The object which is present to my consciousness, as we have said, is the same one. The glass that I now perceive, that I remembered earlier and that I will later imagine is the same one. It is the same in the sense that the glass carries in itself the synthesis of what I have been, that is of my past experience of glass and it is up to me to see it in the knowing, imaginative or temporal mode of consciousness: the glass in itself remains what it is. However, although the object is always the same, *the* objects are not always the same among themselves. And not because they distinguish themselves by shape, colour, function etc., but by *how much* and by *what* it is of my consciousness that they represent. This point needs clarification. In my knowing consciousness of this pack of cigarettes what does the pack of cigarettes represent? We have seen that the pack of cigarettes, as object of my consciousness, represents both the synthesis of what my consciousness has been and of what it is not now. Therefore the pack of cigarettes is simultaneously knowledge of what I am made, that is my past consciousnesses of pack of cigarettes, and what I am not now, that is the existential distance which separates me from the object which is in front of me. What happens though is that I only bought the pack of cigarettes a short time ago, and the cigarette that I am now taking out of it is only the third. Clearly, my past experience of this pack of cigarettes is rather limited. If I actually wanted to quantify it I could say that I have three past consciousnesses of this pack of cigarettes: that of the moment when I bought it, that of the first cigarette and that of the second. As past experience of pack of cigarettes it does not amount to much. How can I assert that the object synthetically represents what I *have been,* if that *have been* is limited to three recent experiences? There is a certain ambiguity in all of this, but only apparently. This pack of cigarettes in front of me is both "a pack of cigarettes" and "the pack of cigarettes" I bought not long ago. In the first case it is an indefinite pack of cigarettes, something that belongs to the category of packs of cigarettes, one of the many that I recognise and use correctly because I know what it is. In the second case, however, "the pack of cigarettes" is a definite object, it is this very pack of cigarettes that is in front of me, the one that I bought not long ago and which I will carry around with me until tonight when it will end up empty, in the dustbin. Clearly, in the object which is in front of me there is both a unicity and a generality which I cannot escape. The generality is reflected in its being a pack of cigarettes and not something else. The unicity is manifested in its being that specific pack of cigarettes and not another. But the unicity and generality, or multiplicity of the pack of cigarettes are not contiguous qualities, external to one another. There is a sort of hierarchy which is the basis of the relationship between the object as representative of a multiplicity of objects, all those that make up a certain category, and the object as representative of itself, in its physicality "in the flesh", in being *that* object which distinguishes itself from all the other objects of the world. The unicity of the object, of this pack of cigarettes, of this pen, of this room, of this city is based on multiplicity. These objects we have just mentioned, the pack of cigarettes, the pen, the room, the city, the world, are all examples of a *this*, they manifest a unicity which distinguishes them from *that other* pack of cigarettes, *that other* pen, etc. But their unicity is based on multiplicity, which allows these objects to be present to consciousness as unique but under a certain, already distinct form, namely pack of cigarettes, pen, etc. So the apparent ambiguity disappears: the object is both unique and multiple. Unique because it is irremediably *this*, and multiple because in order to be *this*, it must have been *those*. It follows that the pack of cigarettes that I bought not long ago, fully represents what I have been, that is my previous experience of packs of cigarettes, because in this object I recognise a precise object, that is a pack of cigarettes. Its unicity comes afterwards, its being *this* cannot prescind its being what it is, that is a witness to what I have been. If we consider the opposite condition, we see that for the indefinite object there is no need to represent unicity. I can think of a flower, a love, a city, a world, without them having to be that flower, that love, that city, that world. I somehow think of them as *neutral* objects, as pure essences which stretch out before me and which do not invade my existential space. At most they are entities which are resolved on a linguistic level: am I required to define a flower, love, a city, the world? Well, I shall put myself to the test and try to unite in an abstract definition, the abstract entity which I am required to define. But even if language is excluded from the matter things do not change: I can think of the object in non-verbal terms without the object becoming *that* object. It is clear then that unicity requires multiplicity while multiplicity does not require unicity.

But what happens when in front of me there is a new object which I have no experience of? At first sight one would say that any object that I see for the first time is unique and does not carry in itself the multiplicity that we attributed to known objects. And yet, as we have already seen, even an object that I have no experience of represents what my consciousness has been in the mode of negation. The multiplicity on which the new object is based is represented by its not being what consciousness has been, or if you wish, by being what consciousness has never been. But in actual fact, as soon as an unknown object shows up, all the multiplicity of which it is made manifests itself instantaneously. This geometric form that I have never seen before is *already* "geometric form that I have never seen", that is it summarises and represents in the negative all that my consciousness has been. And this happens without my needing to notice the unicity of the object. So the object, be it known or unknown, is first the expression of a multiplicity of my past consciousnesses and then becomes *this* object, that is it declares its unicity.

However, for there to be unicity of an object, it must be seen by consciousness in the temporal or imaginative mode. In other words, in order to achieve the passage from the multiplicity to the unicity of an object there has to be an act of consciousness that selects its object as *this*, which can only happen if consciousness transcends the knowing mode to put itself at the level of the temporalization and of the imagination of the object. It is only in the temporalizing and the imagining act that the object appears to me in the definite mode, namely as *this*. It could certainly be argued that also in what we have called knowing consciousness the object somehow appears to me as unique, as *this*. The glass in front of me is in any case *this* glass, it is with this glass that I interact and not with a generic glass when I pick it up and bring it to my lips. Of course, but the unicity of this glass somehow falls into the anonymity of its being any glass, one of the many that I have come across in my life. It is only when that existential space, which we have already described with the idea of presence, opens up between me and the glass, that the glass comes out of its anonymity and becomes that glass which is not me and with which I am contemporary. In short there is a continuous possibility of changing the relationship from multiplicity to unicity of the object, and this possibility depends on the very way in which consciousness addresses the object. Besides, in the sphere of the psychology of memory it is, for instance, well known that the probability of remembering a certain object depends on what is called depth of encoding of the object. But what is depth of encoding if not the degree of consciousness of the unicity of the object which is in front of me? In Tulving's hypothesis of co-ordination this idea is made explicit, though in slightly different terms, when he says that the probability of remembering a certain object depends on the degree of awareness of that object at the moment it is encountered. But, you may ask, where is the proof that in temporal and imaginative consciousness the object is present to consciousness as unique and not as general or multiple? I can easily remember, for example, a generic walk along the shore, without being able to locate it in any specific time but only the past in general. But that does not mean that the walk I remember is not a particular walk but the general idea of walking along the shore. In reality memory, what Tulving rightly called episodic memory, cannot be anything other than memory of an object-episode in its unicity, because the unicity of an object is one of those very elements that describe the ontological relationship between remembering consciousness and its object. In the same way, in the imagination it is the object in its unicity which is present to my consciousness. It is that object, that centaur I am imagining now, and I would not be able to imagine the idea of centaur without returning to knowing consciousness and thus annulling the imaginative act. And the level of knowing consciousness is that of generality-multiplicity. A multiplicity which is based on repetition of an experience.

When I say "a glass", "a friend", "a walk", I am generically describing the synthetic category which describes all the objects that I give those names to because I have had repeated experience of them. What is that which in psychology is called categorising ability if not the generalisation that repeated experience of the world encourages me to use on the objects of which it is composed? As we have already said, repeated experience tends to annul consciousness, that is reduce the space which separates consciousness from the object, without however being able to truly annihilate it. So the balance between multiplicity and unicity of an object also depends on repeated experience, on what we have also called familiarity. The more familiarity there is with an object, the more the balance moves towards multiplicity and the less probability there is of seeing the object as unique. When there is no repeated experience, the balance moves towards the unicity of the object and the probability of the object being seen in the temporal mode increases. This is why sometimes memories seem to come "from outside", to appear spontaneously without an act of volition. A smell, an image, a sound can make the memory "come to life" inside me because in that smell, that image, that sound, it is unicity which has the better of multiplicity, because that existential space which separates me from the object is amplified. That is why a sunset, a new walk "move" me, because their unicity emphasises what separates me from them and pushes me to say that I am *here,* that I exist as a being which denies being the object of which it is conscious.

The hypothesis we have described is an attempt to synthesise what a phenomenological investigation of consciousness and of the reductive necessities implicit in any hypothesis which proposes itself as scientific, have demonstrated. It is therefore a somewhat paradoxical hypothesis since it tends to reduce the irreducible, but this problem has already been emphasised in the first part of this chapter.

Before proceeding any further to see the extent to which the hypothesis we have described can account for empirical reality, that is prove itself to be a scientific hypothesis, let us summarise its main points:

1) Consciousness is not a unitary dimension that passively receives what comes to it from outside, but is the set of distinct and original modes used to address an object. Among the modes of consciousness there is knowing consciousness, imaginative consciousness and temporal consciousness. Each of these represents an original, irreducible mode of seeing the world. Each mode of consciousness has a reflexive and non-reflexive form.

2) Knowing consciousness describes the mode of addressing the object *in order to know it*, that is in order to discover its quality and quantity. Knowing consciousness roughly corresponds to what in psychology is generally referred to as semantic memory. Unlike semantic memory, however, knowing consciousness does not presuppose any mental representation of the object or of its parts. Knowing consciousness is the synthesis of past consciousnesses and this synthesis enables knowledge of the object. As synthesis of past consciousnesses, knowing consciousness is temporal, but at the same time atemporal in the sense that it is not consciousness *of* time.

3) Imaginative consciousness, like knowing consciousness is an organised, irreducible form of consciousness. The image which manifests itself to imaginative consciousness is not a faded copy of a real object, but

the reflection of an original relationship between consciousness and the object. Unlike knowing consciousness, the aim of imaginative consciousness is not to know and so it is completely indifferent to the values of certainty and truth. The aim of imaginative consciousness is "unrealising", namely that of seeing the object as not belonging to objective reality.

4) Temporal consciousness is the third organised and irreducible form of consciousness described in our hypothesis. Temporal consciousness is consciousness *of* time, that is it temporalizes its object according to the subordinate structures of temporality. Temporal consciousness locates its object in the past, present and future. When it locates its object in the past, temporal consciousness corresponds to what in psychology is referred to as episodic memory. However, consciousness of the past distinguishes itself from episodic memory in that it does not require the existence of memory traces.

5) Both temporal consciousness and imaginative consciousness require and are based on knowing consciousness. In other words, for the object to be present to consciousness in the temporal mode or that of the imagination, it must already be a certain object, that is it has to represent knowledge.

6) Since consciousness must be consciousness *of*, every type of consciousness is consciousness of an object. The object which is present to consciousness in its three forms represents the synthesis of what consciousness has been and of what consciousness is not. The object is synthesis of past and present experience. The object of consciousness represents the definite and the indefinite, generality-multiplicity and unicity. The multiplicity of the object represents what consciousness has been in the past and its unicity what the object is for present consciousness. However, the unicity of the object is based on its multiplicity. The relationship between multiplicity and unicity of the object varies according to the mode of consciousness in which the object is seen and the degree of repeated experience of the object itself. The balance between multiplicity and unicity moves towards unicity when the object is addressed in the mode of temporal and imaginative consciousness and when the degree of repeated experience is low. It moves towards multiplicity when it is addressed in the mode of knowing consciousness and there is a high degree of repeated experience.

The ideas schematised in our hypothesis allow us to make some predictions:

1) Since knowing consciousness, imaginative consciousness and temporal consciousness are three organised and irreducible forms of consciousness, they should also be able to be distinguished in pathology, that is it should be possible to observe specific deficits that reflect the reciprocal organisation of the different types of consciousness. Furthermore, the activity of distinct cerebral structures may correspond to these three different modes of consciousness.

2) However, since temporal consciousness and imaginative consciousness are based on knowing consciousness, it is unlikely that deficits in knowing consciousness can be observed without there being deficits in the other two types of consciousness. Nevertheless, it should be possible to observe deficits in temporal consciousness, imaginative consciousness, or both without deficits in knowing consciousness. Since imaginative consciousness and temporal consciousness are based on knowing consciousness, it is likely that the activity of the neural structures which correspond to temporal consciousness and imaginative consciousness is generally shared by knowing consciousness.

3) A deficit in temporal consciousness should impair, although to different degrees, all three dimensions of temporality. In other words a patient with an episodic-memory deficit is also likely to have a deficit in consciousness of his personal present and future.

4) Since knowledge of the quality, quantity and function of an object is the reflection of distinct relationships between knowing consciousness and its object, it should be possible to observe specific deficits in knowledge of quality, quantity and function.

5) Since every mode of consciousness has a non-reflexive and a reflexive form, it should be possible to observe specific deficits in the reflexive form. The opposite should not be possible because the reflexive form of consciousness is the reflexive of the non-reflexive form.

6) In phylogeny and ontogeny, the development of knowing consciousness should precede that of temporal consciousness and imaginative consciousness. While in progressive degradation of

consciousness, the deficit in temporal and imaginative consciousness should precede that of knowing consciousness.

7) Since multiplicity and unicity of the object of consciousness are functions of both the modes of consciousness and the degree of repeated experience, temporal consciousness may see multiplicity as unicity, and knowing consciousness may see unicity as multiplicity.

In the following chapter we shall attempt to demonstrate the extent to which some of the predictions of our hypothesis have been confirmed by available clinical and experimental data. But let us first provide a method for the verification of our hypothesis, a method which does not fall into the same traps as those described earlier.

3. TOWARDS EXPERIMENTAL PHENOMENOLOGY

Consciousness, as we have strongly emphasised, manifests itself for what it is in its relationship with an object. When I observe a landscape, when I remember last night's argument, when I imagine a centaur galloping along the shore, my consciousness is completely directed towards the object of which it is consciousness. It is all "outside me" and is realised as consciousness precisely because it is consciousness of its object in a certain mode. In what is also called conscious experience, it is the object which reigns, without there being room for anything else, an ego which lingers in the background, a consciousness, a being. When consciousness selects its object in the mode of the past, for example, there is no consciousness before me, but just the selected object down there, where *it was*. There is not even an ego who selects that object, there is only that object which presents itself to the past and the distance which separates me from it. When we described the different types of consciousness we insisted on their *irreducibility*. Consciousness of knowledge, temporal consciousness and imaginative consciousness, we said, are organised, irreducible structures of consciousness. What did we mean? Simply that which should be taken for granted but in reality is not, at least in the sphere of science, because on the long journey both the starting-point and the destination have been forgotten. Conscious experience is in fact the starting-point for every theory of the mind, and the place towards which the results of scientific research should converge. The irreducibility of conscious experience, as we have already said but it is worth repeating, resides in the fact that conscious experience is the concrete reality of human existence, a reality that can perhaps be represented in the abstract terms of theoretical and abstract models but which cannot be reduced to these, just as the sensation of heat cannot be reduced to the variations of an expansible element inside a glass column. This consciousness we are talking about, that is conscious experience of an object, is what we have called non-reflexive consciousness, and what we could now call first-hand consciousness. This first-hand consciousness is the central aspect of mental life, the nucleus from which all the questions that man asks himself, including the scientific ones, arise. Now, it is paradoxical that science itself, or a large part of it, which is based on being consciousness of its own object, hastens to negate *tout court* conscious experience as a relevant aspect of mental life or tries to negate it in another way by reducing it to a physiological or psychological *elsewhere*. We have already analysed the paradoxes of this reduction and shall not go back over them. But science's negation of conscious experience as irreducible is not only surprising, but precludes *a priori* the possibility of knowing anything about non-reflexive consciousness, that is of the way in which consciousness, in its entirety, manifests all its characteristics. Actually, science's negation of first-hand consciousness stems mainly from a badly concealed fear, that of not having the means available to study it. There is a sort of respectable Puritanism in science together with a guilt complex which consists in not wanting to ignore its self-imposed method and in that unconfessed embarrassment about the method's inadequacy in describing most of what is fundamental in mental life. This *a priori* negative behaviour of science with regard to non-reflexive consciousness has, in reality, made scientists uncertain about the actual significance of their work. In other words, scientists have not realised, and continue not to realise, that most of what they do in their psychological experiments is actually measuring and describing non-reflexive consciousness. And so, paradox upon paradox, on the one hand any relevance to the starting-point of scientific investigation in psychology is denied, while on the other it is the starting-point itself which is studied. Indeed, what psychologists study in their experiments is non-reflexive consciousness, though in an indirect way. Let us take a classic test of recognition memory as an example. The subject, first of all, is shown a series of words. He is then presented with the same words mixed up with words which were not presented before. The subject's task is to distinguish the words seen before from those seen for the first time. What is this if not an example of research on non-reflexive consciousness. In fact, what is required of the subject is to indicate when his consciousness is consciousness of an object *as already seen before*. Of course, what the experimenter obtains from this sort of test is indirect information on non-reflexive consciousness of recollection and this information will certainly tell him nothing of what it is like to recognise a word as already seen. The fact remains though that non-reflexive conscious experience of the object is used in the experimental sphere to draw conclusions about the functioning or dysfunctioning of memory. Therefore the results of this sort of experiment indirectly refer us back to non-reflexive consciousness because this is where they stem from. This does not apply only to experiments on memory. When the experimenter asks the subject to press the right-hand button on seeing a red light, and the left-hand one on seeing a blue light, what the experimenter is addressing is, once again, non-reflexive consciousness *of red and blue*. Therefore science, in spite of itself, already indirectly studies non-reflexive consciousness, which makes any negation of consciousness on its part all the more absurd.

We are thus able to have indirect knowledge of conscious experience, or non-reflexive or first-hand consciousness. It is however somewhat incomplete knowledge and the information gathered from it tells us nothing about the quality of conscious experience. The subject who claims to recognise a certain stimulus as "already seen" in a test of recognition memory indicates that he is remembering, that is recognising an object as past. But his reply does not tell us anything about what it is like to remember[1]. In the same way, the subject who was taught to press the button when the red light appears tells us nothing about what it is like, from his point of view, to see a red light come on. Of course the observer will be able to make inferences about what it is like to recognise an object or perceive a red light. Indeed he probably knows from his personal experience what it is like to recognise an object which was seen a few minutes earlier, or to see a red light come on. Thus through inference, he will be able to "recognise" his own experience in the subject's. But it is a matter of approximate recognition which at best is limited to selecting the most general aspect of the conscious experience of recognising or of perceiving a red light. The subjective aspect of experience will once again pass unnoticed since conscious experience only shows all of its characteristics on a direct level.

---

[1] see Nagel, T., 1974; Nagel, T., 1986; Nagel, T., 1993.

A second way of studying consciousness consists in asking subjects, while they are performing a certain experimental task, what they are doing, that is what type of consciousness they have while doing a certain thing. As in the previous case, it is a question of an indirect method and thus the information that can be drawn from it is incomplete and limited. But, unlike the previous method, this one permits the study not of conscious experience but of consciousness of experience, that is of that second-hand consciousness which we have called reflexive consciousness. In other words, in this type of experimental situation, the phenomenology of the experience is reported by the subject thanks to a reflexive, that is second-degree, act which allows him to glance at his own conscious experience. I am now drinking from this glass and at this moment mine is non-reflexive consciousness of glass-to-drink-from. There is nothing else in my consciousness. And yet if someone, or I myself, were to ask "what are you doing?", then my consciousness would take a step back to observe itself. That is it would perform a reflexive act and become consciousness of consciousness which drinks from the glass. This reflexive mode of consciousness can then be translated into verbal terms and I will say "I am drinking from this glass". The type of information that can be gathered from this sort of investigation is certainly less direct than that provided by the previous method, but in some ways it is more complete. It is less direct in that it comes indirectly from consciousness of experience, that is from reflexive consciousness and not from conscious experience, that is non-reflexive consciousness. It is more complete in that it gives us more details on the quality of conscious experience. For example, to take up, once again, the case of recognition memory, when a subject claims to recognise a certain stimulus, non-reflexive consciousness, the observer can only indirectly infer that the subject is consciously experiencing the memory. In fact he may only have a vague sense of familiarity with the stimulus or he may find himself in the situation of guessing, that is of operating a probabilistic estimation of the possibility that that particular stimulus belongs to the series of stimuli seen before. As you can see, his reply tells us absolutely nothing about the quality of his conscious experience and the inferences that can be made are contaminated by a high probability of error. If, however, when he claims to recognise a stimulus, the subject is also asked to say whether recognition is accompanied by consciousness of the memory, that is consciousness that that particular stimulus had previously been seen, or alternatively whether recognition is accompanied only by a vague sense of familiarity with the stimulus, or whether recognition is only fruit of a probabilistic inference, the information that can be drawn will tell us more about the quality of the experience of recognition. It is precisely these types of reflections which led Tulving[1] to propose an experimental paradigm which permitted the distinction of different types of consciousness associated with recognition memory. According to Tulving, recognition memory is indeed composed of at least two distinct elements: a stimulus can be recognised by having, to use his terminology, *autonoetic consciousness* of it, that is by fully recognising it as an element of one's personal past, or it can be recognised with a vague sense of familiarity, that is without autonoetic consciousness of the stimulus as belonging to one's personal past. This distinction can be brought to light experimentally by asking subjects, while they are performing recognition tasks, to identify under which aspects of consciousness recognition of the stimulus takes place. This experimental paradigm is an example of the successful application of the method of experimental phenomenology. This method of Tulving's, initially criticised for not being scientific, has been used and developed by various scholars[2], producing a corpus of important new information, though indirect, on what it means to recognise a previously seen stimulus. This information could not have been provided by previously existing paradigms.

The paradigm introduced by Tulving to study consciousness of experience in recognition memory represents an important starting-point inasmuch as it introduces the phenomenological aspect of experience as a variable. It is a starting-point since what Tulving outlined for the study of recognition memory can not only be extended to other spheres of memory, but also to the indirect study of consciousness in other spheres of human experience. As regards memory, the method should be extended to free recollection, that is, asking subjects when recalling a certain previously presented stimulus whether recollection is accompanied by subjective experience of the memory or whether it occurs without this type of experience. The other aspects of temporal consciousness should also be studied with this paradigm or versions of it. As regards consciousness of the present, for instance, it is completely unknown whether and to what extent the presence of an object to consciousness is accompanied by a sense of

---

[1] Tulving, E., 1985.
[2] Dalla Barba, G., 1993; Dalla Barba, G., 1997; Gardiner, J.M., 1988; Gardiner, J.M. & Java, R.I., 1990; Gardiner, J.M. & Java, R.I., 1991; Gardiner, J.M. & Java, R.I., 1993; Gardiner, J.M. & Java, R.I., 1993; Gardiner, J.M. & Parkin, A.J., 1990; Parkin, A.J., 1993; Rajaram, S., 1993.

contemporaneity with the object, that is under what conditions the present object reveals itself as *contemporary* in what William James called the psychological present. Then the future, as a dimension of temporality, should also be studied from the point of view of experimental phenomenology. What happens in subjective experience when somebody says "tomorrow I am going to the barber's"? Is it the placing of a personal act in the future or merely a *semantic* reply, dictated by what I know of myself and my future without there having to be experience of the future in itself? The only way of knowing this is by directly asking the subject who is being questioned.

Important results are also expected from the application of experimental phenomenology to the study of imaginative consciousness and its deficits. What is someone who is imagining a centaur imagining? Is he really imagining a centaur or does he only have the *semantic* idea of a centaur in mind, that is does he become conscious of the centaur only as a verbal-conceptual entity without his subjective experience being accompanied by any mental image? And what happens in subjective experience, that is in indirectly studied reflexive consciousness, of the patient who cannot say if a cherry is redder than a strawberry? We need to ask him. Consciousness of knowledge is also totally unknown in this respect. When you are in front of a picture of a rose, what do you see? A distinct object which qualifies as a *rose* through an image-word association, an object of a certain shape, colour, a particular smell, a function, that of pricking with its thorns or of being given as a present? And what is a rose for those who cannot name it and who do not recognise its shape, colour, or function? Who knows? Yet again, the person who is being questioned needs to be asked. The indirect study of reflexive consciousness according to experimental paradigms which investigate, in a controlled way, what are also known as third person reports, can provide a lot of important information about the structure and organisation of conscious experience, information which science has not been able to provide until now.

The third experimental way to study consciousness is that of phenomenological reduction. There seems to be a contradiction here since Husserl places the origins of phenomenological reduction as propaedeutic to science and thus by definition as not belonging to science itself. As we shall see, this contradiction can actually be overcome, and talking of experimental phenomenological reduction is neither paradoxical nor arbitrary. Phenomenological reduction in its classic form means going back to the objects themselves, that is returning to direct experience of the world as it presents itself in its pre-scientific dimension, prior to knowledge. Varela[1] who claims this method as his own, calling it neurophenomenology, quotes Merleau-Ponty[2] on this subject: "Going back to the objects themselves means going back to this world prior to the knowledge of which knowledge always *talks,* and compared to which every scientific definition is an abstract, dependent sign like geography compared to the landscape in which we originally learnt what a forest, a field and a river were." But Varela, perhaps out of diplomacy, avoids quoting Merleau-Ponty's previous words: "The first task that Husserl foresaw for his debutant phenomenology, which was to be a 'descriptive psychology' or to return to 'the objects themselves', is above all a disavowal of science. I am not the result or the convergence of the many causalities which define my body or my 'psychism', I cannot think of myself as part of the world, as a simple object of biology, psychology and sociology, nor can I close the universe of science on me. All that I know about the world, even through science, I know first from my point of view or from an experience of the world without which the symbols of science would be meaningless. The whole universe of science is constructed on the real world we live in and if we want to think of science itself, to assess its exact meaning and significance, we must first of all reawaken this experience of the world of which science is the second expression. Science does not have, nor will it ever have, the same sense of being as the perceived world, simply because it is neither a definition nor an explanation of it. I was not formerly a 'living being' or a 'man' or a 'consciousness', with all the characteristics that zoology, social anatomy or inductive psychology attribute to these products of nature or of history - I am the absolute source, my existence does not come from my antecedents, from my physical or social environment, but it goes towards these and supports them, since it is I who make being for me (and thus being in the only sense that the word can have for me) this tradition that I choose to take up again or this horizon whose distance from me - not belonging to it as property - would disappear if I were not there to glance over it. The scientific views according to which I am a moment of the world, are always ingenuous and hypocritical, because they leave out, that is they do not mention, the other view - that of consciousness - for which a world

---

[1] Varela, F.J., 1995.
[2] Merleau-Ponty, M., 1945.

originally arranges itself around me and begins to exist for me." In Merleau-Ponty's description it is clear how the phenomenological method, at least in its classic intentions, set itself directly outside science, unmasking the naivety and hypocrisy. This still holds today since science certainly has not given proof of having overcome that behaviour denounced by the phenomenologists. However, what neither Merleau-Ponty nor classic phenomenology in general have considered is that phenomenological reduction is not only propaedeutic to knowledge, scientific knowledge included, but can be scientific itself inasmuch as it is capable of providing reproducible information "on the things themselves". As we shall shortly see.

The method of phenomenological reduction is a reflexive, introspective method, even if it is introspection which does not exhaust itself in the introspective method adopted by psychologists of the beginning of this century and is not to be confused with this. Indeed, in phenomenological reduction, introspection is an attitude of thought which starts by eliminating beliefs and judgements "on things" with the aim of grasping their essence. Putting "in brackets", as suggested by the phenomenologists, the world which appears to us according to lines of sight of what we already know of it, that is our prejudices against things, has as a consequent the "suspension of judgement", which allows us to perceive the things themselves "in the flesh" as Husserl says. In this way phenomenological reduction allows direct information to be obtained on non-reflexive consciousness. Indeed, since it is a method which uses reflection, its result is a glance that consciousness takes at consciousness. Phenomenological reduction allows one to know non-reflexive consciousness in the mode of reflection. But here there is perhaps a misunderstanding nourished by phenomenology itself, and partly resolved by the philosophy of existence which was seen as its development and counterbalance. In phenomenological reduction, things do not actually appear "in the flesh" as Husserl says. What appears in the flesh is consciousness of things. It follows that phenomenological reduction does not produce information on things but on consciousness of things. A phenomenological analysis of perception, for instance, does not, by any means tell me what direct perception of a rose is, rather it tells me what my perceptive consciousness of rose is. In short, phenomenological reduction, as emphasised, requires a second-degree act, that stepping back we have already mentioned, which allows consciousness to take a look at itself. The information on consciousness that phenomenological reduction can provide is thus, once again, second-hand. First-degree consciousness, or non-reflexive consciousness, continues to escape the notice of qualitative investigation as it always will since its very being is *towards* the object, and in its relationship with the object it exhausts and completes itself. When I tell myself, or someone else, what I feel on perceiving a rose, on making love with a woman, on remembering a landscape, on running for the bus, what I am doing is describing from outside consciousness what is somehow exterior to me, in the sense that when I describe these situations I have a view of what I have never been since my consciousness when I perceived the rose, made love, contemplated the landscape, caught the bus, was direct consciousness of what I was conscious of and nothing else. This does not stop phenomenological reduction from providing information of a better quality on non-reflexive consciousness than that which can be obtained with the first method mentioned in this part of our study. Indeed in the first method it was a matter of situations in which non-reflexive consciousness was seen *from outside*, that is by an observer who, for instance, recorded the replies of a subject who claimed to recognise a certain stimulus as *already seen*. In that situation the observer's position could only be inferential: he could infer that since the subject claimed to recognise a certain stimulus as already seen, his subjective experience was *probably* an experience of recognition, that is of the placing of an object in the past. However in the case of phenomenological reduction it is the subject himself who asks and answers himself about a certain phenomenon, for example "what does that stimulus which I seem to recognise mean to me?". In short, there is more quality in phenomenological reduction than in the indirect investigation of non-reflexive consciousness described earlier.

We proposed the three methodological approaches just described as experimental methods. We soon realised that there was a possible contradiction in considering these methods, largely based on phenomenological hypotheses, as experimental and thus scientific methods. However we also realised that experimental and therefore scientific phenomenology is possible provided that not only what positivist science considers to be scientific is taken into consideration. Yet the data and information provided by the phenomenological method must be reproducible for there to be an experimental phenomenology and for the three methods described to be considered scientific. In other words, for phenomenology to become established on an experimental level, the results of the investigation itself must be reproducible under exactly the same conditions of investigation with a significant degree of invariance. As regards the first method, that is the one already in general use in experimental psychology and neuropsychology, there is nothing much to add: the reproducibility of an experience has already been demonstrated and is in fact the basis from which the conclusions of these sciences are drawn. If, for example, it is believed that, with some exceptions, it is easier to recognise a certain stimulus than to freely recall it, it is because a certain amount of data which show that recognition is systematically superior to free recollection have been consistently reproduced. But something more about the quality of conscious experience can be learnt from this method. The data obtained with the classic method of experimental psychology and neuropsychology should be compared with those from the second method, that is from the indirect study of reflexive consciousness. It is the degree of convergence between the two series of data that should be compared. In other words it is a question of establishing whether, and to what extent, the response of a subject on a task which involves non-reflexive consciousness coincides with the response that the same subject makes when doing a task which involves reflexive consciousness. As far as the second method is concerned, that is the indirect study of reflexive consciousness, it has already produced reproducible data in the sphere of recognition memory. The method, as we have already said, can be extended to other spheres besides memory and in these too, what is required of the method is the reproducibility of the data and their convergence with the data provided by the first method. The indirect study of reflexive consciousness must also provide and be able to reproduce information on the influence of an object and its characteristics of multiplicity and singularity on conscious experience. In other words, one of the aims of the application of this method is to show to what extent the characteristics of the object we have previously described determine the unveiling of one type of consciousness or of another. In order for the method of phenomenological reduction to be considered experimental, it too must provide reproducible results. Since it is a purely reflexive method, the result of reflection must first of all be communicable, that is become a first-person report, which can then be compared with other first-person reports on the same subject. In this case too, convergence with the results of the other methods is of prime importance.

The question we asked ourselves at the beginning of this chapter was about the possibility of a scientific theory of consciousness which could account for and overcome the theoretical problems discussed in the earlier sections of this work. The answer is: yes, a scientific theory of consciousness is possible on condition that the limits that any scientific reduction involves are accounted for. Indeed we have seen that we have to content ourselves with an indirect study of consciousness and so the information we can draw from, by definition, does not grasp consciousness in itself. The hypothesis we proposed is not intended to consider all types of consciousness, just some of them. And again, those types of consciousness described are certainly rather approximate, in the sense that for the aims of this work we have put aspects of consciousness, which in reality are quite clearly distinct, together under labels which are perhaps too general. But again, the aim of this work was first of all to produce some distinctions within consciousness, distinctions which science and theoretical reflection have until now ignored or traced back to unlikely explanatory idols: the memory trace, representation, the *homunculus,* for example. For however (deliberately) partial and incomplete, our hypothesis is an operative hypothesis which demands experimental falsification. We have even suggested an experimental method, perhaps making Husserl, and others who maintain that phenomenology should have nothing to do with the narrow world of science and experimentalism, turn in his grave. In reality, science and experimentalism have for too long been considered as synonyms. Experimentalism is only an (unlucky) aspect of science, not science itself. Science in itself is a method, not an ideology. It uses experiments and the reproducibility of their results to confirm the hypotheses it poses. Nothing more, nothing less. It is against a science without hypotheses, or with such ingenuous hypotheses that even a six-year-old could easily confute them, that this work demands a return to hypotheses as the result of reflection which puts aside the conformist prejudices, totems and explanatory idols we observe today and which are reflected in the acritical adherence to the totem of the neurosciences and its presumed and unreal developments, at least as regards the explanation *from below* of human experience. And against an illusion, the functionalist illusion which sees the concreteness of experience as stemming from an abstract elsewhere. In the following pages we will show how the hypotheses proposed can account for some of the current data on the pathology of the so-called cognitive functions without having to fall, once again, into the paradoxes of the interpretative paradigms of functionalism.

CHAPTER 7

CONSCIOUSNESS AND REALITY

In the preceding chapter we described a hypothesis regarding the organisation of consciousness or the modes of consciousness, as we have called them. We also proposed a method, that of experimental phenomenology, to verify this hypothesis. Future studies which apply this method will prove whether or not we were right, but in the meantime, the hypothesis we have formulated allows us to interpret experimental data from some existing psychological and neuropsychological studies on memory.

1. AMNESIA

The amnesic syndrome is a serious pathological condition of memory loss following cerebral damage. Amnesia is a devastating condition, perhaps one of the most debilitating neuropsychological syndromes. Patients suffering from it are unable to recall or recognise anything after only a minute or so. Usually they claim not to recognise their doctor or the experimenter with whom they may have only just ended a long session. Sometimes they can recall events which took place many years earlier, for example, they may remember the school or the house of their childhood, but in the most serious cases retrograde amnesia, i.e. amnesia for events which took place before they became amnesics, can be global. In this case they do not remember, for example, having children, being married, or else they believe their parents are still alive. It is as though their present life had disappeared from consciousness into nothing. The result is that they are lost in a *no time*. Psychologists prefer to say that these patients are locked inside a permanent present, but we shall see further on that this is not the case: there is no present in the conscious experience of amnesic patients. These patients, however, do not usually present any general degradation of their intellectual capacities, they may maintain an absolutely normal intelligence quotient, resolve complex problems, including problems of arithmetic, as long as these do not require the use of memory. There are various causes which lead to this condition. The most classic is chronic alcoholism, and in this case it is called Korsakoff's syndrome, from the name of the Russian neurologist who described it a century ago. Among the other causes, the most frequent are encephalitis from herpes virus simplex, certain forms of cerebral infarction, cranial-encephalic traumas. These same patients, whose ability to remember is so devastatingly damaged, have what psychologists call normal implicit memory.

The term implicit memory indicates a collection of phenomena which are well known in psychology and neuropsychology. It is used to describe the fact that past experience implicitly influences present experience, without there being any memory of this. Nothing odd, you will say, about this implicit memory. Basically, every action we carry out is an expression of implicit memory since it is based on "knowledge", acquired knowledge of which there is no memory. When I write, speak, brush my teeth, light a cigarette, I am able to carry out these actions because I learned them without, however, there being any memory of the moment or moments in which I gradually learned to perform them. What surprises psychologists and neuropsychologists is that so-called implicit memory is not only used for actions learned gradually and repeated *ad infinitum*, like writing, speaking, brushing your teeth or smoking, but also for unique experiences. The fact that the so-called implicit expression of experience is also observable in amnesic patients is considered even more surprising. We have already spoken about Claparède [1] who, nearly a century ago, described an experiment carried out on a severely amnesic patient. During one of his sessions with that patient Claparède had hidden a pin between his fingers and when he shook hands the patient was painfully pricked. The pain, like any other event, was immediately forgotten by the patient. However when, at the end of the session, Claparède once again held out his hand, the patient

---

[1] Claparède, E., 1911.

refused to shake it. When asked why, she answered that she simply did not feel like shaking his hand because at times there are pins hidden in a hand you are about to shake. But this was an idea that "went through her head", a totally impersonal idea which made no reference at all to the episode of the prick which had been totally forgotten. Korsakoff [1] had made a similar observation some years earlier. In his original article on the syndrome which is named after him, he describes a patient who had undergone an electric shock and was later presented with the box containing the instrument used to produce the shock. Even though the patient did not explicitly remember the episode of the shock, when he saw the box he asked the experimenter if by any chance he intended to use it to give him a shock. What happens in these patients? Who is Claparède's patient and what is happening to her when she withdraws her hand to avoid being pricked once again? You will say that she is implicitly expressing her past experience of being pricked. But what does this mean? What does implicit mean and *why* is the patient's behaviour implicit? And what type of consciousness is that of Claparède's patient when she avoids being pricked again? It is clear that there is absolutely nothing implicit in her behaviour. What indeed is implicit behaviour if not a way of facing others and the world, which along side the explicit meaning places an implicit meaning which deliberately represents the true message to be transmitted? In other words, behaviour is implicit when there is consciousness and intention to hide the implicit message behind a different explicit message. Bateson[2] spoke well and at length on this when he presented the double link as one of the probable origins of schizophrenia. The double link is a type of relationship between people in which an explicit message is set against an opposing implicit message. But in Claparède's patient, as far as we know, everything is explicit. When she refuses to take her sadistic interlocutor's hand, she is hiding nothing. She has no memory of the pin prick and when she withdraws her hand it is because she is afraid of hidden pins in hands, nothing more, nothing less. What is implicit about this? Absolutely nothing. If we are looking in her behaviour for the effect of past experience, namely implicit memory, this effect is to be found in Claparède, not in the patient. All that is implicit in this situation is to be found in Claparède, it is he who attributes the expression of an earlier experience to the woman's behaviour. As far as the woman is concerned, withdrawing her hand is simply her explicit behaviour,

---

[1] Korsakoff, S.S., 1889.
[2] Bateson, G., 1959.

nothing else. In brief, finding it to be implicit behaviour and deciding that this is implicit memory is simply a decision taken by the observer who finds himself in the condition of recognising past elements in the behaviour of the patient under observation. Therefore, implicit memory is entirely on the part of the observer and not of the observed patient, for whom there is absolutely nothing which is implicit.

But, you will say, Claparède's patient has "registered" the past experience, since she carries the signs of it in her present reaction. Certainly, it is clear that the patient's consciousness is a consciousness which continues to be a synthesis of the consciousnesses which preceded it. This patient's consciousness continues to be its own past, and precisely because it is her past she manages to avoid a new pin prick. However, what she is missing, the nucleus of her amnesia, lies in the inability to thematize that past, not in the impossibility of being it. In short, in the light of our hypothesis, there is nothing which should surprise us in this patient's behaviour. What she can no longer do is turn to the world in the temporal mode. Her temporal consciousness, to use our terms, has disappeared. She is no longer capable of placing her experiences in the temporal mode of consciousness, in this case in the past. It is not a question of lost information or memory traces which have been destroyed, but of a disorder of consciousness which is no longer able to place its own past as thesis and thematize it. But at the same time this patient's consciousness continues to be temporal, to carry within itself the signs of its past. In as far as it is consciousness, it is still a synthesis of all past states of consciousness, even that of pin-that-pricks-hand. What is missing in this patient is the possibility to thematize time, namely the ability to trace herself through the past. But time continues to be a founding structure of her consciousness since consciousness cannot but be temporal. In other words, Claparède's patient has lost the ability to address the world in the mode of temporal consciousness, but continues to be able to turn to the world in the mode of knowing consciousness: consciousness which is synthesis of the past without being consciousness *of the* past.

The case described by Claparède and analogous cases described by Korsakoff, more or less in the same period, were experimentally confirmed in the 50s with the research on the famous patient H.M., who was a young engineer who suffered from a serious and untreatable form of temporal epilepsy. Since drug treatment was ineffectual, a neurosurgeon, William Scoville, decided to intervene surgically on H.M. by removing the epileptogenic centre, namely the medial part of both temporal lobes of the brain [1]. Scoville's operation was successful from the point of view of the epilepsy which was thus kept under control, but it also had the devastating result of transforming H.M. into the serious amnesic case which he is still today. Despite his severe amnesia, it soon became apparent that H.M. was able to acquire and retain, even for long periods, a series of tasks and information which were new to him. He was capable, for example, of learning and retaining complex motor skills like following a moving target on top of a rotating disk with a stylus, or mirror drawing, that is not having visual control over his own hand and the sheet of paper, but of their reflected image. The performance of these tasks got better and better by the day without, however, H.M. ever remembering having carried out the tasks before. In short, like Claparède's patient, H.M. proved to have implicit memory, namely the influence of previous experience on his present behaviour. The results obtained on H.M. were later repeated also in other forms and in other patients[2] and today it is generally accepted that amnesics preserve their implicit memory. The aim of all these experiments is to demonstrate that amnesic patients are capable of retaining and implicitly expressing past experience. But what they actually demonstrate is that temporal consciousness and the possibility of bearing the signs of your past are independent. Indeed implicit memory is nothing other than the result of a temporalizing act of an observer's consciousness on the observed. It is the observer who perceives the past in the behaviour of the observed just as he can discover the past in any sign he is presented with. The wear and tear on the keyboard I am using, the crumpled cigarette in the ashtray, the half-empty glass are signs that refer to the past if I bother to see them as such. In themselves those signs are nothing other than what they are. And so implicit memory could be attributed to the signs as much as to amnesics, but that

---

[1] Scoville, W.B., & Milner, B., 1957.
[2] Butters, N., 1987; Cermak, L., Talbot, N., Chandler, K., & Wolbarst, L.R., 1985; Hayman, C.A.G., & Tulving, E., 1989; Heindel, W.C., Salmon, D.P., & Butters, N., 1990; Salmon, D.P., Shimamura, A.P., Butters, N., & Smith, S., 1988; Schacter, D.L., 1989; Schacter, D.L., & Church, B.A., 1992; Shimamura, A.P., 1986; Tulving, E., Hayman, C.A.G., & Macdonald, C.A., 1991; Tulving, E., & Hayman, G., 1995; Tulving, E., & Schacter, D., 1990; Tulving, E., Schacter, D.L., McLachlan, D.R., & Moscovitch, M., 1988; Tulving, E., Schacter, D.L., & Stark, H.A., 1982; Warrington, E., & Weiskrantz, L., 1968.

only confirms the fact that every element in the world is its own past, amnesics included, every element is the result and the continual synthesis of what it was before. But if each of us is the synthesis of what he has been, without there necessarily being temporal consciousness of this, why is implicit memory also lost in some cases. We know, for example, that some serious cases of Alzheimer's do not present the semantic priming effect, namely a form of implicit memory, or that patients with Huntington's chorea do not have implicit learning of specific motor skills. Certainly, but this does not mean that these patients have lost the ability to register memory traces which are then *implicitly* expressed while in amnesic patients the trace of experience can be registered and implicitly expressed. The absence of implicit memory in these patients does not imply that their present consciousness is not the synthesis of the states of consciousness which preceded it. Indeed it continues to be so in every way, and if no effect of implicit memory is observed in these patients, this is because their present consciousness is revealed through an incapacity or a deficiency which is the expression of what they are at present, and the synthesis of what they were. The result is that the observer no longer sees the past in their behaviour, but this does not mean that they do not continue to be that past and that their consciousness is not the synthesis of their states of consciousness that preceded it. In short, implicit memory does not represent a condition in which the memory trace is expressed in behaviour without passing through consciousness, as certain functionalist models claim, a consciousness which, among other things, is generic[1]. It reflects the impossibility of seeing the object in the past, namely in the mode of temporal consciousness. The result is that the object in its unicity is seen in the atemporal and impersonal mode of consciousness, namely in one of those modes that we have described as knowing consciousness. However, our interpretation does not intend to underrate the importance and interest of the studies on implicit memory, but only to demonstrate that the results of these studies can be interpreted differently, without there having to be recourse to explanatory stratagem like the memory trace and its implicit expression.

One of the predictions of our hypothesis concerned the possibility to observe specific deficits of temporal consciousness, or of imaginative consciousness or of both, without deficits of knowing consciousness. This

---

[1] Moscovitch, M., 1989; Schacter, D.L., 1989.

affirmation was based on the hypothesis that these two types of consciousness are based on knowing consciousness, and consequently the functions of knowing consciousness prove necessary for those of temporal and imaginative consciousness but not vice versa. We are not going to deal with imaginative consciousness, about which little is known in amnesics. But amnesia does represent one of the conditions predicted by our hypothesis: a disappearance, or a specific deficiency, of temporal consciousness. Amnesia represents the condition in which an object can no longer be thematized in the temporal mode, namely in the past, present or future. Amnesia then is not a deficiency of memory, nor of that particular type of memory which is referred to as episodic memory, or at least, not only. Amnesia has nothing to do with the loss of a hypothetical episodic memory trace nor with the impossibility of accessing it, because such a trace quite simply does not exist. Despite the theoretical ingenuity of those who go as far as considering (episodic) memory as the result of the re-activation of an unconscious consciousness (sic)[1], it is clear that not only is an unconscious consciousness a mere figure of speech, but the very idea of trace carries in itself that paralogistic stratagem which we have already described in the first chapter of this work, namely the idea that the past can derive from elements borrowed from the present. The habit of considering the mind to be a container often leads to the analogy between what happens in the mind and what happens between a supermarket and one of its customers. Memory traces, or information, are the goods that the supermarket offers, the "recovery mechanisms" are the customer interested in buying the goods. The attempt to take possession of the merchandise may fail for two reasons: because the merchandise is no longer there, or because the supermarket is closed and the customer cannot get in. Nothing could be more misleading. There are neither traces nor goods in the mind, just as there are no mechanisms for recovering information nor customers. What does exist is consciousness which turns to its object in a certain way, in the modes we have already described at length. One of these modes is the temporal mode and with amnesia it is the ability of placing the object in the temporal mode that is lost. Tulving is right, and others with him, when he says that amnesia reflects a deficiency of episodic memory. But that is not the whole story. Indeed not only do amnesics not remember their own past, that is they are unable to place themselves (reflexive mode of temporal consciousness) and an object (non-reflexive mode of temporal

---

[1] Moscovitch, M., 1995.

consciousness) in that dimension of temporality called the past, but neither are they able to place themselves and their object in the present or in the future. Whoever is familiar with amnesics will understand what we are saying. These are patients whose consciousness is in some way lost in a non-time, in a sort of instantaneous present. Take the amnesic patient described by Tulving and co-researchers for example [1]. That patient, as is usually the case in amnesics, had preserved all his so-called semantic knowledge, namely knowing consciousness, but was not capable of recalling any episode of his own past nor of saying anything at all about his future. When he was asked what he had done shortly before or the previous day, or what he would do the following day his answer was "I don't know". When asked to describe his state while trying to remember the past or to predict the future he would say that it was as though there were a blank . When asked to describe this blank which characterised his state when he thought of the following day, he would say that it was "like being asleep" or that it was "a kind of empty thing". When asked to make an analogy with his state, he would say "it's like being in an empty room and someone asks you to find a chair that isn't there". Or else "it's like swimming in the middle of a lake where there is nothing to grab onto." When asked to compare his state when thinking about the past with when he thought about the future, he would answer "the same type of blank." The temporal "blank" of which this patient is a prisoner represents the inability of consciousness to thematize time. Past and future have disappeared as possible objects of consciousness and the patient finds himself enclosed in an instantaneous non-time. In this patient it is not the past which has been lost. Just like Claparède's patient, the past is there, intact, and is manifest in all the knowledge that the patient has not lost and in that which he is still capable of learning. In other words his consciousness continues to be knowing consciousness and, as such, synthesis of the states of consciousness which preceded it. What is missing is the ability to thematize time, to carry out that recognising synthesis which enables one to place an event there where it took place or there where it will take place. The patient of Tulving and his co-researchers is not the only proof that amnesia represents a loss of the ability to thematize an object in the mode of temporal consciousness. Indeed it has been generally observed that amnesics are often "disoriented in time and space", having lost, that is, the ability to place themselves in a present temporal space. Certain recent observations demonstrate that even in

---

[1] Tulving, E., 1985; Tulving, E., Schacter, D.L., McLachlan, D.R., & Moscovitch, M., 1988.

patients with Alzheimer's disease, the inability to remember your personal past is systematically associated with the inability to plan your personal future[1].

Earlier we saw that an object which is present to consciousness is the synthesis of what consciousness has been and of what consciousness is not. The object therefore is the synthesis of past and present experience. At the same time the object of consciousness always represents the definite and the indefinite, which we have also called multiplicity and unicity. The multiplicity of an object represents what consciousness has been in the past, its unicity what the object represents for present consciousness. We have also seen that unicity is based on multiplicity and that the balance between the multiplicity and unicity of the object varies depending on the mode in which the object is seen by consciousness and the degree of repeated experience of the object. The balance between multiplicity and unicity moves towards unicity when the object is seen in the mode of temporal consciousness and imaginative consciousness and when there is little repeated experience of it. On the other hand, it moves towards multiplicity when the object is seen in the mode of knowing consciousness and there is a high degree of repeated experience. Considering the nature of the object of consciousness in this way enabled us to foresee the possibility that temporal consciousness see the multiple as unique and that knowing consciousness see the unique as multiple. One of the terms of this prediction is seemingly confirmed by what happens in amnesics. What is referred to as implicit expression of memory in amnesic patients may indeed be seen as the reflex of knowing consciousness that sees the unicity of an object as multiplicity. In other words, past experience is not seen by amnesic patients in its unicity, as it would be if it were seen in the mode of temporal consciousness, but as multiplicity, namely in the knowing mode of consciousness. Claparède's patient who refuses to shake hands "because at times there are pins hidden between the fingers of hands that you shake" translates the unicity of the object, that is the past experience of being pricked, into an impersonal generalisation, that is into multiplicity. The amnesic patient who performs a certain task better the fifth time than the first, but believes it to be the first, is proof of acquired "knowledge" of which there is no temporal consciousness but which reflects the relationship between knowing consciousness and the object seen in its multiplicity rather than its unicity.

---

[1] Dalla Barba, G., Nedjam, Z., & Dubois, B., 1999.

But we said the unicity of an object could also be seen in the mode of knowing consciousness, without its temporal thematization. The following case study will clarify this situation.

One winter afternoon, MM, a girl of 17, was found by a friend, motionless in the street[1]. On speaking to her, her friend realised that MM did not recognise him and remembered neither her name nor who she was. On getting home, she recognised neither her parents nor her home. Since then, though her learning ability has remained perfectly normal, MM has not remembered anything of her life before the moment she was found motionless in the street. The origin of MM's amnesia has never been understood even though the lack of direct or indirect signs of lesions to the nervous system suggest it is of a psychological nature. But this is not what we are interested in. By the time she had reached us MM was in reality aware of a large part of her past before the episode which had caused her amnesia. Thanks to her normal learning ability she had in one way or another "re-learned" her own biography from her parents and friends. And so, for example, she could recount many episodes from her life without though having any recollective experience of them. It was information, she would say, that she had learned from others and that therefore did not belong to her. Even though it represented her personal past, this for her was knowledge lived impersonally and that she did not recognise as "memories" in the usual sense of the word. Nothing strange, you will say. Indeed, since MM had re-learned her own past from others, this information ended up as knowledge and so it is of no surprise that this acquired information was not accompanied by the subjective phenomenal experience of memory. However, that is not exactly how things stand. Indeed, MM could not say from whom and on which occasion she had learned about many of the episodes that she could recount without recognising them as memories; quite strange for a girl with excellent learning capacity. Furthermore, her parents confirmed that while MM had been told about certain episodes by them or by friends, of others it seemed that there had been no mention. And so it is plausible to think that the amnesia hadn't erased all the episodes of MM's life, but had saved at least a part. However, the episodes which had been saved from the amnesia had lost the status of real personal memories and had assumed that of impersonal knowledge, as though MM in some way knew the personal past of another person. In other words, it is probable that

---

[1] Dalla Barba, G., Mantovan, M.C., Ferruzza, E., & Denes, G., 1997.

the case of MM represents a condition in which the unicity of past experience is seen in the mode of knowing consciousness and not in that of temporal consciousness.

This brief description of certain aspects of amnesia confirms at least three of the predictions of our hypothesis: 1) the impossibility of seeing an object in the mode of temporal consciousness, in its three subordinate structures, while the object can be seen in the mode of knowing consciousness; 2) the possibility that knowing consciousness sees the unicity of an object as multiplicity; 3) the possibility that the unicity of an object be seen in the mode of knowing consciousness and not in that of temporal consciousness. The following examination of confabulation will confirm other aspects of our hypothesis.

2. CONFABULATION

Confabulation is a phenomenon found at times in amnesic patients. These patients who are usually unaware of their memory deficit, sometimes present and often to a great degree, so-called "false memories". They recall episodes and facts which never actually took place, or that took place in a completely different context, but which, as we shall see, are experienced by them as real memories. Even though it is clear that the subject who confabulates has no intention of deceiving his interlocutor, nor is he aware of how inappropriate his behaviour is, when the definitions used to indicate this phenomenon are considered it becomes clear that there is a more or less explicit tendency to make an analogy between confabulation and lying. Confabulation has been defined, for example, as "falsification of memory" [1], "an extreme form of lie or deceit" [2], an "honest lie" [3]. If then we look further back we discover that the analogy between confabulation and the act of lying is stated in explicit terms in the classic idea which sees confabulation as an attempt to fill in mnesic gaps and becomes real identity when Talland, commenting on this idea, says "the reasoning is plausible,

---

[1] Berlyne, N., 1972.
[2] Joseph, R., 1986.
[3] Moscovitch, M., 1989.

and amnesics are not all examples of virtue" [1]. This type of explanation of confabulation, far from capturing its real nature, reflects in one way or another the common tendency to reduce the "scandal" of abnormality to normal terms. And so the patient who confabulates produces false memories because the real ones have disappeared with his illness and, even though he does not realise it, he is considered some sort of liar. Or else his confabulation is seen as the result of a loss of control over his memories due to the damage of certain mechanisms which usually like guards make sure that only real memories get to consciousness by keeping the false ones out [2]. This is clearly a case of what we described in the second chapter as the "*homunculus* fallacy", namely the belief which is common to many theories that the brain and the mind have mechanisms and processes endowed with unconscious intentionality, a type of guard who allows "real" memories to pass and stops the false ones on the doorstep of consciousness. According to these theories the monitoring mechanisms work in the background, outside of consciousness and are not accessible to it. And so, as we have seen, the *homunculus* fallacy falls into the paradox of attributing intentionality, which is a characteristic of consciousness, to unconscious processes which, by definition, are not accessible to consciousness. This is the same as saying unconscious consciousnesses inhabit the mind with the complicity of the brain. Not even spiritualism has gone that far. We will not come back to this point.

The question we must now ask is: what is confabulation? Why under certain conditions do some people invent "another" past for themselves and, as we shall see, also "another" present and "another" future? A past, present and future to which they are so totally attached that they do away with the ability to judge what is true and what is false. Indeed what is seen as false by the interlocutor, who sees the patient living in his world of confabulation, is seen as being absolutely true by the patient who confabulates. In the following pages an attempt is made to answer these questions. We will begin by describing the case history of two patients and try to identify the characteristics of their confabulatory behaviour and to understand the role this plays in the concreteness of their lives.

---

[1] Talland, G.A., 1961.

[2] This type of explanation of confabulation is common to many theories which hypothesise the existence of mechanisms of control localised in the frontal lobe. See for example: Baddeley, A. and B. Wilson, 1986; Johnson, M.K., 1991; Moscovitch, M., 1989.

AB[1] is a man of 75; he worked until his retirement as the sales manager for an airline. He had a good education and is an amateur novelist, some of his works have been published. He is married with two children. He has never suffered from psychiatric or neurological disorders. One day, getting out of the car, AB loses his balance, falls down and fractures his femur. He does not lose consciousness and has no cranial trauma. He is hospitalised in the orthopaedic ward, undergoes surgery and is then transferred to another ward for rehabilitation. It is at this point that the staff begin to notice that AB has problems with his memory in the day to day life of the hospital and this is when our sessions begin. AB was completely disoriented both for people and as far as time and space were concerned and his disorientation almost always assumed the characteristics of confabulation. When questioned, unlike many disoriented patients who usually keep quiet out of embarrassment or give only very slightly imprecise answers, AB clearly gave wrong answers. At our first meeting, for example, he treated me as though we had known each other for some time and when I actually asked him if by chance he remembered having already met me, he answered that we had known each other for years and that he was not yet so far gone that he could not recognise acquaintances. When I asked him if he remembered where and when our first meeting took place, he answered that he thought it had taken place in Bologna many years earlier, but he could not remember the circumstances. We were not in Bologna but in Paris, AB was not Italian but French and as I later found out from his children, he had perhaps been to Bologna once in his life. I had just arrived in France and I spoke French with a heavy Italian accent, as I still do (alas). His answer may have been influenced by my presence. AB knew I was Italian, because I had told him so, and he was exposed to my accent in continuation. And so it is possible that when I asked him where we had first met, "Bologna" came out as a plausible answer and one that was consistent with the Italianness of my accent. Besides, Bologna came up at other times. More than once during our meetings, I would ask him where we were and he inevitably would assert that his hospital room (where we were) was the studio of an Italian doctor in Bologna. We do not know what happened to AB in Bologna and we never will. Perhaps nothing special, but this city was casually and unwittingly "chosen" as part of his past and as the momentary theatre of his present.

---

[1] Dalla Barba, G., 1993; Dalla Barba, G., 1993; Dalla Barba, G., 1995; For a similar case see: Dalla Barba, G., Cipolotti, L., & Denes, G., 1990.

AB was disoriented in time and in this case, unlike most patients disoriented in time, his disorientation took on the form of confabulation. Our meetings took place in the autumn and AB, when questioned about the date, answered without hesitation that he could not remember the day but that it was certainly June. It is worth noting that autumn in Paris is usually quite grey and so we can exclude the possibility that AB's confabulation was the result of deduction. Even though he was hospitalised, all he needed to do was to glance out the window to understand that it could not possibly be June weather. But AB did not use the compensatory strategy. As far as he was concerned it was June in Bologna and not autumn in Paris.

AB's confabulatory behaviour was not limited to his present but also involved his future. On one occasion, for example, when I asked him what he was going to do at the end of our session, he said he was going to spend time putting his bookcase in order and that then he was going out with friends for an aperitif. On another occasion he said that he hoped our session would end early because he had to go to the shops to buy new clothes, since he had not been able to the day before because he had got lost in the centre of Paris where luckily he had run into a nurse who had kindly brought him back to the hospital. On that occasion he did actually try to leave his hospital room saying that there was a taxi waiting for him.

Other examples of AB's confabulatory behaviour regard his past. AB lived a confabulatory past, that is he was conscious of a past that he had never lived. Consider the following examples. His wife (having suffered for some years from a serious illness) died while AB was hospitalised. Even though he sometimes showed he was perfectly aware of this tragic event, at other times he claimed to have seen her the day before when he had gone with his mother to see her in hospital (his mother had actually died many years earlier). Sometimes he claimed his mother had died the Wednesday before, and would complain about having arrived at her deathbed too late because she lived on the other side of Paris and he had got caught in a traffic jam. When I asked him why he was in hospital AB would answer "When I retired they put me here. Perhaps they think I'm mad, but I'm not in the least. Not yet anyway." If I asked him who he had seen that morning, he would inevitably answer that he had seen his wife, his children and the maid, as usual.

Despite this confabulatory behaviour from which neither the past, the present, nor the future were exempt, AB was perfectly aware of past and present public events and was particularly worried about the latter. It was the autumn of 1989 and Central and Eastern Europe were undergoing the well-known political upheavals. Not only did AB follow these events daily in the newspapers, but he was obviously quite worried about them: he had been deported during WWII and now claimed not to understand how the European nations could underestimate the risk of allowing German re-unification.

The second patient, CD [1], is a man of 37, employed as a bank teller; he had an average to below-average education and is married with two children. He has never had neurological or psychiatric problems. More or less during the same period of time as when AB fractured his femur, CD, walking in the mountains, slid down about 200 metres. This caused a serious cranial-encephalic trauma with multiple cerebral contusions, besides other fractures and contusions. After this accident CD spent about 40 days in a coma.

Our first meeting took place about ten months after his accident. CD displayed definite emotional incontinence and a tendency to moria and to laugh for no reason at all. His degree of orientation in time, in space and for people fluctuated considerably and never was perfect. On some occasions his spatio-temporal disorientation was complete and accompanied by flourishing confabulatory behaviour. And so, for example, on one occasion, instead of at the hospital of Padua, he claimed to be in Milan in a church probably dedicated to St Anthony. One of the recurring themes of CD's confabulations were races and walking races, probably because he was actually an enthusiast of this kind of activity to which he dedicated a great deal of his free time. Another favourite and recurring theme in his confabulations was physiotherapy which he actually had undergone for months and continued to do so. However, often the theme around which the confabulations were built was inserted and used in what we could call "anomalous semantic contexts". And so, for example, on one occasion he claimed to have participated the day before in a race, to have won and to have received as a price a piece of meat which had been placed on his right knee. On another occasion, having been asked to define the word

---

[1] Dalla Barba, G., 1993.

"synagogue", he answered "it has to do with physiotherapy". The word "phrase" meant "a field in the mountains" for him.

This particular type of semantically anomalous confabulatory behaviour was also associated with confabulatory behaviour in every way similar to that expressed by AB, which was semantically appropriate though. Besides, like AB, CD was also completely unaware of his deficiency. What do these confabulations in these two patients mean?

According to a by now classic explanation, confabulation reflects the tendency of patients to fill the gaps in their memory with confabulatory memories[1]. In other words AB and CD produce confabulatory memories wherever their memory is weak and has deteriorated. AB has a deficit in episodic memory and therefore confabulates when he has to recall a specific episode from his personal past. Since CD's memory deficiency also includes semantic knowledge, he confabulates when general knowledge also comes into play. But this hypothesis does not specify whether the tendency to fill memory gaps with confabulation reflects an explicit, conscious choice or whether it is the result of a sort of unconscious automatism. If it were conscious behaviour then there would be no difference between the subject who confabulates and the one who lies. But we have seen that in confabulation there is no intention to deceive. Our two patients, and in general patients who confabulate, are not only unaware of the confabulatory nature of their behaviour, but they totally adhere to their confabulations. Indeed these are not limited purely to the verbal sphere but are often translated into non-verbal confabulatory acts, as for example in the case of AB who attempts to leave his hospital room saying a taxi is waiting. If on the other hand you believe that the tendency to fill memory gaps with confabulation is the reflection of a sort of unconscious automatism, then this needs explaining. There are however other reasons why this type of interpretation should be rejected. AB's performance in traditional learning tests was very low, however he confabulated only rarely during these tests. Furthermore, he never confabulated during tests on semantic knowledge where his performance was perfect. In the same way, even though CD confabulated in semantic memory, his most frequent answer to this type of question was "I don't know". Besides, confabulation is quite rare and most patients with memory disorders do not confabulate at all. Why then are only

---

[1] Barbizet, J., 1963; Kopelman, M.D., 1987.
Talland, G.A., 1965.

certain mnesic gaps filled with false memories and not others, and why do only certain patients with memory disorders and not all behave in this way?[1] Finally, as we have seen in AB, confabulation does not concern only the past, namely memory, but also involves the present and the future. More than a specific disorder of memory, it is therefore a phenomenon that involves all subjective temporality. The following case study demonstrates how confabulation involves all the subordinate structures of temporal consciousness.

EF [2] is a fifty-two-year-old woman, married with two children; she has always been a housewife. After a brain haemorrhage she fell into a coma for nearly three months and when she came out of it she was suffering from a serious amnesic-confabulatory syndrome, without her intelligence having been compromised. The most interesting aspect of EF's case was that her confabulation did not only involve her past, that is the recollection of personal memories, but also her present and future. The extension of EF's confabulation to all three dimensions of temporality certainly represented something more than simple coincidence. EF confabulated when asked questions of the following type: "What did you do yesterday? Where are you now? What are you going to do tomorrow?" But she never confabulated when answering questions about historical events or news items (for example "What happened to Kennedy?") In this case her most frequent answer was "I don't know". What is more, EF never confabulated in learning tests. If, for example, she was asked to memorise a list of words or a short story of one or two lines, at the moment of recollection she would simply state that she did not remember anything, without producing any list of words or a confabulatory story. In other words, EF confabulated only when her subjective temporality was involved, that is when she was forced to set elements of her life into a subjective temporal context. "What did you do yesterday?" "I went to the market as usual". "Where are you now?" "At home". "What is a doctor doing at your house?". "I don't know, they say I'm crazy but actually they are the crazy ones". "But isn't this a hospital?". "Well, it could be a hospital, but it is my home". "Why am I wearing a white coat and you a dressing gown?" "I often wear a dressing gown in the house, the white coat is your business". "What are you doing tomorrow?"

---

[1] We have already discussed in the second chapter the theories which see confabulation as the result of a deficiency in the monitoring mechanisms of memory. We have also proved that these theories are victims of the homunculus fallacy. We will not go into it again.
[2] Dalla Barba, G., Cappelletti, Y.J., Signorini, M., & Denes, G., 1997.

"Tomorrow I'm going to the market". "How will you get there?" "As usual, by car". "By yourself?". "Of course, why?". This patient had been hospitalised for several weeks and from the onset of her illness she had never done anything she claimed she had nor anything that she proposed to do. A recent explanation of confabulatory behaviour[1] sees confabulation as the result of a dysfunction of the ego due, yet again, to a deficiency in the monitoring mechanisms situated in the frontal lobe of the brain. According to this explanation, confabulation is *motivated by the aim to protect the ego in a moment of stress and isolation.* The problem with this explanation is that none of the elements invoked to explain confabulation is conscious: the ego, the monitoring processes and the aim of protecting the ego are all unconscious elements. An explanation of this type clearly falls into the *homunculus* fallacy and the theoretic problems that this poses.

Actually, when EF confabulates, she behaves like someone who is consciousness of her past, present and future. The problem though is that EF is conscious of a past, present and future which are "false", in that they do not represent a past, present and future which are consistent with her present situation. What then is EF's confabulatory reality? It is at once clear that her confabulation is always plausible, she describes facts that could have happened or could happen. Indeed, a hypothetical observer who did not know EF's biography or her current situation would have no way of deciding whether or not her stories were confabulatory. EF might state that the previous day she had gone to do the shopping or that after our meeting she would make dinner for her family, acts which conform to her daily life before the onset of her illness. In short, in EF's case, it is clear that she is perfectly aware of her personal temporality but confuses her habits with her real past, present and future. In other words, EF's confabulatory temporality, like AB's, reflects the condition predicted in our hypothesis whereby temporal consciousness sees an object's multiplicity as unicity. Evidently, it is a situation in which temporal consciousness is still present despite brain damage, but can no longer recognise the unicity of an object. In short, it is the specular condition of amnesia. In the case of amnesic patients, as we have seen, it was an object's unicity that was seen as multiplicity by consciousness. In the case of patients that confabulate, temporal consciousness is preserved and habits, the repetition of life, in a word multiplicity, is seen as unicity. Like the purely amnesic patient, the

---

[1] Conway, M.A., & Tacchi, P.C., 1996.

patient who confabulates continues *to be* his past. However, unlike the amnesic, the confabulator, besides being time, thematizes an object in the temporal mode.

The past of the patient who confabulates is, however, by definition, a confabulatory past, the memories he reports are *false*. But it is not only the memories which are false, the present and the future of the person who confabulates are also *false*. And so it is a matter of a whole confabulatory temporality which takes, so to speak, the place of real temporality. In short, the patient who confabulates thematizes a confabulatory temporality. But where does this confabulatory temporality come from? If temporality, as we have affirmed, is not external to consciousness, since there cannot be a given time which consciousness *then* selects, but is a basic structure of consciousness, it then becomes clear that in the case of the patient who confabulates, we are faced with a confabulatory consciousness in which past present and future are somehow distorted. Distorted with respect to what? The truth, you will say; with what *actually* took place, is taking place or will take place. But who establishes the truth? If temporality, and therefore its subordinate dimensions, are inherent to consciousness, what relationship of truth can there be between what you suppose to *actually* have taken place, to be taking place or to be going to take place and the reality of temporal consciousness? And yet for a witness, the doctor or the psychologist observing the patient who confabulates, his stories about the past, his perception of the present and his future plans are confabulatory, in that they are totally at variance with what the listener expects as an answer, so much so that they push him to consider the patient's answers as not normal, namely as confabulatory. Where does this discrepancy between what the observer expects and the answers he receives come from? In other words, what is the origin of this confabulatory temporality? We have already seen how current theories of confabulation resort to the hypothesis of the *homunculus*-watchman which under normal conditions blocks false or inappropriate propositions on the threshold of consciousness and only allows true or appropriate ones to pass. But we have also seen that such a position is untenable for a series of reasons, the first of which is the attribution of intentionality to a mechanism, process or whatever you want to call it, which is not conscious and by definition inaccessible to consciousness. If you consider consciousness as a temporal being, you see that there is no need to bring unintelligible hypotheses like that of the *homunculus* into play. We have already stated that remembering the past is the result of an act of consciousness which transcends the present to select an event down there where it took place. In the same way consciousness which plans the future transcends the present to project itself there where the event will take place. We have also called these acts of consciousness re-cognitive synthesis. Let us suppose this re-cognitive synthesis is possible, that this spontaneous act of consciousness is preserved in the subject who confabulates, but that the target of this re-cognitive synthesis, the object of consciousness which is temporalized, is no longer available or is so only in part, namely in its multiplicity. What will happen? Temporal consciousness will select its object as it always does in the mode of unicity, but it will be an unbalanced object leaning towards multiplicity. In other words, consciousness which confabulates sees the multiplicity of an object as unicity in the temporal mode. You cannot say that it is the object of temporal thematization which is missing in confabulation. The object is there, thematized in the form of time. Is something missing? Yes and no. Indeed on one hand, if I say that yesterday I ate with my parents, who in reality have been dead for some time, it is my past of yesterday that is missing as the object of the thematization of my consciousness that recalls. But at the same time, this thematization is true *for me*, in that at the very moment I make the statement, it becomes my thematized past. A past to which I adhere totally and of which I am absolutely certain, as though it were a real memory. In other words, I am remembering another past and it is the *otherness* of this past which makes it confabulatory in the eyes of those who are observing me. In the same way the hospitalised patient who affirms that in a while he is going to buy some new clothes when it is certain that he will not be leaving the hospital, is planning another future. Confabulatory consciousness is therefore a totally temporal consciousness which thematizes past, present and future. However these in some way are missing and what is thematized is "other". How can we get around this contradiction? In reality it is only an apparent contradiction. First of all what is this "other" that is thematized by consciousness that confabulates, and also with respect to what is it other? When I say that yesterday I ate with my parents I am stating something which is impossible, which for me though, constitutes a real memory. Where does this type of thematization of my past come from? Thinking about it, it becomes clear that I have eaten with my parents innumerable times in my life and what I am doing when I talk of the impossible meal of the previous evening, is nothing other than thematizing a habit or, in neuropsychological terms, semantic knowledge, as a memory. In the same way when the confabulatory patient talks of an improbable or even impossible future, he is simply thematizing in the future what his being of that moment is suggesting to him. And this temporal thematization of what psychologists call "personal semantic knowledge" is nothing other than the thematization of multiplicity in the mode of unicity. You will say that not all confabulation is of this kind, but that sometimes it is of such a bizarre nature that it is impossible to follow it back to the thematization of multiplicity, of a habit or of semantic knowledge. As we saw earlier, for example, one of our patients claimed to have won a race and to have won the prize of a piece of meat which had been placed on his right knee. In reality there is no contradiction here. What the patient affirms always reflects his knowledge, or his habits. We know that running races were his favourite pastime and that in the accident which caused his amnesia, among other things, his knee was injured. The fact is that in this patient, as in other patients who produce confabulations of this sort, the relationships between the various elements of his knowledge seem inappropriate. In other words, in this case it is a question of thematization of knowledge which has somehow been damaged, which has lost the semantic ties that normally rule conversation, the temporal thematization of damaged multiplicity. In this sense patients who confabulate thematize another past, another present and another future. Past, present and future which are other with respect to a particular past, present and future because they are thematizations of a general past, of their most common gestures and actions, in short, of the life that they are. And when this life, the knowledge of which they are made, is altered, the content of their confabulation will become more or less bizarre without there being any difference in nature between the bizarre confabulation and the more plausible one: they are both temporalized thematizations of the patient's knowledge. What is missing, the specific time, the ability to select an object's unicity as unique, that particular event that I lived yesterday, my present of now and my future of tomorrow, is only missing for an observer who witnesses the enormity and the scandal of my confabulation. Nothing is missing for me who is confabulating: my past, my present and my future are there in front of me, thesis of my consciousness which thematizes them. Besides, my consciousness cannot be missing anything since it is not the sum of anything. It can be *other* but it will always be totally whole. And so yet again it is evident that past, present and future are not in themselves separate from consciousness and that time is not of the consistency of stone, which remains unchangeable. Thematized temporality is nothing other than an act of consciousness, one of the many acts that consciousness in its total freedom carries out in its continuous condemnation of not being the *en-soi* which it thematizes. And so memory ceases to be a pure external relationship between an event which took place and consciousness which selects it, but becomes a free act of consciousness that thematizes the *en-soi* in the temporal mode of the past.

That memory is an act of consciousness which in its total freedom thematizes the *en-soi* in the past is confirmed not only by confabulation, namely by the thematization of a past which does not completely coincide with the effective experience of the subject who confabulates. For example, among Buddhists, who believe in the reincarnation of the soul, a common meditation exercise aims at remembering the past lives in which the soul lived before reincarnating itself in the person meditating. It is well known that this exercise in meditation often obtains the result it sets out to, and the subject who is meditating manages to remember what he was, for example, a warrior, a harlot, a dog or a bat. There is no doubt that this type of phenomenon is neither the result of banal mystification nor of a circus trick, but that rather it is something which is extremely serious. However, for those of us who do not believe in metempsychosis, it seems difficult to believe that someone is able to remember a past life since we do not believe in that life. And yet here there is no difficulty in comprehension, nothing mysterious. If, as we have said, recollection is a free act of consciousness that thematizes an event in the past, it is easy to understand how *any* event can be thematized in the past and therefore recalled, including having been a warrior or a harlot, a dog or a bat. We do not intend to discuss this here, but it is clear how the choice of memory in these cases, harlot or princess, warrior who died as a hero in battle or stray dog, reflects and in some way summarises the anguish present in the person remembering, who by remembering enacts various roles which are essentially cathartic. But it is not necessary to resort to Buddhist practices to understand that memory is an act of free consciousness. One day a friend told me, for example, that one of her favourite pastimes when she is bored or sad is *to remember* pleasant events that have never taken place but that she lives as though they really had. In short, with extreme facility she remembers *another* past, which she recognises as false but that to all effects she manages to live as real and to enjoy.

In the light of these observations, confabulation assumes another aspect and becomes in some way more *normal*. Indeed, it is only an act of consciousness which thematizes time. Basically, it is a desperate attempt on the part of consciousness to remain consciousness of time, meant here as consciousness that remembers, that is present and that plans its future. Only that the cornerstones of the thematization have disappeared and what is thematized is no longer a past event, the present condition or a probable future, but a somehow altered and impoverished life whose only points of reference are what has been repeated, what by stint of repetition has become encrusted in the being and which lacking a precise re-cognitive synthesis becomes sole theme of the temporal existence. This is often a desperate attempt, because often confabulation is not a chronic symptom but disappears after a day or two, a couple of weeks or months at the most. It is desperate because in the end it is an attempt which fails and the consciousness of the subject who confabulates returns to being the consciousness of a subject who is no longer able to thematize time, that time which he is unable and which he never ceases to be. But what do we mean when we speak of an *attempt*, a desperate attempt, which however fails, to maintain time as the decisive thesis of consciousness? An attempt, in its common everyday meaning, means that the subject is aware of no longer being able to thematize time and yet he tries to thematize it all the same. Confabulation in this case is an inauthentic act, carried out in bad faith. The act of someone who has lost something, the ability to thematize time, and who continues to pretend he is still able to do so. This is clearly not the case. Attempt also means *to tend towards something*. It is consciousness in its entirety that *tends* towards time, which is still, despite everything, consciousness *of* time. There is no bad faith here. If anything there is a pathological consciousness of time. But adding the adjective *pathological* is not of much help in understanding unless what is meant by this term in this specific instance is clarified. What does pathological mean in this case, apart from being a summarising judgement by a witness who has taken this liberty? In other words is there something wrong with this consciousness that thematizes time in a confabulatory way, and if so what is it that is wrong? Put in these terms, yes, confabulatory consciousness in some way reflects something wrong. We have, after all, already said that consciousness that confabulates is "other", different from consciousness that does not confabulate. Good, this having been established, we must now find out what it is that is wrong and why.

First of all for there to be confabulation, for this something that is out of place, this deficit, this pathological element to exist there must be a "normal" subject to witness the "pathological" behaviour of the person confabulating. In the absence of a relationship of this type, the confabulation is no longer such, it simply ceases to exist, since, as we have seen, it is a question of thematization of time to which the subject totally adheres without seeing anything out of place in it. Consciousness that confabulates, once again, is not missing anything, it is consciousness full of time in its unity and coherency. Indeed, the patient who confabulates is described as *anosognosic* which is a term coined in the field of neurology to indicate someone who is unaware of his deficit. And who but a witness can decide whether or not another person has a deficit and whether he lacks consciousness of said deficit? Therefore if there is something wrong, a deficit, a sign of pathology, we must look for it in the witness of this confabulation, and it is he, that is we, that should ask what is wrong. If we ask this question, we see that what makes us consider confabulation such is a substantial separation, a deep *jatus* which divides us from the person who confabulates. Where is the cleavage through which this *jatus* passes? It is clear that this separation runs along a line which separates the real from the false. The person who confabulates, in all good faith and with all our possible comprehension, says things that are false. But what does "false" mean here? It means saying something, in given circumstances, which is completely different from what you would say if you were not confabulating. It is therefore obvious, without having to consult anthropologists who would tell us that in some forgotten tribe of American Indians the true and the false do not exist or if they do they are different from ours, that the separation lies wholly in the witness, in the person who decides the course of the line which separates the true from the false. The concept of norm, from which the word normal is derived, and of which abnormal and therefore pathological is the antonym, is clearly crucial in this type of situation. Whoever establishes the norm also arrogates the right to judge as abnormal the person who transgresses it. When the norm establishes the limits between true and false, the person who remains on the other side of the barricade is seen as abnormal. What we need to ask ourselves is how, on the basis of what criteria is the boundary between true and false set in the case of confabulation? You will say that those who confabulate pass off episodes that have never taken place for ones that have and therefore the "false" in this case is crystal clear and there is therefore no need to resort to concepts of norms, of separation or of boundaries. Those who confabulate simply talk about a past they have never lived. We will take this simplistic objection as our starting point also because it is the most intransigent point. Firstly, those who confabulate do not simply pass off episodes which have never taken place for ones that have. Their activity is far more sophisticated. Indeed, they also pass off a present which does not exist and a future which will never be. Let us take the present. If someone in hospital tells me they are in a church dedicated to St Anthony, it is still an objective contradiction as when the same person told me he had spent the afternoon of the previous day with his mother who actually had been dead for many years. But how can there be objectivity about the future? The future, being a continuous possibility of existence, cannot by definition but belong to the category of the probable. And yet even the future is given as being without a doubt false in the case of those who confabulate. Where does the apodeictic certainty come from which makes us consider the thematized temporality of those who confabulate as false when, at least by right, we should only have jurisdiction over what "in reality" has happened and is happening but not over what will happen? To answer this question we need to pose another: how can we be certain of our memories, of our present and of our plans? On the basis of which criteria of truth can I say with a considerable degree of certainty that at this time yesterday I was writing another paragraph of this book or that last Sunday at this time I was walking through the Luxembourg gardens? Why can I say that I am in my office and not in a church and why do I state with certainty that in a couple of hours I will go home? You will object that both my memory and present perception and my future are so vivid and obvious that there is no need for further justification. I "see" myself walking through the park on Sunday, the place around me is certainly my office and when I have finished working, unless something unexpected comes up, I will go back home. I am so absolutely certain of all of this that nothing could ever convince me of the contrary. The certainty with which I state my memories, my present and my future cannot in any way become a perhaps. In other words, if, for example, I am convinced Kennedy died in 1964 but everyone affirms that no, he died in 1963, I will recognise my mistake and accept 1963 as the year of Kennedy's death. But no one will ever convince me, not even the greatest number of eye witnesses, that I did not have coffee at breakfast, that I am not at the moment writing and that tomorrow I do not plan to take the train to a certain place. But the fact that I am absolutely certain of my memories, of my present and of my future is used as a criterion of veracity, we will not be able to distinguish normal thematization of time from confabulatory thematization. Indeed, those who confabulate are also absolutely certain of the veracity of their memories, of their present and of their plans. It is therefore clear that if we adopt this criterion, the distance between those who confabulate and those who do not is reduced by a mere millimetre. Apparently there is no way out of this vicious circle. I am certain of my memory since it presents itself to my consciousness with all the apodeicticity of what I really lived. The same thing happens to those who confabulate, and so the gulf that separates us will never be closed. However, it is only a vicious circle from which it is apparently impossible to get out if we insist on linking time to an object and not to an act of consciousness. In other words the contradiction stems from wanting to make time at all costs coincide with the real *facticity* of the remembered episode, of present reality or that of the future. The fact that normally thematized time and real facticity coincide adds nothing to the act in itself, namely to consciousness that thematizes time. What distinguishes normal thematization of temporality from that which is confabulatory is not a difference in the nature of the act, but in the degree or level of knowledge reflected in the two acts, normal and confabulatory thematization of time. Earlier we said that CD's implausible and bizarre confabulations reflected the disintegration of the semantic ties around which a proposition is normally built. CD's confabulation became bizarre and highly implausible because his level of knowing consciousness, or of semantic knowledge, had deteriorated and this affected his propositional capacity. To use neuropsychological terminology, in the case of CD, a semantic memory deficit was responsible for the type of confabulation produced by this patient. But CD had kept his ability to thematize an object in the temporal mode of consciousness, though the object's multiplicity, which has deteriorated on the semantic plane, is seen as unicity. While in the cases of AB and EF temporal thematization sees multiplicity in which the semantic links are intact as unique

This description of confabulatory phenomena demonstrates that temporal consciousness reflects an act which is free and independent of the object which is addressed, or rather, any object may be seen by consciousness in the temporal mode. And since the object of temporal consciousness manifests itself by definition in its unicity, the multiplicity of an object can also be seen by temporal consciousness as unicity. And so another two predictions of our hypothesis have been confirmed by the concreteness of confabulatory existence in the cases described.

3. CONSCIOUSNESS AND EXISTENCE

In the course of this work we have found ourselves in the position of having to assign a central role to temporal consciousness in the psychic life of man. Our aim has been to reject the paradoxes and explanatory illusions which, by tracing the origin of conscious life in various ways back to an unconscious elsewhere – either physiological or psychological – have only put off the problem of consciousness creating a *solutio ad infinitum*. And so this work has led us to re-assign a central role to consciousness in psychic life. Consciousness, in its various modes, cannot be the effect of something which precedes it in a causal chain which develops backwards into infinity. Consciousness is not the effect of anything since it is the very origin of the cause-effect relationship, the relationship consciousness itself offers in an attempt to explain things and *itself*. But our description is missing the answer to a question we have been avoiding: "Why do we have a temporal consciousness and what role does it play in our psychic life?" The answer is complicated and would take more than a few lines at the end of this book. What we can say though is that the centrality of consciousness, and in particular of temporal consciousness in our psychic life is not only the result of theory but has a definite significance in the concreteness of the existence of each of us. Having temporal consciousness means transcending the immediate and placing yourself along the path that establishes the plot and meaning of life. A path which starts in the darkness of that being that I was, that foetus, that infant, a being without consciousness, *immediate*, not even instantaneous because the instant demands that duration which did not yet exist. My relationship with the world - a world which was not yet the distinct world which would surround me later - was immediate. Darkness then began to fade in the dawn of temporal consciousness and a past, a present and a future began to take shape and that being that I was became inter-worldly. A subject which is radically separated from the object in the middle of that temporal path to be pursued - with a past behind me, a concrete present and a possible future. I move along this path knowing that the darkness I rose from is waiting for me down there, in death, in that future that I will be without the possibility of not being it and, in which I will no longer be without the possibility of being. Temporal consciousness therefore is the very need for the inter-worldly being that I am to express itself as such. The path I examine behind me and the one I have in front of me are the very meaning of my existence. But temporal consciousness is not only the meaning of my existence but it is also the condition necessary for existence to come about. How could I love a woman, work well, have political ideas without a consciousness which allows me to place love, work, political ideas along the path of time, of my time? Temporal consciousness enables me to recognise myself, to project myself, for better and for worse. Not only, but by means of temporal consciousness I take full responsibility for myself and the entire world because universal time, of which the world is made, is not given, but stems from the temporal consciousness of each of us. There is a moral responsibility to which temporal consciousness recalls us continually, from which we can hide but not escape. Temporal consciousness engages us constantly as is seen in the questions we always answer unwillingly: "Who are we; who were we; who will we be?" There is a sort of amnesia which persecutes us as individuals and as a society: we soon forget what we have been and what we have done and are ready to re-become what we were even if that being that we were should cover us with shame. Heidegger's *dasein*, being-there, sends you to a having-been and to a will-be, namely to a consciousness which is articulated by means of all the subordinate structures of temporality. There can be no *dasein*, consciousness of the present, without consciousness of the past and of the future. There can be no life without a consciousness which takes full responsibility for the past, the present and the future. And yet, you will say, there is existence, without there being a need for each of us to be obsessed by our thematized past, present and future. Certainly the past, present and the future of each of us are often in the background of concrete consciousness, sometimes they are completely missing, and yet there is life, there is existence all the same. But it is an existence which hides from itself, an existence which in some way or another is in bad faith, in which the liar and the lied to coincide. For this reason temporal consciousness is not only a necessity, but a necessity to be reached, a necessity which escapes us continually, a condition towards which we should tend not as a sterile exercise, but to give concrete and full meaning to our existence, to define it. But what does this tension towards temporal consciousness lead to, what is there at the end of the path? A discovery. The discovery of existence and of how much of it is irremediable, not the bitter, desperate discovery that seriousness imposes on us. The discovery "that all human activity is the same – because it all tends to sacrifice man to give birth to the cause of itself – and all of it is, on principle, destined to fail. And so getting drunk on your own or being a political leader amount to the same thing. If one of these activities wins out over the other it will not be because of its real aim, but because of the degree of consciousness that it has of its ideal aim, and, in this case, the quietism of the lonely drunk will win out over the useless commotion caused by your political activism.[1] But there will be the discovery of the freedom of the path of consciousness, freedom that is neither expected nor determined by things but which comes into being in the moral agent which, forced to exist, invents the free values of its own existence every step of the way. Not without pain. Not without the pain of the anguish which is discovered to be the only source of values. It is through anguish that the world manifests itself as possible infinite, in the past, in the present and in the future and it imposes itself as a continual choice against which every attempt to hide yourself is humanly pointless. This is where we must restart.

---

[1] Sartre, J.P., 1943.

REFERENCES

Baddeley, A. (1982). Your memory. A user's guide. London, UK: Multimedia Pubblications.

Baddeley, A., & Wilson, B. (1986). Amnesia, autobiographical memory and confabulation. In D.C. Rubin (Ed.), Autobiographical Memory, (pp. 225-252). Cambridge, UK: Cambridge University Press.

Barbizet, J. (1963). Defect of memorizing of hippocampal mammillary origin. Journal of Neurology Neurosurgery and Psychiatry, 26, 127-135.

Bateson, G. (1959). Cultural problems posed by a study of schizophrenic process. In A. Auerback (Ed.), Schizophrenia - An integrated approach, . New York: Ronald.

Bergson, H. (1896). Matière et mémoire. Paris: Alcan.

Berlyne, N. (1972). Confabulation. British Journal of Psychiatry, 120, 31-39.

Bock, G., & Marsh, J. (Eds.). (1993). CIBA Symposium on experimental and theoretical studies of consciousness. London: John Wiley and Sons.

Brentano, F. (1874 (1973)). Psychology from an empirical standpoint. London: Routledge and Kegan Paul.

Burgess, P. W., & Shallice, T. (1996). Confabulation and the control of recollection. Memory, 4, 359-411.

Caramazza, A. (1984). The logic of neuropsychological research and the problem of patient classification in aphasia. Brain and Language, 21, 9-20.

Chalmers, D. J. (1995). Facing up the problem of consciousness. In J. Shear (Ed.), Explaining conscousness: the hard problem, . Cambridge, MA: The MIT Press.

Changeux, J. P. (1983). L'homme neuronal. Paris: Librairie Arthème Fayard.

Churchland, P. S. (1981). On the alleged backwards referral of experiences and its relevance to the mind-body problem. Philosophy of Science, 48, 165-181.

Churchland, P. S. (1981). The timing of sensation: reply to Libet. Philosophy of Science, 48, 492-497.

Churchland, P. S. (1986). Neurophilosophy. Cambridge, MA: The MIT Press.

Churchland, P. S. (1988). Reduction and neurological basis of consciousness. In A. J. Marcel & E. Bisiach (Eds.), Consciousness in contemporary science, . Oxford: Oxford University Press.

Claparède, E. (1911). Recognition et moïté. Archives de Psychologie, 11, 79-90.

Coltheart, M. (1978). Lexical acces in simple reading tasks. In G. Underwood (Ed.), Strategies of information processing, . London: Academic Press.

Coltheart, M. (1981). Disorders of reading and their implications for models of normal reading. Visible Language, 15, 245-286.

Conway, M. A., & Tacchi, P. C. (1996). Motivated confabulation. Neurocase, 2, 325-339.

Crick, F. (1996). Visual perception: rivalry and consciousness. Nature, 379, 485-486.

Crick, F., & Koch, C. (1990). Towards a neurobiological theory of consciousness. Seminars in The Neurosciences, 2, 263-275.

Dalla Barba, G. (1993). Confabulation: knowledge and recollective experience. Cognitive Neuropsychology, 10(1), 1-20.

Dalla Barba, G. (1993). Different patterns of confabulation. Cortex, 29, 567-581.

Dalla Barba, G. (1995). Consciousness and confabulation: remembering another past. In R. Campbell & M. Conway (Eds.), Broken memories, . Oxford: Blackwell.

Dalla Barba, G. (1997). Recognition memory and recollective experience in Alzheimer's disease. Memory, 5(6), 657-672.

Dalla Barba, G., Cappelletti, Y. J., Signorini, M., & Denes, G. (1997). Confabulation: remembering "another" past, planning "another" future. Neurocase, 3, 425-436.

Dalla Barba, G., Cappelletti, Y. J., Signorini, M., & Denes, G. (1997). Confabulation: remembering "another" past, planning "another" future. Neurocase, 3, 425-436.

References

Dalla Barba, G., Cipolotti, L., & Denes, G. (1990). Autobiographical memory loss and confabulation in Korsakoff's syndrome: a case report. Cortex, 26, 525-534.

Dalla Barba, G., Mantovan, M. C., Ferruzza, E., & Denes, G. (1997). Remembering and knowing the past: a case study of isolated retrograde amnesia. Cortex, 33(1), 143-154.

Damasio, A. R. (1994-1995). L'erreur de Decartes. Paris: Odile Jacob.

Dennet, D. (1978). Brainstorm. Cambridge, MA: The MIT Press.

Dennet, D. C. (1991). Consciousness explained. Boston: Little Brown.

Dennet, D. C., & Kinsbourne, M. (1992). Time and the observer: The where and the when of consciousness in the brain. Behavioral and Brain Sciences, 15, 183-247.

Descartes, R. (1637). Le discours de la méthode. Paris.

Dreyfus, H. (1979). What computers can't do. (revised edition ed.). New York: Harper and Row.

Dreyfus, H. (Ed.). (1982). Husserl: Intentionality and cognitive science (A Bradford Book ed.). Cambridge, Massachusetts: MIT Press.

Dreyfus, H. (1983). Michel Foucault: Beyond Structuralism and Hermeneutics. Chicago: University of Chicago Press.

Dreyfus, H. (1989). Alternative philosophical conceptualizations of psychopathology. In H.A. Durfy & D. F. T. Rodier (Eds.), Phenomenology and beyond: The self and its language., . Dordrecht: Kluwer Academic Publishers.

Dreyfus, H., & Dreyfus, S. (1986). Mind over machine. New York: Macmillan, Free Press.

Dreyfus, H., & Dreyfus, S. (1988). Making a mind versus modeling a brain: Artificial intelligence back to a branchpoint. Daedalus(winter), 15-43.

Dreyfus, H., & Dreyfus, S. (1990). What is morality A phenomenological account of the development of ethical expertise. In D. Rassmussen (Ed.), Universalism versus Communitarianism, . Cambridge, Massachusetts: The MIT Press.

Edelman, G. M. (1987). Neural Darwinism: The theory of Neuronal Group selection. New York: Basic Books.

Edelman, G. M. (1989). The remembered present: A biological theory of consciousness. New York: Basic Books.

Edelman, G. M. (1992). Bright air, brilliant fire: On the matter of mind. New York: Basic Books.

Fodor, J. A. (1983). The modularity of mind. Cambridge, MA: The MIT Press.

Gardiner, J. M. (1988). Functional aspects of recollective experience. Memory and Cognition, 16, 309-313.

Gardiner, J. M., & Java, R. I. (1990). Recollective experience in word and nonword recognition. Memory and Cognition, 18, 23-30.

Gardiner, J. M., & Java, R. I. (1991). Forgetting in recognition memory with and without recollective experience. Memory and Cognition, 19, 617-623.

Gardiner, J. M., & Java, R. I. (1993). Recognising and remembering. In A.F. Collins, S.E. Gathercole, M. A. Conway, & P. E. Morris (Eds.), Theories of memory., (pp. 163-187). Hillsdale: Lawrence Erlbaum Associates.

Gardiner, J. M., & Java, R. I. (1993). Recognition memory and awarenes: An experimental approach. European Journal of Cognitive Psychology, 5(3), 337-346.

Gardiner, J. M., & Parkin, A. J. (1990). Attention and recollective experience in recognition memory. Memory and Cognition, 18(6), 579-583.

Globus, G. (1990). Heidegger and cognitive science. Philosophy Today, Spring, 20-30.

Hintzman, D. L. (1978). The psychology of learning and memory. San Francisco: W.H. Freeman.

Husserl, E. (1893-1917). Zür Phänomenologie des Inneren Zietbewusstseins. (Alfredo Martini, Trans.): Milano: Franco Angeli.

Husserl, E. (1950). Ideen zur einen reinen Phänomenologie (Giulio Alliney, Trans.). Hen Haag: Martinus Nijhoff.

Jacoby, L. L., Kelley, C. M., & Dywan, J. (1989). Memory attributions. In H.L. Roediger III & F.I.M. Craik (Eds.), Varieties of memory and consciousness: Essays in honour of Endel, Hillsdale New Jersey: Laurence Erlbaum Associates Inc.

James, W. (1890). Principles of psychology. New York: Holt.

Johnson, M. (1988). Discriminating the origin of information. In F. Oltmanns & B. Mahers (Eds.), Delusional Beliefs, (pp. 34-65). New York: Wiley.

Johnson, M. K. (1991). Reality Monitoring: Evidence from Confabulation in Organic Brain Disease Patients. In G. P. Prigatano & D. L. Schacter (Eds.), Awareness of Deficit After Brain Injury, . New York-Oxford: Oxford University Press.

Johnson, M. K., & Hirst, W. (1991). Processing subsystems of memory. In R.G. Lister & H.J. Weingartner (Eds.), Perspectives in cognitive neuroscience., . New York: Oxford University Press.

Johnson, M. K., & Raye, C. L. (1981). Reality monitoring. Psychological Review, 88, 67-85.

Joseph, R. (1986). Confabulation and delusional denial: frontal lobe and lateralized influences. Journal of Clinical Psychology, 42, 507-520.

Kopelman, M. D. (1987). Two types of confabulation. Journal of Neurology, Neurosurgery and Psychiatry, 50, 1482-1487.

Korsakoff, S. S. (1889). Etude médico-psychologique sur une forme des maladies de la mémoire. Revue Philosophique, 28, 501-530.

Libet, B. (1965). Cortical activation in conscious and unconscious experience. Perspectives in Biology and Medicine, 9, 77-86.

Libet, B. (1981). The experimental evidence for subjective referral of a sensory experience backwards in time: Reply to P.S. Churchland. Philosophy of Science, 48, 182-197.

Libet, B. (1982). Brain stimulation in the study of neuronal functions for conscious sensory experience. Human Neurobiology, 1, 235-242.

Libet, B. (1985). Subjective antedating of a sensory experience and mind-brain theories. Journal of Theoretical Biology, 114, 563-570.

Libet, B., Wright, E. W., Feinstein, B., & Pearl, D. K. (1979). Subjective referral of the timing for a conscious sensory experience. Brain, 102, 193-224.

Marcel, A. J. (1988). Phenomenal experience and functionalism. In A.J. Marcel & E. Bisiach (Eds.), Consciousness in contemporary science, (pp. 121-158). Oxford: Oxford University Press.

Merleau-Ponty, M. (1942). La structure du comportement. Paris: Presses Universitaires de France.

Merleau-Ponty, M. (1945). Phénoménologie de la perception. Paris: Librairie Gallimard.

Milner, B. (1958). Psychological defects produced by temporal lobe excision. Paper presented at the Association for Research in Nervous and Mental Disease The brain and human behavior, Baltimore.

Milner, B. (1965). Visually guided maze learning in man: effects of bilateral hippocampal, bilateral frontal and unilateral cerebral lesions. Neuropsychologia, 3, 317-338.

Morton, J., Hammersley, R. H., & Bekerian, D. A. (1985). Headed records: a model for memory and its failures. Cognition, 20, 1-23.

Morton, J., & Patterson, K. E. (1980). A new attempt at an interpretation, or, an attempt at a new interpretation. In M. Coltheart, K. E. Patterson, & J. C. Marshall (Eds.), Deep dyslexia, . London: Rutledge.

Moscovitch, M. (1989). Confabulation and the frontal system: strategic versus associative retrieval in neuropsychological theories of memory. In H.L. Roedinger & F.I. Craik (Eds.), Varieties of memory and consciousness: Essay in honor of Endel Tulving, . Hillsdale NJ: Lawrence Erlbaum.

Moscovitch, M. (1995). Models of consciousness and memory. In M. S. Gazzaniga (Ed.), The Cognitive Neurosciences, (pp. 1341-1356). Cambridge MA: M.I.T. Press.

Moscovitch, M. (1995). Recovered consciousness: an hypothesis concerning modularity and episodic memory. Journal of Clinical and Experimental Neuropsychology, 17(2), 276-290.

Nagel, T. (1974). What is like to be a bat? Philosophical Review, 83, 435-451.

Nagel, T. (1986). The view from nowhere. New York: Oxford University Press.

Nagel, T. (1993). What is the mind-body problem? In G. Bock & J. Marsh (Eds.), CIBA Symposium on experimental and theoretical studies of consciousness, (pp. 1-13). London: John Wiley and Sons.

Parkin, A. J. (1993). On the origin of functional differences in recollective experience. Memory, 1(3), 231-237.

Popper, K. R., & Eccles, J. C. (1977). The self and its brain. Berlin: Springer-Verlag.

Putnam, H. (1988). Much ado about not very much. In S. R. Graubard (Ed.), The artificial intelligence debate., . Cambridge, MA: The MIT Press.

Putnam, H. (1988). Representation and reality. Cambridge, Ma: The MIT Press.

Rajaram, S. (1993). Remembering and knowing: Two means to access the personal past. Memory and Cognition, 21, 98-102.

Ramachandran, V. S. (1987). Interaction between color and motion in human vision. Nature, 328, 645-647.

Ribot, T. (1882). Les maladies de la mémoire. (XVIII Ed 1906) Paris: Alcan.

Robinson, A. L. (1976). Metallurgy: extraordinary alloys that remember their past. Science, 191, 934-936.

Roediger, H. I., & Blaxton, T. A. (1987). Retrieval modes produce dissociations in memory for surface information. In D.S. Gorfein & R.R. Hoffman (Eds.), Memory and cognitive processes: the Ebbinghaus centellian conference., . Hillsdale, New Jersey: Erlbaum.

Rosenfield, I. (1992). The strange, familiar and forgotten. London: Macmillan.

Sartre, J.-P. L'imagination.

Sartre, J.-P. (1936 (1988)). La trascendance de l'Ego. (Vol. 1936 Recherches philosophiques). Paris: J. Vrin.

Sartre, J.-P. (1939). Une idée fondamentale de la phénoménologie de Husserl: l'intentionnalité., Situations I, . Paris: Gallimard.

Sartre, J.-P. (1940). L'imaginaire. Paris: Gallimard.

Sartre, J.-P. (1943). L'être et le néant. Paris: Gallimard.

Sartre, J.-P. (1946 (1949)). Matérialisme et révolution. (Situations III). Paris: Gallimard.

Sartre, J. P. (1938). Esquisse d'une théorie des émotions. Paris: Hermann.

Schacter, D. L. (1989). On the relation between memory and consciousness: dissociable interactions and conscious experience. In H.L. Roediger & F.I.M. Craik (Eds.), Varieties of memory and consciousness. Essays in honour of Endel Tulving., . Hillsdale, New Jersey: Lawrence Erlbaum.

Schacter, D. L., & Tulving, E. (Eds.). (1994). Memory Systems 1994. Cambridge, Ma: MIT Press.

Schacter, D. L., & Tulving, E. (1994). What are the memory systems of 1994? In D. L. Schacter & E. Tulving (Eds.), Memory Systems 1994, . Cambridge, Ma: MIT Press.

Searle, J. R. (1980). Minds, brains and programs. Behavioral and Brain Sciences, 3, 417-457.

Searle, J. R. (1983). Intentionality. Cambridge: Cambridge University Press.

Searle, J. R. (1990). Consciousness, explanatory inversion, and cognitive science. Behavioral and Brain Sciences, 13, 585-642.

Searle, J. R. (1992). The rediscovery of the mind. Cambridge, MA: The MIT Press.

Talland, G. A. (1965). Deranged memory. New York: Academic Press.

Titchener, E. B. (1929 (1972)). Systematic Psychology: Prolegomena. London and Ithaca: Cornell University Press.

Tulving, E. (1972). Episodic and semantic memory. In E. Tulving & W. Donaldson (Eds.), Organization of memory, . New York: Academic Press.

Tulving, E. (1983). Elements of episodic memory. Oxford: University Press.

Tulving, E. (1984). Précis of elements of episodic memory. The Behavioral and Brain Science, 7, 223-268.

Tulving, E. (1989). Memory: performance, knowledge and experience. European Journal of Cognitive Psychology, 1, 3-26.

Tulving, E. (1993). Varieties of consciousness and levels of awareness in memory. In A. Baddeley & L. Weiskrantz (Eds.), Attention: selection, awareness and control., (pp. 282-299). New York: Oxford University Press.

Varela, F. (1991). Principles of biological autonomy. New York: North-Holland/Elsevier.

Varela, F. J. (1995). Neurophenomenology: A methodological remedy for the hard problem. In J. Shear (Ed.), Explaining consciousness - 'the hard problem', . Cambridge, MA: The MIT Press.

Varela, F. J., Thompson, E., & Rosh, E. (1991). The embodied mind. Cambridge MA: MIT Press.

Warrington, E., & Weiskrantz, L. (1968). A new method of testing of long-term retention with special reference to amnesic patients. Nature, 217, 972-974.

Warrington, E. K., & Weiskrantz, L. (1968). A study of learning and retention in amnesic patients. Neuropsychologia, 6, 283-291.

Weiskrantz, L. (1987). Neuroanatomy of memory and amnesia: a case for multiple memory systems. Human Neurobiology, 6, 93-105.

Wittgenstein, L. (1953). Philosofical investigations. Oxford: Basil Blackwell.

INDEX

Alzheimer's disease, 186, 189
amnesia, 182–191
   implicit learning in, 14–16

Baddeley, A., 16, 28, 192
Barbizet, J., 196
Bateson, G., 183
before-after relationship, 117–24
beliefs, 33–41
Bergson, H., 6, 8, 106, 111, 118
Berlyne, N., 8, 191
body
   mind-body dualism, 48, 50, 51, 54–57, 73
brain, 49, 50
   and consciousness, 46-48, 51–57
Brentano, F., 31, 88
Burgess, I., 28, 67
Butters, N., 185

Caramazza, A., 62
censorship, 58, 60
Cermak, L., 185
Chalmers, D., 49
Changeux, J-P., 54
Churchland, P., 47, 120, 121
Claparède, E., 8, 11, 13, 14, 16, 183-85, 188-89
cognitivism

consciousness, 61–71
   memory, 66–69
   reading models, 62–66
Coltheart, M., 63
confabulation, 28, 30, 31, 191–206
consciousness
   autonoetic, 19, 175
   foundations of, 43–71
   imaginative, 94, 97, 153, 155-58, 161, 165-69, 174, 186, 187, 189
   intentionality, 33–34
   knowing, 153–66, 186-191, 206
   neurobiological substantialism, 51, 53, 54, 57, 72
   noetic, 19
   temporal, 121, 122, 124, 142, 144, 153, 154, 157-161, 166-69, 173, 184-89, 191, 197-200, 206-8
   varieties of, 87–104
Conway, M., 28, 198
Crick, F., 46, 47

Dalla Barba, G., 30, 173, 189, 190, 193, 195, 197
Damasio, A., 53
Dennet, D., 33, 53, 79, 122
Descartes, R., 53, 54, 117, 118

determinism, 12, 36, 44, 58, 72, 83, 98-101
double link, 187
duration, 111, 118

Edelman, J., 54
ego, 95–96, 169
episodic memory, 15, 16, 18, 19, 23, 124, 158, 165, 167, 187, 196
  autonoetic consciousness, 19
  deficit, 170
experimental phenomenology, 169–179

false memories, 28, 31, 32, 41, 191, 192, 197
Fodor, J., 62
functionalism, 37, 52, 61, 62, 71, 72, 179
  anthropomorphization of the unconscious, 61–71
  memory, 66–69
  memory trace, 6
  reading models, 62–66
future
  consciousness of, 159-60
  nature of, 114–17

Gardiner, J., 173
Globus, G., 61

Heidegger, M., 144, 208
Hintzman, D., 16
homunculus fallacy, 31–42, 61, 66, 67, 69, 83, 91, 149, 192, 197
Husserl, E., 31, 32, 88, 107, 111, 126, 140, 174, 175, 176, 179

infantile amnesia, 103
intentionality, 31
  consciousness, 33–34
  unconscious, 34–39
intuition, 60, 73, 125-126, 130, 139

Jacoby, L., 18
James, W., 8, 174
Johnson, M., 28, 31, 192
Joseph, R., 191

Kant, E., 117
knowledge, 2-5, 9-23, 25, 27, 30, 47, 50, 52, 60, 67, 69, 70, 73, 79, 83, 96, 98, 102, 103, 124-132, 134, 135, 137-40, 145-162, 166-69, 171, 174-76, 182, 188-90, 196, 200, 201, 206
  and representation, 20–23
  brain damage, 20, 21
  ontology of, 125–38
  phenomenological description, 1–5
  vs recollection, 1–5, 23
Kopelman, R., 196
Korsakoff, S., 14, 182-184

Libet, B., 119–21

Malraux, A., 110, 155
Marcel, A., 61, 66, 85
materialism
  quality vs quantity, 75–77
  science, 71–85
meaning, 19, 20
memory
  and representation, 13–25

cognitivist models, 66–69
consciousness of the past, 7, 19, 23, 70, 101, 122, 123, 149, 152, 154, 158, 159, 167, 184, 208
control systems, 27–32, 67, 69
implicit memory, 182-186
multiple vs single memory system, 15–18
memory trace, 6-12, 17-19, 23, 25, 27, 28, 43, 67, 84, 97, 106, 115, 124, 145, 149, 167, 179, 184, 186, 187
paradox of, 5–13
temporal nature of, 6–9
Merleau-Ponty, M., 7, 45, 54, 56, 78, 101, 109, 110, 117, 175, 176
Milner, B., 14, 185
mind-body dualism, 48, 50, 51, 54–57, 73
monitoring mechanisms, 28–31, 42
Morton, J., 8
Moscovitch, M., 28, 69, 90, 153, 185-188, 191–92

Nagel, T., 74, 76, 78, 171
Nietzsche, F., 4

Parkin, 173
past
problem of, 1–25
patient H.M., 185
perception, 4, 7, 13, 24, 33, 44, 74, 76-80, 92-94, 101-102, 132-134, 136, 152, 154-156, 159, 176, 199, 205

phenomenological reduction, 174-178
Popper, K., 120
presence, 105, 111–13
present
consciousness of, 122, 159, 173, 208
nature of, 111–14
psychoanalytic theory
anthropomorphization of the unconscious, 57–61
Putnam, H., 61

Rajaram, S., 173
reading
two-routes model, 63
representation, 13–25
unconscious, 41
Ribot, T., 14
Robinson, A., 12
Roediger, H., 18
Rosenfield, I., 84

Sartre, J-P., 12, 32, 50, 59, 73, 75, 82, 95, 97, 108, 108, 109, 112, 115, 118, 130, 137, 156, 209
Schacter, D., 15, 69, 90, 102, 153, 185, 186, 188
schizophrenia, 183
Searle, J., 33–37, 39, 47, 48, 50, 61, 62, 72, 92
semantic memory, 15–18, 23, 124, 153, 166, 196, 206
noetic consciousness, 19
Shallice, T., 67
Shimamura, A., 185
Spinoza, B., 10

Talland, C., 191, 192, 19

temporality, 9, 39, 101, 104, 105-124, 138-140, 142, 143, 144, 146, 149, 167, 168, 174, 188, 197, 198, 199, 201, 205, 206, 208
   confabulation and, 191-201
   ontology of, 117–24
   phenomenology of, 105–17
Titchener, E., 95
Tulving E., ,15–18, 66, 87, 102, 158, 165, 173, 185, 188

unconscious
   functionalist anthropomorphization, 61–71
   intentionality, 34–39
   psychoanalytic anthropomorphization, 57–61
   unconscious subject, 35, 39, 40, 43

Varela, F., 61, 175

Warrington, E., 14, 185
Weiskrantz, L., 14, 16, 189
Wilson, B., 28, 192
Wittgenstein, L., 56